ON
TRIAL
IN
CENTRAL
AUSTRALIA
TROUBLE
KIERAN
FINNANE

UQP

First published in 2016 by University of Queensland Press
PO Box 6042, St Lucia, Queensland 4067 Australia

uqp.com.au
uqp@uqp.uq.edu.au

Cover design by Sandy Cull, gogoGingko
Cover photo: 'Glass Midden' by Mike Gillam/www.vanishingpointgallery.com.au

Typeset in 11.5/16 pt Bembo by Post Pre-press Group, Brisbane
Printed in Australia by McPherson's Printing Group, Melbourne

Cataloguing-in-Publication Data
National Library of Australia
Cataloguing-in-publication data is available at http://catalogue.nla.gov.au

ISBN 978 0 7022 5403 1 (pbk)
ISBN 978 0 7022 5717 9 (pdf)
ISBN 978 0 7022 5718 6 (epub)
ISBN 978 0 7022 5719 3 (kindle)

University of Queensland Press uses papers that are natural, renewable
and recyclable products made from wood grown in sustainable forests.
The logging and manufacturing processes conform to the environmental regulations
of the country of origin.

CONTENTS

A NOTE ON NAMES AND USAGE

The given names of the Aboriginal dead are not used except where permission has been received. Even though the customary avoidance of given names does not last indefinitely, I choose to be cautious. I have used the initial and family name or else a bereavement name, spelled variously Kwementyaye, for Arrernte people, for example, or Kumunjayi for Warlpiri people. There are other terms as well as other spelling variations, which reflect the subtle sound differences in the various languages of the region, but I have adopted these two for the sake of clarity.

In Central Australia Aboriginal people generally refer to themselves in English as 'Aboriginal', unless they are being more specific about their particular affiliations. I follow their example. The term 'Indigenous' is often used in official contexts and always in statistical reporting; where appropriate I have followed suit, even when the reference is still to local Aboriginal people and does not include Torres Strait Islanders.

INTRODUCTION:
ONE STONE ROOM

The day of trouble begins like other days, out in the camps, the flats and houses, the river, bars and bottle shops, on the streets, off the highway. It may be hot or desert winter cold. Months pass, a year or maybe more, before memory of the trouble is revived for a re-enactment of sorts in the Alice Springs courthouse. This is where my stories begin.

Back when the courthouse was built, in 1980, somebody was thinking about the character of the local jurisdiction: Aboriginal paintings hang on the lobby walls, earthy pigments on small boards, works from the first decade of the Western Desert art movement. But what kind of signal are they? For the knowing, they may well lay out Aboriginal laws that still have a hold in this region although little heed is paid to them in the courts. Even if it were, they would often be hard to distinguish and deal with – so much else, alcohol not the least, gets in the way. The paintings are faded now due to natural light falling through the opaque glazed roof above. The light is welcome. It's claustrophobic enough in the lobby, often very crowded, the air heavy with people's worries and the boredom of waiting.

Outside, the building is a double-storey concrete blockhouse. The only time its stern face has softened was during an arts festival when it was wrapped in bright knitted blankets. From a distance the coloured squares and concentric circles looked like the Aboriginal acrylic paintings of more recent decades. Lately graffiti has appeared on the footpath in front of the entrance stairs, small letters stencilled in black: 'This is the front line,' it says. It's discreet enough for nobody to bother scrubbing it out. I'd like to know who did it, and what kind of battle they think is going on inside.

Across the road are watered lawns, brilliant green. On busy court days they are dotted with groups of Aboriginal people – whole families, children of all ages, old people, lots of women usually. They sit on the ground. There's a shape to these groups, a settled spreading. This shape is my earliest memory of Alice Springs. I know I came by air from the coast but I can't remember it. I just recall seeing a circle of women, dark skin and hair, black skirts, coloured tops, under the strong March sun, settled into the green lawns around the town council chambers. I knew then that I'd arrived in a part of Australia quite different from the one I'd grown up in with my brother and four sisters, first in the Blue Mountains where our father taught high school, later in Sydney. A circle of women was an important part of our young lives – our mother, her two sisters and their mother. They enjoyed each other's company, sitting together around their kitchen tables, over cups of tea or coffee, talking, endlessly it seemed to us, and laughing a lot. My fond memory of them in that mode may be partly why I noticed the circle of women in Alice Springs, but it was the long, patient sitting on the ground that was so striking.

If the groups on the lawns look east, past the low-slung original courthouse with its iron roof and empty verandahs, past the construction site of the new Supreme Court, towards the river, they can see the grand old river red gum that has survived almost miraculously in the middle of what was once a through road. Its significance is appreciated in folkloric names like 'Grandfather Tree' and 'Tree of Knowledge'. Margaret Kemarre Turner OAM prefers to call it the 'Foundation Tree'. An important Arrernte cultural go-between in Alice Springs, Kemarre was asked, at a public spaces planning forum some years back, how she relates to Todd Mall, the pedestrian strip in the middle of town. Her answer made no mention of buildings, paving, seating, shade structures, the things the forum was thinking about. 'That old tree is still standing,' she said. 'It represents the people of this place.' She also talked about the many other trees like it found still in the town centre as well as in and along the river. She recalled that the area was once a good place for finding yalke – a tiny wild onion that springs up after summer rain. Could she still feel 'the energy of the land' underneath the built town? 'Yes, the foundation is still here, that's how people see it.'[1]

A friend of mine says the town is so racist that when it's not, it has to be remarked upon. Many agree with him. But the recent work around the tree is worth remarking on nonetheless. It had been surrounded by exotic shrubs, fences, regulatory signs, bins, shade structures. It was alive but almost lost from view. All this was cleared away. You can walk or sit now in its presence. A small sign at ground level explains that it is part of the story of the kwekatye (uninitiated) boys travelling north. From the shade of its branches you can look through to the banks of the river where another significant tree, not quite so old, grows tall and straight. On a winter's afternoon the long rays of the sun, slanting in from the west, fill the street and light up the white bark of the far tree like a beacon.

Architects and artists have done design work around the tree through to the river, referencing Arrernte traditions. At a civic occasion to mark the work's completion, another Arrernte woman, Barbara Satour, put this in perspective. She was doing the 'Welcome to Country' honours. It was AFL Grand Final time and she made jokes about football and showed her team colours before getting down to business. There was now all around 'a bit too much cement' for her, 'not enough bitumen and dust'. She recalled the Alice of her youth, when there was less separation between bush and town, and a horse could still be ridden lickety-split down the main street. She didn't have anything to say about the new, culturally respectful shade structures and public artworks. It was to the Foundation Tree towering above her that she pointed: 'That's our statue, it represents all us Arrernte people of Central Australia.'[2]

The town is full of sacred sites and trees.[3] They usually come to public attention only when they are being complained about for getting in the way of some new development. I sat with custodian Doris Kngwarraye Stuart in her flat one day, not far from the eastern edge of town, listening to the sound of jackhammers as they gouged out the side of a small sacred hill nearby. Somehow it had fallen through the cracks of sites protection legislation. She was sick with distress. 'This is why we live short lives,' she kept saying.

When I look at sites I wish they weren't overgrown with feral grasses, covered in broken glass, fenced off, carved up, trampled on. Why do we tolerate this? Doris thinks a low profile is the best strategy, at least until it gets to the point of a site's threatened destruction. She does quiet background work, usually with artists. She finds artists are more receptive to the stories, and it pleases her when they make something of them that is beautiful and respectful. I got on a bus one day with her and two of her long-time friends and supporters, Dan Murphy and Lucy Stewart, both artists, both white. Lucy teaches art at the public high school and had brought along some of her students, local Aboriginal girls. She was also driving the bus. Other passengers included a group of artists visiting from interstate. We went on a sites tour. No money changed hands. 'This is my sacred duty,' said Doris. 'It's priceless.'

We stopped in front of a small hill opposite the hospital, part of Ntyarlkarle Tyaneme (Caterpillar Dreaming). It's surrounded by cyclone mesh and overgrown with feral buffel grass, though a few gums and other native species survive. I can remember when a derelict house sat on top of it, known variously as the Judge's or Magistrate's House. Doris spoke of walking in the vicinity when she was a child: 'We used to have to cross the road. Our father was in front and we would follow him. We crossed the road out of respect for the site. No questions asked.' They were distressed when the house was built on the hill. Then, a few years back, a telecom tower was erected on top of the range without custodians' permission. The company proposed a compensation payment. Custodians asked instead that the company organise and pay for the demolition of the Judge's House, revegetate the site and put up the fence. 'They got out of it lightly,' said Doris.

Generally she doesn't like to see sites fenced – 'They need to breathe'. They can seem so vulnerable though. On the tour she showed us a caterpillar egg site, a low mound scattered with quartz stones right at the edge of what is now a suburban road. You wouldn't look at it twice, unless you knew. There's a path cutting across it, made by people taking a shortcut from a nearby town camp. 'They've got no respect,' said Doris.

The path worn by feet is easier to accept than the deliberate destruction of the tail of the caterpillar during roadworks to build Barrett Drive back in 1982. A plan was being negotiated with custodians for the road to go over the top of the caterpillar – a low ridge. Without notice the intruding section and a sacred tree growing on it were destroyed by a government contractor.[4] 'When I saw that I stood and cried. Not just the tears coming out of our eyes. Our stomach cried,' Doris was reported as saying.[5] It would be harder for something like that to happen now, or would it? I think back to the jackhammers. That was in 2011. And to the trees at Traeger Park, the town's premier sportsground. In the view of some they were in the way and it was suspected they had been poisoned in 2009. Custodians have firmly resisted removal of the dead trees; they're not going to reward bad behaviour. Let them stand as a reminder.[6]

Everyone got off the tour bus at Heavitree Gap – Ntaripe to the Arrernte. Dan, one of the artists supporting Doris, walked off a bit. Turning his back to us, facing the Gap, he scooped up a handful of sand and threw it into the air, singing out: 'We're sorry, we've come through, broken the rules, we didn't know, we're sorry. But we have your Kngwarraye here, your apmereke-artweye. We'll try to learn.' I hadn't expected to be so moved. I'd lived in town for more than two decades; I felt I had taken a long time to be standing there and hearing those words. Do I think about this now as I drive through the Gap, which, as I live on the south side, I have to do whenever I come to town? Sometimes. Especially when I see a woman walking head down through this important site, which once women were prohibited from entering. If she's with a man, she stays well behind him.[7]

'Apmereke-artweye' is the term for what I have been calling loosely 'custodian'. Doris doesn't like the English term. She prefers that we learn to use the Arrernte. 'Kngwarraye' is her 'skin name', describing how she fits into her kinship group. She won't do 'Welcome to Country'. 'Did you ask before you came here and decided you wanted to feel welcome?' she challenges. Then she goes on to explain: in the past, visitors from the south would stop on that side of Ntaripe and wait to be invited into Mparntwe by the right people.

These days if Doris is invited to speak at a formal occasion she'll talk only about sites being acknowledged, not about welcome. She'll say something about the stories, point to some of the features – the dancing trees of Ankerre Ankerre (Coolibah Swamp), the head of the caterpillar that is Tharrarltneme (Annie Meyer Hill), the nose of the wild dog, Alhekulyele (the peak of Mount Gillen). She'll also say, putting trusted people on the spot, that they can do the acknowledgment: 'You don't have to be Aboriginal to respect sites.'

~

Doris is named as one of the fourteen applicants in *Hayes v Northern Territory*, the 2000 Federal Court decision that determined native title exists over more than 100 parcels of land in the Alice Springs municipality. Her late brother, Robert Stuart, gave evidence during the claim. He was a genial man who liked to make people laugh. You can hear it even in the transcript.[8] The questioning was getting at the day-to-day activity by the Arrernte Mparntwe on their lands – had they maintained their traditional knowledge and practices? Robert gave the first part of his evidence at Akngwelye Antere, near the present-day Desert Park, west of the town, where he used to hunt with his father. He was asked if he still went there, into the valley. He said he could if he wanted to. But could he go hunting there? By Arrernte Mparntwe law yes, but there would be complications. What were they?

A: The buildings.

Q: Yes?

A: And the restrictions.

Q: Are there restrictions from the Desert Park?

A: Yes.

Q: What are they?

A: $12 fee.

Even if he paid it though, he knew he wouldn't have been able to hunt at this tourist park, not even with a pea rifle. Asked about water sources, he said there was a soakage just behind him, coming off the range. His father had showed it to him and showed him how to get water from it, digging with a yam stick.

Other witnesses spoke about the places they used to camp, the places where they used to look for tucker and meat and water. There are myriad places right across the town, all named, areas and features that non-Arrernte would not necessarily recognise as 'a place'. Places in the footsteps of the ancestor creators who passed that way, forming the land as they went. Rocks, even small rocks, named.

Trees, single trees and groups of trees. Mounds. Hillocks. Soakages. Conception sites. Places for gathering firewood, for collecting plants to make bush medicine, for collecting bark that is burned, its ash used to chew with native tobacco. All named. They make for a very different map of the broad valley north of the range where a town grew with its grid of streets and lot numbers.

Doris had a son who was a painter. He signed his works as David Mpetyane. In 1992, years ahead of the determination of native title, he made a painting about the two maps. In it his bird's eye follows a long swoop north from the Gap – Ntaripe. He takes in the grid of streets, painted in thick black lines, sitting harshly on Mparntwe, yet unable to obliterate its great structures – the ranges, the river and creeks – and its ground seething with life. I wonder, with the explosion of feral grasses since the heavy rains at the turn of the century, whether he would have been able to see the ground in the same way today. I can't ask him as he died well before his time, in 2008.

He called this painting *Fertility* and wrote a poem in English to go with it, under the same title. This is the first verse:

Alice lost her virginity
Witness by
The old man gum tree
While the dog sat confused
Paternity licking its wounds
She gave birth
To one stone room
Next a shed then a house.[9]

The title and the birth suggest a generative coming together, something that is not often said about the town's history. But there's no getting away from what else is there – the loss, wounds, confusion, confinement. That's what the town lives with, and everything good that happens is still against that backdrop.

The trace of Arrernte stories of the land can occasionally be seen in the present-day urban and commercial landscape of Alice Springs. The Yeperenye Shopping Centre, for example, is named for one of the sacred caterpillars and is owned by Yeperenye Pty Ltd, a company made up of Aboriginal interests. The company also has a substantial portfolio of other real estate across the Alice Springs CBD, including the Kmart site and buildings.[10] These assets are part of the bricks and mortar manifestation of a rising local Aboriginal middle class, rarely paid attention to. An Aboriginal investment company, Centrecorp, through an intricate network of proprietary limited companies, has an even larger portfolio of assets.[11] Centrecorp's shareholders are three prominent Aboriginal organisations, including the Central Land Council. Native title holders, through a company associated with their body corporate, have a share in Yeperenye Pty Ltd and other significant assets, including a chain of suburban supermarkets.[12]

Social and economic change is also reflected in statistics produced by the Census, which since 2001 has collected separate Indigenous-specific data for the town camps and the rest of Alice Springs. People are often surprised to learn that roughly four times as many Aboriginal residents of Alice live in the suburbs rather than in the camps. And on many indices measured by the Census the two groups show a significantly different profile, with marked differences again compared to the local non-Aboriginal population. A higher proportion of Aboriginal 'town dwellers' are engaged with mainstream education, with paid employment, with home ownership (not yet a possibility in the camps);[13] their median incomes are higher, by almost twice; proportionally fewer of them live in over-crowded households; proportionally fewer speak an Aboriginal language in their own home.[14] Clearly processes of adaptation and transformation are under way, with their gains and losses.

Statistics distil; they can't show the many faces of the lived change. An address in the suburbs, for example, does not necessarily entail a material turn for the better, as illustrated by a story I covered a few years back. It involved a young Aboriginal couple and their child, a toddler. Neither adult had a paid job. At the time they were living with the woman's relatives in an ordinary suburban street in Alice, where public housing and homes of the middle class sit side by side.

It was winter. The house the young couple were in had had the power cut off; that day there was nothing to eat for breakfast. They had no money; they were hungry and cold. The wife left to look for food. It was about ten in the morning. Pushing their little boy in a pram, she went first to a nearby hostel, looking for an uncle who might be able to help out. He couldn't. So she walked across town for some twelve blocks to a town camp where she hoped to find an aunty. She was told the woman was playing the pokies at a neighbourhood hotel. She stood out on the street and waited. Eventually her aunty came and took her to a supermarket. From there the young woman traipsed back to her husband, with five shopping bags in tow. It was by then about three in the afternoon.[15]

Apart from their stretched resources, the couple's situation also shows the connection between many 'camp dwellers' and 'town dwellers', with members of the same family living some in the suburbs, some in camps, others in supported accommodation. On this day it was a camp dweller who provided material assistance to town dwellers.

Families also move between town and bush communities or their homelands, in both directions. Many remote-living people come into Alice Springs for a whole range of reasons. They stay with family, or in hostels, or sleep rough, for days, weeks, even months and years. In the case of the young couple, the husband came from the Top

End, and they moved to and fro over the great distances between his community and Alice. Things were not working out very well for them, but it is not always so.

Camp living also does not necessarily spell disadvantage, especially following a recent building and refurbishing program (a legacy of the federal government's Intervention / Stronger Futures). Living close to family is highly valued by many and can be difficult to achieve in the suburbs. In one of the camps, a colleague and I met a single man in his thirties who was very pleased to have been allocated one half of a duplex, sharing it with a young relative. He showed us over it, all neat as a pin; he had flowers growing by the front door and trees along the fence. In the past he had chosen not to live in the camp, but he was glad that he did now. Another young relative lived in the other half of the duplex. His sister, her partner and baby lived in a new house on one side; on the other, his two brothers and their families were in two new houses. Out front from all of them, in a refurbished house, lived their ageing mother, cared for by the sister. Across the road an elderly aunt. Formerly she had been 'stressed out' living in a house with twelve adults and five or six small children; now she was much happier living in a new four-bedroom, two-bathroom house shared by two adult grandchildren and eight young children. Her older married daughter was her carer and lived in a house nearby. At the time of our visit, most of the adult men in this family group were employed.[16]

The artist Mervyn Rubuntja lives with his family in Larapinta Valley town camp. He paints the landscapes around there as well as around his homeland, west of Alice, from where he can see Rutjipma (Mount Sonder). Going back to his homeland, or at least spending more time there, is always on his mind, he says, but then he laughs: he is 'too much needed' in Alice Springs, in demand for exhibitions but also as a senior man in his clan, for family matters and representational roles, such as attending land council meetings. 'The land's there for everyone,' he says genially to a largely white exhibition audience. 'We share the land.' He draws the line at sharing it with Chinese mining companies though. If, through the land council, he has to negotiate with mining companies, he says they should at least be Australian. He has visited China, on an artists exchange. He couldn't get over the crowds, the dirty skies, the suspect water, the lack of open space. The experience made him more certain than ever of the good fortune of Australians. And of how he paints, of the strong clear colour he uses to render his landscapes – the way he sees them in unpolluted light.[17]

Margaret Kemarre Turner lives in the suburbs but devotes a lot of time and energy to maintaining her family's links to their homeland east of the town, to their language and traditional knowledge. Widely and affectionately called MK, she has a wonderful memory for faces and contexts and great personal warmth. If she knows you, she will touch your arm or hand or embrace you. She'll express her pleasure in seeing you and ask how you are. One morning, running into her in the town centre, I had something more to say than the usual: I told her our house had burned down. This had happened just two days before and I was still dealing with the shock. She was surprised and thought for a moment: she had seen smoke on the horizon as she returned from her country the night before last. 'Maybe that was your house?' It was possible, the Santa Teresa road passed not that far from where we lived. Then she moved on to what was on her mind that day.

She was worried for a relative, a man who had done long years of gaol time for murder. He had finally become eligible for release on parole. In the Northern Territory for someone convicted of murder, parole can be considered only after serving a mandatory minimum of twenty years. MK grieved for this man, for his decades lost. She so much wanted to see him free, back with family, but there were obstacles. She asked me to come and talk to her with a view to reporting on his situation. I wasn't offended to have my loss gently pushed aside. I had plenty of support and was aware of how widely her responsibilities stretched. We made a time for the day after next.

I arrived at her house in the suburb of Gillen at around 9 am. She asked me to come in, offering me the only chair in the room. There was a small TV set on a milk crate and a small image of the Holy Mother and Child high up on one wall. (MK is a devout Catholic as well as a devoted Arrernte law woman. I have seen her in the little Ngkarte Mikwekenhe church on South Terrace, getting it ready for Mass with flowers and candles; I have seen her returning to town with the traces of red ochre on her skin and her eyes lit up with the deep satisfaction of ceremony.) The floor was mopped and bare. There were two double mattresses pushed against opposite walls. On one a young woman was trying to sleep with her baby. On the other a young couple pulled their heads under the covers; it was mid-winter and bed was a good place to be in the unheated house. I could hear the washing machine going in another room. MK sat opposite me, cross-legged on the floor. As we talked there were people coming and going, all of them young. Sometimes MK spoke to them in Arrernte but never lost the thread with me in her expressive English. I went away with my notebook full, though later she changed her mind about wanting me to do that story at that time.

I was glad to have sat in MK's house after I had lost mine. It was so stripped down to the essentials, it sheltered so many people and she made so much of it possible by her personal authority and generous heart. It put what I needed to do for my small family in perspective.

That year was 2003. I had first come to Alice Springs in 1986, with a television crew covering an off-road race known as 'The Finke'. Then it was just for bikes, now it's for bikes and cars, racing in several categories over more than 400 kilometres of tough desert terrain. It's the town's biggest annual event, attended by more than

10,000 people camping along the race track each Queen's Birthday weekend. Preparation for filming gave me another sharp memory from that early time. A photo of a trackside camp shown to the crew as an example of the high times to expect as part of race weekend: a men-only camp, lots of booze and hilarity and a blow-up life-size doll, a black one. She had a salami sausage stuck in her plastic vagina.

I met another man on that first trip, Erwin Chlanda, a journalist then working as a freelancer, shooting his own stories for television. He'd been in Alice Springs since 1974. He'd raised a family there but was now divorced. I'd not long come from five years living in France, was still smoking French cigarettes; he asked for one. He was Austrian by birth and upbringing; European affinity had something to do with why we were drawn to one another when our paths crossed on the other side of the world. And I was looking for change, for a reason and a place to live back in Australia; he set about showing me that I'd find both with him in Alice Springs.

Erwin started working for our production as a cameraman. The Finke was not our only Outback shoot and he came up with more, so we got to see quite a bit of one another over the following months. One story he pitched as the 'Black Olympics' – the annual sports weekend in Yuendumu. This took me into Aboriginal lands for the first time and put me in contact with remote-living Aboriginal people. It also introduced me to dirt roads and swags, to dry creekbeds and glittering night skies, to making fires, cooking on them, going unwashed for days on end. I loved it. We drove out to Balgo in Western Australia, and from there followed a family group back across the Tanami Desert to Yuendumu. I made friends with a little girl in the group called Pamela, who was travelling with her grandparents. Soon she was spending the days holding my hand. I loved that too. Then the shoot was over and I went away.

On the trip from Balgo we overnighted at the Rabbit Flat roadhouse. I got my first visceral taste of Outback segregation.

Aboriginal drinkers were served through a hatch and had to stay outside; white drinkers, including us, were served in the bar. Some of the time, though, we spent with the Balgo family outside; they were the people we were travelling with after all. It was probably one of the things that got us offside with the proprietor, Bruce Farrands. Another thing was that we drove across his newly graded airstrip to make camp on the other side. The tyre tracks were visible but we did no damage. Early next morning he drove up and told us to clear off or he'd 'shotgun the whole outfit'. He was carrying a rifle and had a reputation; Erwin took him at his word. We bundled everything into the car, but Erwin needed to collect the camera batteries that he'd left on charge in the bar. Before he'd even put the key in the ignition we heard shots. Sure enough, when we pulled up at the roadhouse, Farrands was sitting out front, rifle across his lap, and the charger and batteries were on the ground, full of bullet holes. I felt unnerved, but once we got out of firing range, excitement took over. The place – the whole big desert – in all sorts of ways made me feel alive.

Erwin moved to Sydney, crewing for other shoots we were doing. His teenage son Laurie worked for us too, while his daughter Lesley was finishing school in Adelaide. By the middle of the following year I was ready to come back to Alice Springs to live, with Erwin and in this country. We put my stuff in his trayback and drove. It took four days. I remember listening to a tape of Paul Simon's *Graceland* too many times, and reading AB Facey's *A Fortunate Life*, propped on a pillow on my knees to hold it steady. It was probably a good thing to start my reading about 'the bush' with such a strong dose of optimism. Sometimes I just gazed out the window, enjoying the physical sense of distance rolling out between what I had ever known and what was to come.

I gave up smoking and we had our daughter Jacqueline a year later, our son Rainer after that. Erwin and I worked together in a stringing business, selling news and current affairs to television networks.

He could pilot a single-engine light plane and we often used one to get around the bush. We covered a lot of country that way. In 1994, with Jacquie at school but Rainer just three, we launched into something different, setting up our own newspaper, the *Alice Springs News*, a free distribution weekly with serious editorial ambitions. For Erwin it gave greater rein to his own brand of fearless reporting. For me it started with arts reviewing. I'd made my first forays into film-making and arts writing in Paris; before that I'd studied for a Fine Arts degree in Sydney. There was a serious arts culture in Alice Springs, especially in the visual arts. There were many fine practising artists, black (most famously) and white; they had reasonably good exhibition opportunities, but there was next to no critical culture in the public domain. To my knowledge my reviews were the first of their kind locally.

Over time I expanded into reporting across a broad range of subjects, but years passed before I went into the courts. Court reporting is very time-consuming, and our newspaper didn't have the resources to do it. It was the death of Kwementyaye Ryder in 2009 that finally took me there – too big a story to ignore. It must have been while waiting for an early hearing in this case that I sat through a few hours in the Magistrates Court for the first time. I filled my notebook with the stories. There was nothing I was going to do with them, but there was a lot of detail that my mind hooked on. What people looked like to start with, their demeanour, their physical state, where they lived, how they spoke (if they spoke), what was said for them, who was there with them, what kind of a day they had been having when the trouble occurred, a glimpse perhaps of the kind of life they had lived until then, how relieved or upset or indifferent or dazed they looked when they were told they could leave or were led away to the cells. As a mostly phantom presence there were also victims to think about. Most of the defendants were Aboriginal; most of the victims too. Heavy drinking, despite all the controls imposed on it, was commonplace. Driving offences, including the most serious, were endless. An impression of lawlessness accumulated, though at times it looked like an anarchic resistance to settler law or at least an absence of assent to its dictates. In tandem there grew an impression of an over-policed people.[18] There were many examples of people, particularly women, turning to the law to help, then having to suffer the consequences. They might have wanted, for instance, the violence against them to stop but didn't necessarily want the solutions the law proposed – too late. There was a husband and wife. Each had a 'no contact if intoxicated' domestic violence order (DVO) against the other. Still they would drink together. One night the husband became violent with the wife when a police car passed in the vicinity. She ran for help. She got it, her husband was arrested, but so was she, for being in breach of her DVO. She spent the rest of the night in the cells.

These impressions were bare bones but they were putting together a kind of body, a distressed body, one that I'd not really found a way of getting close to before. In journalistic fashion I could recognise how this 'body' was both shaping the town and being shaped by it – crudely speaking, its distress was turning Alice Springs into a giant casualty ward, while the town's thriving liquor trade was hooking up the body to an alcohol drip. It fitted: the big budget items were in the areas of health and law and order; the big policy debates, enactments and failures were around alcohol control. And yet there was more to these stories than could be subsumed into a generalised framework, rendered only for some kind of foregone conclusion. They had their own life, their own terrible attraction, while within and around them could be glimpsed the larger, painfully changing, occasionally impressive, deeply interconnected life of the town and the region.

My interest sparked, I started to read judges' sentencing remarks. They are a particular kind of literature. The language is often stilted in both its formality and plainness but because no effect is being sought, or only the effect of stern fact and judgment, the stories stand out in their starkness. One in particular. The crime had happened at Whitegate, a camp on native title land to the east of town. It's not a town camp, its infrastructure is much more rudimentary; in official parlance it is 'unauthorised'. There, at the end of a long day's drinking and dope-smoking, a young man had stabbed his wife, the mother of his child, eleven times. Finally her uncle put a stop to it. The young man missed bones and vital organs and she didn't die. The attack was said to have happened with no word spoken.

Eleven thrusts of a knife and not a word. That struck me; so did the young man's background: he had grown up seeing his father being violent with his mother; he had been beaten himself; his father had died in a fight when he was only eight or nine; when he was in his teens his brother died from a heart attack. He had four previous convictions for assault on the young woman. In one incident he had dragged her by the hair along the ground; in another he had struck her twice on the head with a rock. A psychologist prepared a report for the court, describing him as 'an extremely and perpetually angry young man with a short fuse who can rapidly become violent whether drunk or sober. He is highly stressed and anxious due to inter- and intra-family conflict.' I ran the judgment almost verbatim, under the headline 'A short history of violence'.[19]

A fact about this young man, which is true for many but not all of the perpetrators of violence encountered in this book, is that he was not a permanent resident of Alice Springs, but moved between the town and bush communities to the west where he'd been raised. He had boarded in town for three years of high school but went back to the bush after leaving school during Year Ten. He had a job there for a while but at the time of the stabbing he was living mostly in Alice, with his wife's family; he hadn't been employed for four years.

Later I saw a painting intimately linked to this story. It had been made by the artist Rod Moss just a few days before the stabbing. Rod has been painting the Whitegate families for three decades and has published two volumes of memoir about his relationships with them, which have been demanding yet loving and rich.

The painting shows the young man, severely handsome, in a circle of light in the lower left-hand corner of the canvas. He holds a burning candle. The tension in his grip can also be seen on his face. Behind him stands an older man, arms spread to come between the candle-bearer and the small group further back – a young woman watching intently, her full mouth settled into resignation, a child leaning into her, and at her side another young man. There are the attendant dogs and the shadowy shapes of the tin sheds that serve as housing at Whitegate. Last light is receding at the horizon. The painting is titled *And Dark Was the Night*. Rod saw it as depicting 'an internal test of faith and psychic endurance in the face of formidable pressures'. He wasn't to know that the candle-bearer would so soon fail the test nor how he would make the young woman suffer. When Rod learned of the stabbing he wondered at the prescience, in his painting, of her father's 'protectively flung arms'.[20]

At first I hardly noticed the little boy just off-centre in the painting. He clings to his mother, looking past his father into the distance, as if to the future and what it will bring. His face already looks old. I trace him through a few of Rod's later works (his realist portraits are based on photographs). The boy grows taller but doesn't lose that anxious look. There are a lot of children in the wings of the trouble described in this book, although they are rarely visible. I dedicate it to them, to all the children, including my own.

Mine count themselves lucky to have been born and raised in Alice Springs. They loved their childhoods. We lived, still do, on a five-acre rural block and spent a lot of our leisure time out in the bush, walking, camping, often with other families, including Rod's.

It was peaceful and safe and once the children had done their share of firewood collecting, they would be free to go off on their own, make their own fires, build their bush shelters or forts (no parents allowed), go rock-climbing, lizard-chasing, find caves; we'd make them swings, tying ropes into the branches of tall trees; we'd sleep in swags, no tents, even on the freezing nights of winter, a child in with each of us to make sure they stayed warm.

In his art and his writing Rod is unflinching in showing the children of his Arrernte friends not only in the wings of trouble, but sometimes right in the cauldron. A strong strand in his work shows other facets of their lives – their exuberant easefulness in their bodies and in their country, bounding joyfully in the flowing river on a hot day, dogs and family all around, prancing in a band across the landscape, and then in a quieter moment, deeply absorbed by the stories of elder Arranye Johnson, Rod's own fair children sitting there with them. These images are an important reminder of the gamut of life here, even as I embark on telling the stories of trouble that follow.

My children don't need the reminder, they know something of this in their bones. They call Alice Springs 'home' in a way that I can't; they are easeful with it. If home is a place childhood memory makes dear, then for me it is in the Blue Mountains of New South Wales. But now these decades later, it must also be where there is a piece of earth I care for, where I lay my head, have my kitchen, my desk, where my thoughts turn, where it feels like things are happening that are worth remarking upon.

~

So, why these stories of trouble when there are so many other stories to tell?

I've written the basic court reports for the *Alice Springs News*, the who-did-what, the determination of guilt and punishment, but still there is more to say. Violence, often fatal, is at the heart of these stories, yet go into any courthouse and you will find examples of the same. If they demand attention here, it is in part because of their prevalence. The Northern Territory has the worst homicide rate in the country. The national rate in both 2010–11 and 2011–12 was 1.1 per 100,000. In the NT it was 4.8 and 5.5 respectively.[21] For Alice Springs on its own, population 29,000, it can be a multiple of that. For the 12 months to November 2015 the rate was 14. In raw numbers the total from November 2009 to November 2015 was 25 homicides. This compares to a total of 27 for Darwin, a city with almost three times the population.[22]

The NT also has the highest offender rate in Australia for 'acts intended to cause injury': in 2013–14 it was 1,673 offenders per 100,000 persons aged ten years and over.[23] In Alice Springs the rate was more than three times that.[24]

The NT has the highest per capita alcohol consumption in the country: about one and a half times the national figure. Excessive consumption goes for black and white, although higher numbers are reported for Aboriginal drinkers compared with non-Aboriginal.[25] Central Australian consumption showed a modest decline in the first decade of this millennium, but in 2010 Central Australians were still estimated to be drinking at 1.36 times the national level.[26]

The consumption of alcohol, especially at high levels, is a significant risk factor for violence. Nationally around half of all homicides are alcohol-related. Estimates for alcohol involvement in assaults vary considerably, from 23 to as much as 73 per cent.[27] In the NT over the last six years alcohol has been reported by police to be involved in around 60 per cent of assaults, with a modest decline in 2015. In Alice Springs the figure has been closer to 70 per cent, declining to just under 65 per cent in 2015, while around 60 per cent of all assaults are associated with domestic violence.[28] Nationally more than one-third (38 per cent) of victims of alcohol-related violence have also been drinking.[29] In the NT the proportion has been reported as 45 per cent for all victims, similar for Indigenous women, but as notably higher, 56 per cent, for Indigenous men.[30]

The Indigenous offender rate in the NT dwarfs the non-Indigenous rate for crimes of violence. In 2010–11 for homicide it was 36.5 compared to 2.2; for acts intended to cause injury, it was 3007.7 compared to 214.8.[31] Facts far more widely recognised and decried are that Indigenous prisoners make up 86 per cent of the NT prison population and the NT has the highest imprisonment rate in the country: 829.4 per 100,000 in 2014, compared to 185.6 nationally, both figures representing a ten-year high. For over half (53 per cent) of all prisoners in the NT, acts intended to cause injury account for the most serious offence or charge; this is more than double the national figure of 21 per cent.[32]

Indigenous people, especially women, are also over-represented among victims of violence. Between 2013 and 2014 two-thirds (66 per cent) of all assault victims in the NT were Indigenous. The victimisation rate for Indigenous women was more than three times that of Indigenous men, and for almost three-quarters (73 per cent) of Indigenous women the assailant was a family member (for men the percentage was 48.7).[33] As Carly Ingles, a defence lawyer practising in Alice Springs, has powerfully put it: 'The imprisonment rates in the NT, as well as reflecting particular policing and sentencing practices, also reflect the exceptionally high rates that Aboriginal women are victim/survivors of family and domestic violence.'[34]

Their vulnerability to violence is not only established by crime statistics. In a study across the states of Queensland, Western Australia, South Australia and the NT, the hospitalisation rate of Indigenous women for intentionally inflicted violence was found to be 38 times the rate of non-Indigenous women (for Indigenous men the figure was 27 times).[35] Looking at the NT on its own, the rate of hospitalisation for assault of Aboriginal women has been reported as high as 80 times that of non-Aboriginal women.[36]

The numbers, though, are not what prompted me to write this book. I didn't go looking for stories to match them; the relationship was the other way round. The stories I found made the numbers speak to me, just as they opened up with specific substance and depth the worn phrases of popular and policy debates. At the same time the stories do not correlate one to one with the numbers. All of them deal with crimes of violence, almost all being homicides; in all of them alcohol plays a major role; fewer than would be warranted by the numbers are concerned with female victims (although there is evidence of serious violence towards women in the criminal histories of several of the men who have killed other men); the majority of the stories involve Aboriginal victims and offenders; there is only one reference to a crime in which both victim and offender are non-Aboriginal, which is not to say that serious crimes in this category have not been committed in Alice Springs.

In some instances my choice to follow a case was guided by community interest in it: obvious examples, when the interest went well beyond the local, are the killing of Kwementyaye Ryder by five white men, and the proceedings against former AFL star Liam Jurrah for alleged assault causing serious harm. Other cases have had much lower profiles, even in Alice Springs, but in all instances they reflect dynamics that the town and region are grappling with or, it would at times be more accurate to say, are struggling blindly with. The dynamics are not only contained in the facts and circumstances (insofar as we can know them) of the original trouble; they are there also in the court itself, as one stage on which the wider encounter of Aboriginal and settler Australians gets played out, contributing to the shaping of the town and region.

The principle and practice of open court has allowed me a kind of ringside seat for looking into aspects of people's lives that I would otherwise not have had access to. This is a perfect position from which to deliver an 'us and them' story, a prospect repugnant to me.

Empathy alone is not enough to deal with the problem, relying as it does on a likeness of experience, which is sometimes not at all the case. I won't say 'always', however, and this can go for Aboriginal people too. In Central Australia there are many ways in which bonds between people are established across the cultural 'divide', creating families together not the least, but all sorts of other relationships as well. Still, the only way to entirely avoid the 'us and them' dilemma would have been to not write this book. Having chosen to write it, feeling that it was important to do so, I have tried to keep awareness of the dilemma at the front of my mind, and to acknowledge in the writing that I/we may not always really understand what is going on.

Reporting from this ringside seat is also undoubtedly intrusive. One way to avert this problem would have been to either change or not use the names of individuals – and I'm thinking here more of witnesses than defendants. However, it would carry a risk of identities being mistaken and in most instances would be just too complicated and confusing, for me and for readers. Preserving particular identities also accords individuals the basic respect of not being a mere cipher.

The material I gather from the cases is unavoidably framed by legal focus and procedures. It is not the reality of the lived events outside. Even so, between questions and answers, submissions and counter-submissions, charges and verdicts, something of that reality infiltrates – people bring it in, and often quite assertively. Days in court also have their own reality, their own relationships and behaviours and events; they don't just stand in for something else.

My goal has not been to add some other level of judgment to the adjudication of cases but rather, by reporting on them with attention to detail and context, to offer a more nuanced account than is generally available of the kind of trouble faced by not only the individuals and groups involved, but the town and region too. To this end I have sometimes drawn on my personal experience and local knowledge, reported on relevant background events and contexts, and read and talked with other people who have turned their minds to these matters.

For everyone, black and white, much of the lay experience in court is intimidating and mystifying; for many Aboriginal people, living in communities where a distinctly different social order with its own values and law is at least partially intact, and who may speak English as a second, third or fourth language, it is likely to be all the more so. For a long time the courts in the Territory wrestled with degrees of formal and effective acknowledgment of this social context, but in the post-Intervention years, with the judiciary forced by the Commonwealth to turn their backs on customary law even for the purposes of sentencing and bail applications, the message has been that mainstream law is not interested in their difference; it and it alone must prevail.[37]

Recognised or not, however, life as it is lived has a way of leaking into the courts. Commenting on the 'yawning gulf' between court proceedings and the 'subterranean current of traditional law ... alive and kicking in the world of the offenders, the victims, the witnesses – and the interpreters',[38] President of the Criminal Lawyers Association of the Northern Territory, Russell Goldflam, puts it like this: 'Aboriginal people are the mainstream in our courts' – by some 80 per cent. He acknowledges there is no going back to the days when 'our courts gave the nod or turned a blind eye to the use of traditional corporal punishment administered in the bush to settle disputes' but he still sees squaring the circle to work out 'a way of authentically respecting Indigenous culture and law within the moral and legal framework laid down by the High Court and the Commonwealth Parliament' as a fundamental challenge for the administration of justice in the NT. The framework he was thinking about he summed up in this quote from a 2013 landmark High Court judgment, *Munda v Western Australia*:

To accept that Aboriginal offenders are in general less responsible for their actions than other persons would be to deny Aboriginal people their full measure of human dignity … it would be wrong to accept that a victim of violence by an Aboriginal offender is somehow less in need or deserving of such protection and vindication as the criminal law can provide … one of the historical functions of the criminal law has been to discourage victims and their families and friends from resorting to self help, and the consequent escalation of violent vendettas between members of the community.[39]

This tension between the need to do justice to both victims and offenders is a theme common to most of the cases that follow.

~

In the decades I have spent in Alice Springs I have seen the romantic image of a hardy Outback town forced to recede, and with it many of the town's political and social complacencies, its oppressions and discriminations. Though others come in their stead, there has definitely been change, with the old settler ways coming critically under pressure from contemporary Aboriginal ways – both Aboriginal political voice and strength, and the weight of all those things that get summed up as 'Indigenous disadvantage'. In the stories gathered in this book we can see this constant push and pull, willing and unwilling, spoken and unspoken: the courts as crucible through which pass the struggles of this hard and beautiful place.

IN THE MINDS OF MEN

His court appearance was only a mention and likely to be by video link from the gaol. I expected the public gallery to be deserted. As it was, I got the very last spot in the back row. All of the visitors were Aboriginal. The smell of cooking smoke was on their clothing, which suggested to me they either lived in town camps or had come in from the bush.

The defendant, Sebastian Kunoth, entered the small video-link room, wearing an orange t-shirt, prison garb. On remand he was allowed to keep his long hair. It fell in thick waves to his shoulders. His clean-shaven skin was dark and smooth over high cheekbones, eyes dark and deeply set, serious. He was charged with murder. He was shockingly youthful – nineteen years old at the time of his arrest. His wife was twenty-two when she died, three days after receiving severe head injuries at Abbott's Camp on Christmas Day 2012.

As Kunoth sat down he seemed to wave, a low pass of his hand in front of the camera. There was a ripple of response in the gallery. I saw faces all around lifted towards him, smiling. They were not waiting for another case, they were there for him.

The court started its business. It was 8 August 2013. Kunoth's committal hearing had been scheduled to begin the day before, delayed, we learned, by extra matters that the police have been asked to follow up. Now instead of two days, the prosecution asked for three. The magistrate commented about his under-employment that week – no doubt a rare experience in the Alice Springs courts – but set new dates for ten weeks hence.

There had been no discernible reaction to any of this among the visitors or by the defendant. He was told he could go and rose. The video buffering slowed his movement, heightening a sense of submission. His face began to turn from the camera. As one, the visitors raised their arms in a wave to him. There were more eager smiles but not so much as a murmur. As soon as he was gone, they all got up and filed silently from the courtroom.

Who was this for? Kunoth may have been able to see a few of them or at least an impression of their arms raised and moving, but no more than that. Was it for the magistrate, the lawyers – a show of clan strength, of their own judgment of this son, fiercely loved in spite of what he may have done? Was it for themselves – a way of demonstrating their relatedness, of showing support to one another in a time of trouble? They would continue to make their presence felt throughout the hearing. At times they would come close to scuttling it.

The first day of the committal arrived, 28 October, but the extra time had not helped in getting it smoothly under way. Of the original eighteen witnesses, one had died, thirteen had been summonsed but only three had come to court. And of them, only one was present at Abbott's Camp on the night the young woman had been attacked.

The hearing began in Courtroom Four. It is no bigger than a large bedroom and, while there's a witness box, there's no dock. A prosecutions staffer rolled her eyes about it being used to hear a murder charge, having the accused in such proximity to witnesses. Sebastian Kunoth was brought in, wearing handcuffs and civvies – probably the clothes he was arrested in, a sky-blue t-shirt, checked shorts, new-looking runners. In the flesh he was somehow less striking than on the video link. He seemed to have gained weight during his inactive time on remand; his middle was padded and his face had filled out, rendering his expression less intense.

His lawyer pointed out to the magistrate her client's parents. Kunoth's mother stood up, smiling, gesturing to her son. She seemed more assertive than his father. Kunoth takes after him in appearance.

Other relatives squeezed onto the two short benches of the tiny court, among them a man with snowy hair and beard, likely to be Kunoth's grandfather. Tall and broad-shouldered, wrapped in a lumber-jacket, the old man used a walking stick, but this took nothing from his air of authority.

The charge was read, the murder of R Nelson 'on or about' 25 December 2012. We heard the young woman's first name at this time but thereafter, in deference to Aboriginal cultural practice, she would be referred to as 'the deceased' or 'Kumunjayi'.

The first witness was called, Cathy Dean. I recognised her as Kumunjayi's mother. I had spoken to her months earlier on the date of Kunoth's first court appearance. She had dressed quite formally on that occasion, in a draped black dress and gold earrings. On this day she was still wearing black, but her clothes were less formal. Her head was wrapped in a black kerchief and her right forearm was in plaster.

She entered the court and took her seat in the witness box. She had a little girl with her, who looked to be about three years old, with sun-bleached curls, dressed in pink. There was momentary confusion over the child's presence. Kunoth's lawyer said it was not appropriate for the child to be in the witness box – perhaps one of the other grandparents could take her? Kunoth's mother moved forward and attempted to take the little girl by the hand. The child started crying and shrank back behind her maternal grandmother.

Paralysis in the court. The child's cries turned to shrieks. Kunoth's lawyer was furious, pointing out that her client was the father. Whether her concern was for him or the child or both was not clear.

One of the younger female relatives tried to take the child, but the screaming only got louder. The lawyer put an end to it by saying she didn't require cross-examination of this witness. Cathy Dean left with the little girl in her arms.

The next witness was called. He was in custody. Minutes went by. The magistrate looked exasperated. The clerk called down to the cells and reported back that at present there were no prison guards to bring the witness up. More waiting. We would have been able to hear the courtroom clock ticking if it weren't for the child's ongoing screams still reaching us through the walls. Kunoth was visibly upset. He asked his lawyer for tissues.

The witness, Elwyn Brokus, entered the court in handcuffs, which were removed before he took his seat. He looked to be in his mid-twenties, reasonably tall and fit-looking, with the close-cropped hair of a prisoner. In the tiny court the witness box was right next to one of the benches provided for members of the public. Brokus exchanged words briefly with the man nearest to him. Nothing was said about this.

Brokus gave his evidence without an interpreter. On Christmas Eve 2012 he started drinking before noon in 'the Peanut Bar' at the Todd Tavern in the centre of town. Together with the Gap View Hotel, the pub closest to Abbott's Camp, and to a lesser extent the Heavitree Gap Tavern, they were known at the time to conduct an infamous trade, opening in the mornings to sell overpriced drinks to an almost exclusively Aboriginal clientele until closing at 2 pm when their associated bottle shops opened. The three venues were widely known as 'the animal bars'.[1]

Brokus said he drank six schooners at the Peanut Bar. When the bottle shop opened he bought a twenty-four-pack and took a taxi back to Abbott's Camp where he shared the beers with friends. He took a break around five, then resumed drinking around seven. With a mind to the next day being Christmas, just before closing time he went with a friend to the bottle-o at the nearby supermarket where they bought four thirty-packs and a 'four corner' (a two-litre bottle of Jim Beam). Back at the camp they got into one of the thirty-packs. Brokus said he drank half, fifteen cans.

He and his friend were at House Three. A party was getting under way at House Four – loud music, lots of people. When he finished drinking – around ten or eleven, maybe later – he retreated to 'the painting house' to sleep for a while. He woke when a cousin turned up in a car. It was dark except for the beam from the headlights and a streetlight out the front of House Seven. Brokus heard a voice coming from that direction, speaking in Luritja (a Western Desert language). He recognised the voice of Sebastian Kunoth. He could see him dimly, enough to see that he was wearing only shorts. Kunoth was calling out for Lionel Minor: 'Where's Lionel? I want to see him,' was how Brokus translated Kunoth's words. Kunoth was holding what Brokus thought was a stick by his side. Later Brokus saw Lionel Minor, who told him he had had a fight with Kunoth. Brokus knew there was 'trouble' between them, that they were 'enemies', that the problem was 'long-standing'. Minor told him that he had won the fight, that he'd knocked Kunoth out.

The Crown prosecutor pressed Brokus. What did he remember Minor saying about the fight? Brokus hesitated, sighing. Eventually he spoke: 'He said jealousing.'

Who did he say was jealous?

'Sebastian.'

Anything else?

'I can't remember, I think that's it.'

The prosecutor repeated his question. Brokus sighed again, frowning. Looking down, he pressed a forefinger and thumb to the bridge of his nose. He seemed very unhappy. Nothing more was said.

An anthropologist friend explains that 'jealousing' in the Aboriginal domain covers a wide range of reasons for conflict. The reasons include but are not confined to disputes between lovers. The common thread in the other reasons she lists is 'offended entitlement'. The sense of offence, in best-case scenarios, is managed by mediation and negotiation through family networks, even allowing for degrees of violence between parties. But alcohol often escalates 'jealousing' beyond the reach of mediation.[2]

In the criminal cases I have observed I have never heard cultural subtleties like this explored. Any off-the-cuff attempt to do so has been met with a challenge to the speaker's expertise. 'Jealousing' has simply been taken to be an Aboriginal English equivalent of 'being jealous', typically one sexual partner of another.[3]

Brokus's evidence had begun to set the scene: heavy drinking, a party, a jealous fight, a seemingly reluctant witness. That was as close as we got on the first day. The next witness, Glenis Wilkins, was nowhere near Abbott's Camp that Christmas Eve, but she had had some past contact with Kunoth. Wilkins is a non-Aboriginal woman running the aged care service at Mount Liebig, north-west of Alice Springs. This is Kunoth's mother's country where he spent most of his youth.

Although Kunoth's lawyer suggested that a lot of Wilkins's evidence was hearsay, an impression of Kunoth's past began to emerge. Wilkins, who had lived in the community for years, working in a number of different roles, said Kunoth's mother had told her of him smashing things in their home, smoking ganja, getting mad. He had lost a brother when he was in his teens. A visiting mental health worker tried several times to speak with him after this loss but

Kunoth rejected his approaches. Wilkins watched Kunoth getting angrier over the years; she witnessed him in scuffles on the road with family members. She saw him trying to get his little girl away from her mother. She said the mother and child ran to her and she, Wilkins, took the child inside.

There were no further witnesses and it was not even lunchtime. The prosecutor was hopeful that police would find them for resumption at two o'clock. The guard led Kunoth outside but allowed him to linger in the lobby. One by one family members hugged him in silence. The first and longest embrace came from the old man I assumed to be his grandfather.

At 2 pm, the witnesses still hadn't showed up. Warrants were issued for their arrest. I was told by someone familiar with the community that they were hiding from police – they didn't want to speak 'against family'.

Whatever the reason, the prosecutor was up against it. The next morning he told an unimpressed magistrate that while a 'large operation' had been planned for picking up the missing witnesses, police attention had been diverted by a dead body found in the creek.

He meant the Todd River. As I drove home later, I saw the search area on the western bank and extending well down into the dry riverbed, bounded by police tape, with a paddy wagon and a couple of officers stationed there. A small group of Aboriginal women and children watched from a nearby street corner. *ABC News* that evening reported that police were treating the death as suspicious and would continue their investigations into the night.

The hearing moved to Courtroom Three, quite a bit larger than Four, but still without a dock. Kunoth sat sometimes at the bar table alongside his lawyer, sometimes on the bench directly behind her. The prosecutor was able to produce one witness. Stephen Morgan looked to be around forty and seemed unhappy about being there, this impression strengthened by a weeping eye which he continually wiped with a tissue. As he can't read English very well, the prosecutor had read his statement to him and he accepted it as 'a true story'. He spoke through an interpreter.

Morgan had been at the party at House Four with his wife. There were other people dancing and listening to music, among them Kumunjayi and Lionel Minor. Kumunjayi was 'on her own', he said, which I took to mean she was not with Lionel Minor. 'They was all dancing', 'mix up'.

Morgan had been drinking rum and agreed he was 'full drunk' before arriving. At the party he had a couple more beers, standing, watching the dancing. It wasn't that dark when he left, and Kunoth had arrived.

What did you see him do? asked Kunoth's lawyer.

'No, I didn't see that,' he replied through the interpreter.

Did you see him do anything?

'No, I didn't see him, I was full drunk.'

Did you see him holding anything?

'No, I didn't see.'

Did he hit you?

'Yes, just once.'

Did you see any fight between Lionel Minor and Sebastian Kunoth?

'No, I was sitting down in the creek, drinking, I didn't see nothing.'

Did you see Sebastian hit Lionel with an iron?

'No, I was at home asleep.'

Did you see Sebastian with Kumunjayi at any time?

'No, I must have been drunk at that time.'

There was evidence from the police crime-scene examiner and then, 'That's all I've got,' said the prosecutor. He suggested reconvening at 2 pm when 'hopefully there may be more'.

'On what basis are we living in this hope?' asked the magistrate. The police firmly believed that all parties bar one for whom warrants had been issued were in town, said the prosecutor. The magistrate consented to come back at 2 pm.

Kunoth's family had again been in court in good number. They filed out now, but his mother lingered. She was looking quite pleased with the way things were going. She hugged her son and rubbed his back. He was unsmiling.

The prosecutor was out of luck. No further witnesses were produced and the matter was adjourned.

The third day proved a little more promising, but the prosecutor foreshadowed needing a fourth. The magistrate was not happy: three days for a committal was already a lot.

Kunoth attended, again in the same clothes. His mother arrived and had his little daughter by the hand. He smiled at the child. Today she seemed quite comfortable with his mother and other relatives. They slowly filled the single long bench for the public in this courtroom and then began to occupy the bench behind the bar table, usually reserved for legal and court personnel.

The little girl soon became restless and she went in and out at will, pulling at the heavy door until various relatives got up to help and then follow behind to keep an eye on her.

Stephen Morgan's wife, Christine Peterson, was called. She looked around thirty and had roughly cut short hair, possibly following a recent bereavement. Like all other Aboriginal witnesses in this hearing, she looked unhappy to be there. This is not always so. I have often observed Aboriginal witnesses much more at ease in the witness box, including in murder charge proceedings.

Peterson gave her evidence through an interpreter, but it took more than interpretation to get her going. She was very reluctant to accept that she had given two statements to police, one in Alice Springs on

Christmas Day, one three days later at Papunya, a community to the north-west, not quite as far as Mount Liebig. Eventually she agreed.

Are they true stories?

Again, a long hesitation. Then a question came back through the interpreter: 'Is that [the statement] from Papunya?'

Yes, said the prosecutor who told the magistrate that he had read both statements to the witness that morning. Do you remember? he asked her.

She stared uncertainly, finally nodding her head in agreement. At that moment there was murmuring and some movement in the public gallery.

This prompted the magistrate to speak: 'People in court cannot talk and gesture to the witness.'

He asked Kunoth's lawyer if there was a reason for so many people to be present. She said they were members of her client's family. The prosecutor asked for them to be removed. The magistrate enquired particularly about one man who had 'plonked himself' next to Kunoth. That man left.

This seemed to relax Peterson enough for her to agree that the first of her statements, made in town, 'must be right'.

And the one from Papunya, asked the magistrate, is there something in it you don't agree with?

Again she hesitated, looking very worried, holding her hand to her mouth, but she finally accepted it as a 'true story'.

She continued to appear anxious throughout her evidence. It was initially very similar to her husband's – they were drinking, they went to the party at House Four, there were lots of people dancing, including 'Pitjantjatjara mob' whom she didn't know. She saw Kumunjayi there, dancing 'with the girls'. She saw Lionel Minor too, though not in the same room as Kumunjayi.

Was Lionel Minor in the house when Sebastian Kunoth arrived?

No.

Was he there when your husband, Stephen, got hit by Sebastian Kunoth?

No.

Was that the first thing Sebastian Kunoth did, hit your husband?

'He pushed him … just a little push.'

Was Sebastian Kunoth full drunk?

He had been sitting down at House Seven with her and Stephen for a while in the afternoon, drinking Jim Beam. He was 'a little bit sober'.

What else did you see Sebastian Kunoth do?

'He pushed me a little bit. He got angry when he seen his partner dancing.'

What did you see him do?

'He pulled her by the hair, she ran, herself.'

Did Sebastian Kunoth follow her?

'Yes.'

Peterson and her husband went back to House Seven. She saw Lionel Minor there, standing in the dark. Some time 'little bit longer' – time enough for her to be making up a bed – she heard girls sing out for her to call the police and ambulance.

The prosecutor re-examined her on some points. She said when Kumunjayi ran from House Four by herself, Kunoth was still inside. Was he near Kumunjayi or away from Kumunjayi?

'Must be long way, I was drunk too at that time.'

Another couple gave evidence rounding out the picture of the party and the night's drinking but with little more to add. So far, the most damaging eyewitness evidence had come from Christine Peterson but it hadn't gone to more than Kunoth being angry with Kumunjayi, pulling her by the hair, and her running from him.

The prosecutor promised that police were on their way from Mutitjulu with an important witness. She should arrive by 3 pm and her appearance would be followed by the forensic pathologist who had had 'duties' at the hospital. I thought of the dead woman found in the Todd – her autopsy no doubt. By the next day the police were advising that the woman's death was no longer considered suspicious. During the coming week I would encounter rumours around town that there had been a cover-up, that she was battered to death, 'pulverised', that there'd been pressure to cover up because of the obvious failure of the government's reversals on alcohol policy. I would dismiss these suggestions. Monumental evidence of the devastating impact of alcohol is under our noses in Alice Springs day in, day out. Why cover up one case?

I was reading in the back row of the court, waiting for the hearing to resume, when my attention was caught by a defence lawyer saying 'born in 1991'. That's the birth year of my son, Rainer. I looked up to see who this age peer was and found I recognised a childhood friend of his. They had played soccer together and sometimes Rainer would sleep over at his place, enjoying the fun of his large family. Now there he was – a young non-Aboriginal man, educated, a talented sportsman – in the dock. An assault charge against him had been withdrawn, but he was pleading guilty to property damage and disorderly behaviour at a police station. He had been drinking on the night – a bottle of scotch, on his own, topping up with some beers. He got a community work order and had to pay restitution.

When Kunoth's hearing resumed, straightaway the evidence of the 'important witness', Janet Wirri, was more critical than anything heard thus far. The prosecutor clarified a couple of points in the statements she had made on Christmas Day 2012. She told police she could hear a woman screaming and that she walked around the back 'to where that bloke was hitting that girl'. What was the name of 'that bloke'?

'Sebastian,' she said.

There was lighting at House Three, that was how she could see him.

Did you say anything to him?

'Yes … I was telling him to stop.'

Kunoth's lawyer asked Wirri about her drinking on the day. She had started in the afternoon, around 2 pm. Family were shouting her Poker Face Chardonnay – a cheap wine sold in plastic bottles. They had bought four or five bottles from the Gap View bottle shop.

Wirri said there were five of them drinking together, and they finished the wine around 10 or 11 pm. There was also a thirty-pack of beer and a bottle of rum. She drank about four cans of beer on top of the wine.

She was a youngish woman, perhaps thirty years old, solemn-faced in court but with a steady manner. The slogan on her blue t-shirt spelled out in white the word 'Supremacy'.

House Four was hers: 'I pay rent for that house.'

Did you know the people dancing?

Yes, and she named them, quite a list.

Were there people you didn't know?

'Some Luritja people … I only look after the Pitjantjatjara mob.'

Were you full drunk at the party?

'Yes, I was drunk but I could see.'

For a while she danced with 'that woman who passed away'. She didn't know her name. Later her foot was sore and she went outside to sit down on a mattress. Kunoth arrived. He walked through the front gate, past her and in the front door.

After he went in, did lots of people come out?

'Might be, I was outside.'

Later she went in to switch the power off and everyone was gone. Only a couple of women remained as 'company to camp'.

At about this point a man entered the courtroom. I'd noticed him before as he resembled Kunoth's father, his brother perhaps. He walked right up to the prosecutor and appeared to steady himself – he looked drunk. He stepped around him to go and sit alongside Kunoth, who was at the bar table, next to his lawyer. The magistrate told the man that was not a place for the public to sit.

'Sorry,' said the man, 'I wanted to sit next to my son.'

This confirmed that he was Kunoth's uncle. In Central Australian Aboriginal languages, the same word is used to designate your children and your brother's children.

Wirri continued. She was sitting on her mattress when she heard voices screaming. She could see 'them two' fighting.

Which two?

'Them two, husband and wife.'

How far away were they? asked Kunoth's lawyer.

Wirri indicated a distance of around twenty metres, 'a little bit far away'.

The lawyer tried to get more precision on what she saw.

'He was holding her down.'

What else?

'When he was holding her down, that's when I told them to leave it.'

What happened next?

'Sebastian then walked off.'

Did you stay or did you walk off?

'After that I told them to stop it, I came straight back.'

There was muttering in the gallery. It was coming from Kunoth's uncle. The prosecutor wanted him to leave. Kunoth's lawyer turned around and told him to go out. He got up but continued talking quite loudly. In the torrent of Aboriginal speech directed to Wirri I thought I heard the English words: 'I'm going to cut you, you'll be dead.' My jaw dropped and I stared at the magistrate, expecting him to react. He didn't.

But the prosecutor was on his feet: 'I seek that man be arrested ... intimidation of a witness.'

The magistrate was not sure what had been said. The prosecutor asked that the matter be stood down while he made enquiries.

In the foyer the prosecutor spoke to the interpreter. When he was finished, I told him what I thought I heard. Later that day I made a statement to police and they took a photocopy of my notes.

I wondered why the apparent intimidation had been acted out in public. There must have been plenty of opportunity outside the court to put Wirri under pressure, and from the demeanour of some witnesses and the failure to appear by others, it seemed that this might have been happening for them. Was this a further reminder to her or could it be a defiant performance for the court, a challenge to its jurisdiction in this matter?

Following this incident, extended family members were not allowed into the courtroom. Possibly they wouldn't have wanted to listen anyway: the forensic pathologist was giving his autopsy evidence.

Three wounds to the scalp, one in the front, two in the back, had been inflicted on Kumunjayi with 'moderate force' on a scale of 'mild, moderate, severe, extreme'. The fracture to the back of the skull, however, was a 'severe injury', consistent with having been inflicted by a 'large heavy blunt instrument'. (Indigenous women are hospitalised for head injuries at sixty-nine times the rate of non-Indigenous women.[4]) The impact of Kumunjayi's head injury was not 'visible to the naked eye' but had caused subdural and sub-arachnoid bleeding over the brain. There was bruising to the front of the brain – a 'contrecoup injury' – and severe hypoxic damage caused by reduced oxygen supply, most likely the result of swelling caused by the fracture.

At the end of the day, four witnesses of substance were still outstanding, including the most important, Lionel Minor.

It has been a 'frustrating couple of days', said the prosecutor.

'*Three* days,' corrected the magistrate.

The prosecutor nonetheless asked for the fourth 'in the interests of justice'. The magistrate reluctantly agreed. The hearing was adjourned to 12 December 2013, by which time Sebastian Kunoth would have been in gaol for almost a year.

~

Without naming Kunoth, police had announced on 27 December 2012 that the man to be charged over the Christmas Day assault at Abbott's Camp was in custody. They had arrested him during the night at Mosquito Bore, an outstation in the Utopia homelands, north-east of Alice Springs.[5] Kumunjayi was still alive, so at that stage the charges were recklessly endangering life, causing serious harm and engaging in conduct contravening a domestic violence order (DVO).[6] Kumunjayi died the next day, 28 December, and the main charge was upgraded to murder on 31 December. In a statement to media Detective Acting Senior Sergeant Janelle Snigg commented: 'We have been working very hard with a wide variety of agencies in the Domestic and Family Violence sphere over the past twelve months and this death, sadly, proves we have a long way to go before we can put an end to this senseless violence.'[7]

More unusually, the then acting chief minister of the Northern Territory, Robyn Lambley, on the same day made a statement on the death, reported in national as well as local media. In it she expressed her shock that 'despite the mandatory reporting requirement for Domestic and Family Violence in the Northern Territory, women are still being savagely beaten and murdered in domestic disputes'.

She then went further on the specific case: 'I have been advised that family and friends of this woman knew that the victim was being subjected to extreme violence and abuse by her husband prior to her death.' She said she wanted to know how it had happened and to 'form a clearer understanding of what could have been done to prevent it'. Then she muddied the waters by taking aim at the policies of her political opponents, the former Labor government.[8]

A few days later Darwin-based daily the *NT News* reported that Sebastian Kunoth, as the subject of a DVO, had been on the Banned Drinkers Register before it was controversially dismantled by the new Country Liberal government on its very first day in power. The headline ran 'List lapse lets murder accused back on grog'.[9]

In Alice Springs a prominent local commentator, Bob Durnan, took the acting chief minister to task in a piece on the news and opinion site, *Alice Online*.[10] Durnan is an active member of the Labor Party as well as the People's Alcohol Action Coalition and has more than three decades in community development work behind him. He first expressed his sadness over Kumunjayi's death along with the other 'needless deaths of young Aboriginal people over the Christmas and New Year period':

> Another woman, a local town camp resident, was run over by an L-plated motorcycle rider as she lay sleeping on Sturt Terrace, next to the Todd River, in the early hours of New Year's Day.
>
> These deaths came just after a Wallace Rockhole couple and a woman from Hermannsburg were tragically killed in a vehicle rollover three days before Christmas; the rollover followed a police chase near the Ntaria drinking camp 90 km west of Alice Springs on Larapinta Drive.
>
> A Bloomfield Street resident was seriously injured when he was allegedly bashed with baseball bats by two men after he asked his neighbours to turn down their music late on New Year's Eve.
>
> It has been said that alcohol was involved in all these incidents.

Durnan went on to criticise Minister Lambley's implied criticism of the dead woman's family, her omission of the fact that Kumunjayi had taken out a DVO against Kunoth, and her gratuitous politicising of the issues. He also countered her claims that Labor's policies had failed, saying that the rate of killing and serious injury of Central Australian women had declined in recent years and would likely have been higher without the Labor initiatives. The most important of these, he argued, were mandatory reporting requirements, domestic violence intervention teams in hospitals, and some Alice Springs-specific initiatives including close collaborations between police and other agencies dealing with 'actual and threatened violence'.

'Perhaps whilst she has been publicly discounting the mandatory reporting of DV, and abolishing the DV support worker positions which had been stationed in NT hospitals, Ms Lambley is in fact worried about whether the abolition of the Banned Drinkers Register by her government could possibly have been a factor in this tragic situation,' wrote Durnan.

It was this public debate around Kumunjayi's death that initially drew me to follow the case through the courts. Why had her death, more than all the others, attracted such interest? Without suggesting cynical motives, it might have been because it happened in the holiday period, when not much else was going on. The public interest was not sustained as the case progressed. Mine was, though drawn also by the response of Kunoth's family and witnesses to the prosecution of his alleged crime.

~

On the last day of the committal hearing family members were allowed back in. The prosecutor was relieved to finally produce the witness Lionel Minor, Kunoth's 'enemy'.

On Christmas Eve 2012 Minor was drinking at Charles Creek with 'families' – 'beer, Jim Beam, all that'. He had twelve cans and some of the spirit. From there he went on to visit families in

Nicker Crescent, where he had another six cans. He said he was 'little bit drunk'. Next he went to the 24 Hour Store and then to Abbott's Camp where he had more beer. It was dark when he called in on the party at House Four, 'just for a minute, I think'. He named the people he saw there, including Kumunjayi.

Were you dancing?

'No.'

Did you talk to Kumunjayi?

'Not at all.'

Did you stand near her?

'Not at all.'

He said she wasn't dancing but standing next to Christine Peterson. He saw Sebastian Kunoth come in. He agreed that he and Kunoth had been enemies for a long time. He saw Kunoth punch Christine's husband, her brother and 'everybody else' including Christine and other 'ladies'.

'I was talking [to Kunoth], "Don't do that".'

He was outside when Kunoth came at him with an iron bar. He said Kunoth hit him with it on the head. Minor grabbed it and chucked it away, then punched Kunoth, causing him to fall to the ground. Christine then told Minor to leave.

Dwayne Kulitja followed Minor into the witness box. He was also at the party. He was unusually anxious to minimise his drinking on the day. 'Little bit, little bit!' he insisted.

Kunoth's lawyer sought to reassure him: 'I'm not saying it's a bad thing to drink.'

'Little bit Jim Beam, little bit rum, that's all,' he admitted. Then later he had 'four or five cans of beer' but he didn't smoke ganja: 'No, little bit sober, only cigarette.'

He joined in the fighting: 'I was helping.'

He got hit in the face: 'He bin punch me with stick.'

Who?

'My little son.'

This is a classificatory description of their relationship. Kulitja is only older than Kunoth by eight or so years.

The magistrate asked him if the 'little son' was in the room. He pointed to Kunoth.

Someone in the public gallery raised their voice, possibly in anger, but the magistrate ignored it.

Kunoth's lawyer asked Kulitja if he saw Kunoth hit other people.

'All the families,' he replied.

Did you see him hit any women?

'Seen him hit a woman but he stopped. From there I went home and heard news in the morning … I saw it, I told him "Leave it", try to stop my son … She was on the ground but she got up, she was all right. She got up and went.'

Two more witnesses hadn't turned up, but the prosecution had provided enough evidence: the defence accepted there was a case to answer.

Kunoth was ordered to stand trial for murder.

~

Kunoth remained on remand as Christmas and New Year passed, with pre-trial conferences occurring behind closed doors.

On the evening of 20 February 2013 police found a man's body in scrubland off the Stuart Highway just north of town, near where a car had been torched two days earlier. In the following week seven men were charged in relation to the death, six with murder and one with being an accessory after the fact.[11]

The ABC reported police alleging that five men went to New Ilparpa town camp where they attacked the victim. This camp is south of Heavitree Gap; I pass it every day on the way to and from my home in one of the town's 'farm' areas. At the camp the victim was assaulted in 'numerous ways, numerous times ... clubbed with steel bars, tree branches and stabbed numerous times' before being taken in a car back to Charles Creek. Police also believe that the car was set alight as 'a direct result of it being used in the transport of the deceased'.[12]

Rumours flew about the man's ordeal. As if what was being alleged was not enough, I heard some suggestions that he had been decapitated, others that he had been dismembered. A more level-headed Luritja source told me that this was a payback killing for the death of Sebastian Kunoth's wife, although the dead man had no direct involvement in it. The source said he was targeted because he had been adopted by relations of Kunoth, that this adoptee status made him more vulnerable to a payback attack.

In the same week as the arrest of the seven, another man, Everett Wheeler, was charged with the murder of his wife. Wheeler was twenty-seven, his wife was twenty-six.[13] The fatal assault took place just outside the boundary of the Larapinta Valley town camp. This prompted the town camp's service provider and advocacy organisation, Tangentyere Council, to call for an emergency summit to address the rising levels of violence. The meeting descended into chaos when Scott McConnell, the CEO of a rival organisation, was excluded. McConnell, a white man born and raised in the region, headed up the Aboriginal organisation Ingkerreke Outstations Resource Services. Articulate, shrewd and politically active in the Centre, he was openly an ally of the Aboriginal politician Alison Anderson, a loyalty that persisted through her changes of political allegiance. At the time of the emergency summit, having quit Labor while it was still in power and re-won her seat as a Country Liberal, Anderson was the Minister for Indigenous Advancement in the fairly new Country Liberal government.[14] When McConnell was excluded from the summit, Anderson left too. Her walkout captured the headlines, Tangentyere lost the initiative, and for the time being victims of violence dropped from view.[15]

Christopher Kunoth, Sebastian's uncle, accused of intimidating the witness Janet Wirri, was dealt with on 27 February. He had been in custody since his arrest on the day of the incident. Now he pleaded guilty to the charge.

'Once you were able to listen to the tape, you then admitted that it was you and you said those words,' said the magistrate.

His exact words weren't specified, but I later learned from Christopher Kunoth's lawyer that while what was said was threatening it did not include the murderous English sentences that I thought I heard.

'You were drunk at the time,' continued the magistrate, 'but being drunk is no excuse. It provides some explanation but it is the wrong thing to do to …'

He was sentenced to six months, suspended after four – which meant he would be released shortly. To prevent him from further interfering in the trial, he was banned from the town centre on any day that the trial was listed, from approaching or contacting Janet Wirri, and from coming within 200 metres of Abbott's Camp. The conditions would apply for twelve months.

At the end of March Sebastian Kunoth's case was listed in the Supreme Court: he would plead guilty to manslaughter. Murder attracts a mandatory life sentence in the Territory, with a minimum twenty-year non-parole period, so the court very rarely gets guilty pleas to murder charges.

These murder sentencing laws, the most severe of any Australian jurisdiction, are the subject of periodic protest by the judiciary and members of the legal profession. This is primarily because they fail to acknowledge that each murder, like each other serious offence, has its own circumstances, and they remove from judges the ability to take those circumstances into account and thus remove also the discretion to decide on a sentence that 'fits the crime'. The prescribed non-parole period of a minimum twenty years is at least an improvement on the regime prior to 2005, when 'life meant life'. However, the lack of incentive to plead guilty to murder remains, as President of the Criminal Lawyers Association of the Northern Territory, Russell Goldflam, points out:

> When a Northern Territory lawyer acts for a client charged with a serious crime such as rape, the client is advised that if he pleads guilty at an early stage of the proceedings, he can expect to serve a sentence significantly shorter than if he is convicted after a jury trial. The 'discount' given for an early plea is usually around 25 per cent, sometimes higher, depending on the offender's co-operation with the authorities and demonstrated remorse. When the charge is murder, however, no such advice can be given, because of the mandatory life sentence which will inevitably be imposed if the accused is convicted.[16]

Goldflam is aware of only three guilty pleas to murder, out of the scores who have been tried for the charge, and the dozens who have been convicted since the *Criminal Code* came into operation in 1984. As a result, he says, murder trials – 'typically horrendously expensive ordeals' – are far more frequent in the Territory than they need be. On the other hand, when an accused with a reasonably arguable defence is offered a manslaughter plea by the Crown, they often get advised to take it rather than risk losing the trial and being convicted of murder. Thus, some accused 'who have a real prospect of securing a complete acquittal by a jury agree to plead guilty to manslaughter and are given lengthy prison sentences, rather than run the risk of being convicted for murder and getting a life sentence'. Such a prospect applies usually in cases where self-defence is raised.

No such defence had been raised for Sebastian Kunoth but perhaps his drawn-out committal hearing, with all its demands on police and court resources and its anxiety-provoking experience for witnesses, would have been avoided if 'life with twenty' had not been hanging over his head.

On 11 April 2014 Chief Justice Trevor Riley heard the plea.

Kunoth whispered 'guilty' to having caused the death of Kumunjayi, 'being reckless as to causing the death'. Reckless manslaughter, as opposed to 'negligent', is at the more serious end of the spectrum. The court now heard that the critical injury occurred when he picked up a piece of broken concrete – the size of a house brick, weighing around two kilograms – and brought it down on the back of Kumunjayi's head. He also struck her several times to the head with a stick. This was after punching her, pulling her to the ground, punching her a further four times in the back and kicking her twice in the neck and back. A man at the scene pushed him away, but Kunoth punched him in the face and kept going. He dragged Kumunjayi into the yard of House Four. She was sitting on the ground under a tree, with her arms over her head, yelling for help. Bystanders were shouting at Kunoth to stop. After the blow with the lump of concrete, he did. In a strangely deliberate move he put the concrete in the branches of the tree before walking away.

Kumunjayi was bleeding heavily and stopped breathing. Paramedics revived her and she was taken to hospital.

Kunoth gave an interview to police on the day of his arrest, while she was still alive. In it he admitted to punching her three times and to dragging her by the clothing into the yard of House Four. He denied to police striking her with the concrete but now, before the court, he admitted this, confirmed his lawyer.

At the time the two were 'highly intoxicated', according to the Crown facts. Under the terms of his DVO, Kunoth was prohibited from approaching Kumunjayi when he had been drinking or taking other drugs. He had four prior convictions for aggravated assault – three were assaults on her, the fourth on his father.

An eloquent victim impact statement by Kumunjayi's mother, Cathy Dean, was read aloud in court at her request. She invoked her daughter's full name, remembering with delight when she was born 'healthy and perfect'. She grew 'happy in her little world', soon taking to 'being an elder sister naturally'. When she turned five, though, things changed. Dean did not say specifically but it seemed that she had separated from the children's father, when she sent them to her mother's sister in Papunya while she began a job in Alice Springs. From Papunya, their paternal grandfather took them to visit his family in Port Lincoln and Adelaide and refused to send them back. Dean said she had to get help from authorities to have them returned. Six months had gone by. She then took them to Broome to visit her father's side of the family, an important bonding time 'after being forcibly separated'. (From the way she expressed herself and the life she described, it seems Dean was well experienced in moving between Aboriginal and non-Aboriginal contexts.)

As the family moved around, Kumunjayi 'adapted quickly', 'her world and knowledge expanded'. For secondary schooling she was sent to board at Kormilda College in Darwin. Her circle of friends grew and she connected with family members there. Then, at age sixteen, she 'took a turn that would later have a devastating effect on all our lives' – she met Sebastian Kunoth.

Dean said she knew from the beginning that the relationship was not good. The couple's two children 'witnessed the growing violence which was becoming a normal part of this man's way of having control over their mother'. She worried about the impact of this experience on them: 'Will [Kumunjayi's son] become another statistic and continue the cycle of violence?' she asked. 'Will her exquisite daughter too become another number in the books of domestic violence statistics? Will she allow this to happen to her as she grows to become a young woman?'[17] She remembered Kumunjayi as 'precious, smart, beautiful' – 'I am now left with utter sadness and desolation, constantly asking why, how.'

Kunoth's lawyer told the court that her client 'accepts full responsibility for what he has done … he understands the devastation wreaked upon his own children and the family of the deceased'. She said he would have liked to apologise from the dock but she understood that the family 'did not wish to hear that'.

'I can understand why they would not,' said the chief justice.

The lawyer went on. In the six weeks before his crime Kunoth had been in Mount Liebig doing a pre-vocational mechanics course and was 'significantly alcohol and substance free'. This was in contrast to his life whenever he was in Alice Springs and able to get hold of alcohol and marijuana. He had consumed both in large quantities on Christmas Eve and when he got to Abbott's Camp he was 'feeling a bit paranoid and was very, very drunk'. He wasn't expecting Kumunjayi to be there. He caught sight of her through the window of House Four. She was dancing. In the room he also saw a man from a Mount Liebig family with whom there was 'long-standing animosity'.

This man must have been Lionel Minor. Here perhaps we could see Kunoth's actions in the context of the broader meaning of 'jealousing', his sense of grievance in relation to his wife mixed poisonously with his family's wider grievance, the cause of which his lawyer would shortly allude to.

'In his paranoid state he thought she had become entwined with his arch enemy,' she continued, although 'there was absolutely nothing at all [between them] based in fact, beyond being in the same room and enjoying the company of other people'.

Kunoth was raised by both his parents. Together with other family members, they were present in the court for the plea, as they had been for most of the proceedings. His first language is his mother's, Luritja, but he also understands his father's, Alyawarre, and has strong connections to his father's country in the Utopia homelands (a 600-kilometre drive away). He went to primary school in Mount Liebig and at Yipirinya, an Aboriginal primary school in Alice Springs, and he did some secondary schooling at Yirara College, a boarding school for Aboriginal students, also in Alice. He could speak English but couldn't read and write it. He had never had a job.

When the family was in Alice Springs they mostly stayed in town camps. There from an early age Kunoth witnessed the day-to-day problems with alcohol and the use of violence (though never between his parents) to resolve arguments. It led to 'the unfortunate deadening that occurs, that people seem to accept as the normal course of life, you can hit your wife and stab someone, and that just happens all the time', said his lawyer. She and Kunoth had talked a lot about it.

Kunoth had a twin brother as well as an older sister and brother. When he was fifteen his twin became ill and died. For any family and any brother, but perhaps especially a twin, it would have been a terrible loss. It was aggravated for the Kunoths by the feud they had with the other Mount Liebig family. This had its roots in a conflict over royalty payments (due on land affected by mining). The conflict escalated after the death of Sebastian's twin, for which the other family believed they were being blamed – accused of causing it by 'black magic'.[18] There were violent altercations between them, including one in a suburban street in Alice Springs.

The Kunoth family retreated to Utopia to get away from the trouble and the easy access to alcohol and drugs that had become a problem for Sebastian. On a Utopia outstation his older brother, at nineteen years of age, committed suicide. The only place the family could come back to was Alice Springs. Sebastian was the only surviving male child. He felt 'a degree of responsibility due to that', said his lawyer, and wasn't handling it at all, succumbing to the town's 'drinking and drug culture'.

I thought back to the signs of great affection from family members for this young man – the smiles and waving when he appeared by video link, the long embrace by his grandfather, his mother rubbing his back. I had thought of it as a silent assertion of the strength of their family bonds and law, but perhaps it was also that they were dreading more loss for him and themselves, hoping against hope they could hold it off by cleaving to him.

I always listen to these scant biographies of the offender with interest. It is a professional hazard to look for connections between one fact and another, between the crime and a life circumstance. Favourite candidates are past trauma, addictions and un-employment. These are part of the picture that all general studies of the antecedents to offending behaviour point to, according to criminologist Don Weatherburn. He more precisely lists the four key factors that stand out in relation to the onset, seriousness, duration and frequency of involvement in crime: poor parenting (particularly child neglect and abuse), poor school performance / early school leaving, unemployment, and drug and alcohol abuse. The data makes clear, he writes, that Indigenous Australians fare much worse than non-Indigenous Australians in relation to all four, which insidiously 'form a vicious circle'.[19]

The flagship rehabilitation effort of the Territory government was focussed on employment. They called their scheme 'Sentenced to a Job'. A job wouldn't hurt Sebastian Kunoth, I thought, although I recognised the reflex of a culture imbued with the work ethic. There's not necessarily consensus on this among Aboriginal people, perhaps especially not when they are traditionally oriented. In her book *Iwenhe Tyerrtye: What it means to be an Aboriginal person*, senior Arrernte woman Margaret Kemarre Turner discusses 'how you yourself came to be, to grow, wherever you came from'. She sums up the ideal like this: 'To be joyful and loving, to share our food, to guide and care for our loved ones, to understand, to speak only in the correct way to people, and to bear in mind always our kin relationship and obligations. That's respect. That's the way our Rule is now, and that's the way it's always been.' Although Kemarre has worked a lot in the course of her long life, in particular as a teacher and interpreter, departing from that 'Rule', for instance by prioritising paid employment, is not possible, she warns:

> Trying to break away from your relationships as an Aboriginal person, to achieve something in a good job or something like that, well, you're that same person always, and you can never really change anything. And it wouldn't achieve. You might think it can achieve something for yourself, but it wouldn't. You'll always bend. And you wouldn't know where to start. Well, you might start, but [no] further things will hold you.[20]

Anthropologist Nicolas Peterson makes a similar point when he writes doubtfully of the prospects for secular assimilation of people living in remote communities where the basic elements of Aboriginal social and economic organisation are still intact, albeit facilitated by welfare entitlements: 'a person's identity is not defined by a career with the demands of working in the market, but as a kinsperson doing work for kin'.[21]

I would think about this again when a few months later I read the sentencing remarks in the case of Everett Wheeler, the man who killed his wife in February 2013, just outside Larapinta Valley town camp.

Wheeler too pleaded guilty to the reckless manslaughter of his wife. He was sent to gaol for ten years and six months, with a non-parole period of seven years. Similarly to Kunoth's wife, Wheeler's wife died as a result of blows to the head causing subdural haemorrhage and swelling to the brain, although the attack by rock and/or star picket was more frenzied, with eight of twelve scalp lacerations going down to the bone. Like Kunoth, Wheeler was drunk at the time and had a long-standing problem with drinking. The assault also had its roots in a jealous argument but in this instance it was the wife who was jealous. Her furious insults, rooted in her suspicion of his wandering eye (and probably her knowledge of his polygamy), provoked Wheeler to the point of snapping. Justice Brian Martin accepted this, regarding Wheeler's crime 'as a serious example of manslaughter under provocation accompanied by an intention to cause serious harm'.

Unlike Kunoth, Wheeler had a strong work history. Despite limited mainstream education he had worked as a builder's labourer for local government since he was eighteen. On the job, repairing and refurbishing houses around Hermannsburg, an Aboriginal community 130 kilometres west of Alice Springs, he had developed skills as a carpenter. He had a role model in his father who had worked most of his life as a grader operator.

Wheeler's mother died when he was only three but he was brought up by grandparents and aunts on both sides of the family. They were described as 'very supportive' of him, as Kunoth's family clearly were of Sebastian. But Wheeler's family were said to not have had any problems with him over the years, which was not the case with the Kunoths. Wheeler was initiated (there was no mention of this regarding Kunoth, though he may well have been) and he had helped others 'with traditional matters'. His maternal grandfather is a Lutheran pastor in the strong evangelical tradition of the Western Arrernte; Wheeler went to church weekly and continued to attend services in gaol.

In contrast to Kunoth there was no suggestion that Wheeler had been exposed to excessive violence, but like him he had meted it out when drunk. He had four prior convictions for assault on four separate women, with all of whom he was in an intimate relationship, some of them at the same time, and two of them, mothers of his children. On all four occasions he had been drinking.

'Your problems are not just with alcohol,' Justice Martin said to him. 'You have an anger management problem and it is an anger which is too readily aimed at the women with whom you are in a relationship.'

In his essay 'A long weekend in Alice Springs' the psychologist Craig San Roque writes of a man he knows 'in some obscure desert camp at a midnight hour', taking up an axe in a drunken rage and slaying his sleeping mother-in-law, having mistaken her for his wife.[22] After serving his time, the man, now sober, asks San Roque, 'What made me do this thing? What is in alcohol which makes me murder?' San Roque returns the question, 'What is it in your mind which lets you murder, and in such a manner?'

There's no neat answer. San Roque wrestles with the question as does the man. Then he broadens it: 'What is it in our brain that allows us to take axes to our sleeping women and murder our mothers-in-law? From what strange nubs in the minds of men do these repetitive, autonomous acts of violence unfold?'[23]

In the essay San Roque is ruminating on the operation of a 'cultural complex' in Alice Springs. At an individual level 'sharpness of awareness or self-awareness drops', he writes.

At a mob level it is as though a population becomes dazed and addicted to a state of intoxication. A somnambulism operates which simultaneously silences voices of contradiction and revelation. I can discover where a complex is operating in my own backyard by noting when and where I am most inarticulate. When I am fascinated by something but am almost unable to think about it and almost unable to speak.[24]

'Alcohol problem', 'anger management problem': not only sentencing remarks but the broader discussion, public and private, of the 'social problems' of Alice Springs are replete with these very limited articulations of what we are living in.

San Roque takes us to greater depth. With long years behind him of working in Central Australia, he enters the matter more imaginatively: 'The modern town of Alice Springs is built on the site of a mythic event, a rape and a dog fight ... Serious dark men whisper the details, adding sometimes that this event is always being lived out in this place. You can't get away from it, they say.'[25]

The European settler population also can't get away from the legacy of the colonial effort, with the rifle as its major 'tool', Christian righteousness becoming a kind of terror, 'eating other people. Or their country.'[26] San Roque is looking at the ways cultural mentalities are shaped. They may be resistant to change, though not impervious. It takes hard mental work, however, and so many obstacles can get in the way, as he describes in the context of his professional visit to a nineteen-year-old woman in the Alice hospital's psychiatric ward. She is 'trapped in cannabis-induced psychosis' and also sniffs petrol. He evokes her home place:

> An Aboriginal community much like any other – badly designed, badly built, badly serviced, subject to idiosyncratic heroes and missionaries of one ideology or another, an expression of the pathology of the Australian psyche ... Despite the hundred or so funerals which she has witnessed, the spectre of death is not a deterrent to her sniffing. Grandmother's voice rolls away with wind-blown plastic bags. There is no substance in this so recently created nightmare. Nothing stops her drift. A decomposition of self.[27]

It was after the suicide of his older brother that Sebastian Kunoth met Kumunjayi at a football carnival. Kumunjayi was only sixteen.

Kunoth was already the father of a child by another woman, a daughter now five years old. His daughter with Kumunjayi, that little girl with her sun-bleached curls, was now three, and their son, four.

He accepted that the court had previously given him an opportunity to 'deal with [his] demons'. He had entered residential rehab but was evicted when he was caught smoking cannabis. His probation officer then told him to go to Mount Liebig to do the pre-vocational mechanics course, and Kunoth put his name on a waiting list for a job with the shire.

His lawyer admitted that his prospects of rehabilitation were 'concerning' but argued that he was still very young and 'should not be written off'. She said he had developed some insight into his behaviour. She spoke of an incident during the committal hearing when his children were in court with Kumunjayi's mother. The children were 'cowering from my client', she said: 'That made him very upset when he realised his own children were scared of him. He understands why they were.'

She spoke of 'other violent matters occurring which some people believe can be attributed to this incident … possibly other people losing their lives as a consequence of what has gone on'. An allusion, no doubt, to the alleged payback killing of the man whose body was found off the north Stuart Highway and possibly to other incidents not widely known.

'He carries that with him,' she said. 'Nothing he can say will bring her back. He accepts he has to do his time … accepts he needs to be punished and other people need to be deterred.'

Chief Justice Riley sent Sebastian Kunoth to gaol for nine and a half years. He gave a discount for the 'utilitarian value' of his guilty plea from what would otherwise have been imprisonment for twelve years. The non-parole period was set at seven years.

There was the usual outcry that the sentence was inadequate. It was 'a joke', 'a slap on the wrist', 'a living shame for the entire community', wrote the commenters in the *Alice Springs News Online*.[28] They would probably have agreed with the new prosecutor, fresh in town, when he argued that Kunoth's offence was 'one of the most serious matters of this type to come before these courts'.

'Nowhere near it,' the chief justice cut in. 'Unfortunately and regrettably. This is a dreadful crime but we've seen much worse.'

TROUBLE AT THE TURN-OFF

The prospect of a trial for manslaughter hanging over the head of Grace Beasley was ended by a *nolle prosequi* – the proceedings were dropped. The young woman was from Ali Curung,[1] an Aboriginal community closer to Tennant Creek than Alice Springs, although the committal hearing had been held in Alice. The deceased was also a woman, a mother of three children, and also from Ali Curung.

If Aboriginal women die violent deaths in disproportionate numbers in Central Australia, it is predominantly at the hands of Aboriginal men, very often their partners.[2] Here seemed to have been an instance of one young Aboriginal woman dying at the hands of another. This is what had drawn me to the case. Although the numbers are small, the female imprisonment rate is rising in the NT, and the rate is the worst in the country; it involves Aboriginal women disproportionately; it is at least partially explained by an increase in serious violent offending; and the violence is not only being perpetrated by women against their violent male partners – women are often victims too. The nature of the violence, however, even if fatal, tends to be less severe.[3]

In this case, the *nolle* meant that faces would not be put on the numbers: Grace Beasley must be presumed innocent. It was not surprising that the case against her was dropped. Evidence of a criminal act had looked weak by the time all witnesses had been called. What remained seemed to be evidence of something else, not criminal but heedless, unprotective – of self and others.

A few weeks before Christmas in 2012, after a long day's drinking, four carloads of people ended up at the Ali Curung turn-off. Most of them lived at the community and were family or knew one another. Most were drunk or very drunk. Grog was running low, arguing and jealous fights broke out. And a young woman died. Grace Beasley was charged with her murder.

Cause of death: a subdural haemorrhage. The only external injuries were some superficial abrasions, but the autopsy revealed that she had suffered four blows to the head, including two 'relatively minor' blows to the middle of the face. One or all of them may have contributed to the haemorrhage, the Alice Springs Magistrates Court heard. The forensic pathologist from Darwin, Dr Terence Sinton, is a dry man, precise in manner with an appearance to match, bespectacled, clipped beard, trim figure. He would not rule out the possibility of the blows resulting from a fall. They could also have been caused by kicks or punches but were the result of a 'mild' degree of force (on a scale of 'mild, moderate, severe, extreme'); there were no broken bones.

The post-mortem blood alcohol reading was .224. While subdural haemorrhage is always associated with physical trauma, this 'acute alcohol toxicity' may also have contributed to the woman's death. Her self-defence abilities would have dropped, Dr Sinton explained; and there may have been 'a synergistic effect' between the toxic chemical delivered direct to the brain tissue and the trauma from the blows.

The magistrate asked about this conclusion: a .224 reading in the context of the Northern Territory did not seem exceptional.

Dr Sinton could not agree: the mere fact that alcohol abuse is widespread in the Territory does not mean that such a level of toxicity is any less a problem for the individual.

The dead woman, B Nelson, had a pretty French first name but after the charge was read was referred to only by the bereavement term, Kumunjayi. The medical facts of her death stood starkly crisp alongside the foggy recall of its witnesses. After two and a half days, and with the most damaging evidence recanted, the Crown conceded that the charge of murder against Grace could not be maintained: no evidence remained that could indicate an intention on her part to kill or cause serious harm to Kumunjayi.

Grace was visibly relieved even though at that point she was still ordered to stand trial for manslaughter, whether negligent or reckless. She was an attractive young woman in her mid-twenties, bleached strands at the front of her dark shoulder-length hair, an eager manner. She nodded compliantly as the bail conditions were read out: she was to reside at Ngukurr (on the Roper River in the Top End, far from home) and report weekly to police there. She was not allowed to be in Ali Curung, nor Wycliffe Well or Wauchope – licensed roadhouses on the highway that cropped up frequently in the evidence – and she was not allowed to drink.

Her mother, Lucy Jackson, was waiting at the courtroom door. Grace smiled and waved at her to come in. Lucy, a tall confident woman, was employed at Ali Curung as an Indigenous Engagement Officer, liaising between government and the community. Later she was described to me by someone who worked with her as 'a tower of strength and common sense'. She was acting as surety for Grace and was ready to set out immediately with her daughter on the long journey to Ngukurr.

The day of 'the trouble', as it was always referred to in court, was a Saturday. In the early hours Kumunjayi woke her partner, Lance

Brown – she was having difficulty breathing. The nurse called to their home wanted Kumunjayi to go to the clinic, but she refused. Neither would she go later in the morning, saying she was fine, according to Lance. Instead the couple set off for the Wauchope roadhouse, together with four of Lance's relatives. A first round of five six-packs of VB was bought and drunk, followed by two more before they moved on to Wycliffe Well.

When I listened to the evidence in court I had only a vague memory of both roadhouses from previous journeys north. Next time I went that way I took more notice. Wycliffe Well, less than twenty kilometres from the turn-off to Ali Curung, struck me as the more congenial place. The roadhouse has long traded off folklore about local UFO sightings and looks like a cheap movie set, painted black, with ghostly white aliens and spaceships looming among the planets and stars. Colourful cut-outs of alien heads stand up along the roofline, and in the forecourt a little green man has alighted from his spaceship. Across the way a bridge crosses the creekbed, shading its soft sand. There was no-one there when I passed through, but a forty-four-gallon drum provided as a rubbish bin suggested the area was used as a spot to gather. Grog litter further into the creek confirmed it. A line of young gums grew along the bank, something of a screen between the creek and the roadhouse. Nestled into rocks were some faded artificial flowers, usually markers of a place where a person has died. Another Kumunjayi perhaps.

Wauchope is further north. Most of the players in these events spread their purchases between the two roadhouses, to get around the different restrictions on quantity and product sold to any one customer.[4] Take-away liquor was prominently advertised at Wauchope and purchased through a hatch opening onto the front verandah. Apart from the concrete picnic tables out the front, there was no obvious place to drink it nearby, no shaded ground or concealing screen of trees. The door into the bar bore a sign saying 'SEX', followed by the unoriginal 'Now that we have got your attention, NO shoes, shirt, service.'

At Wycliffe Well in the mid-afternoon Kumunjayi and Lance crossed paths with five women from Ali Curung, including Grace, her sister Gabrielle and their mother, Lucy, sitting in the creek sand under the bridge, making their way through four six-packs. They'd started drinking around lunchtime. Lucy 'growled' Kumunjayi and Lance away. They were 'already drunk', she said, and were asking for more grog. In the late afternoon Lucy set off in her grey car to replenish supplies at Wauchope. She bought another eight six-packs and went back to her daughters at Wycliffe Well.

Another group from Ali Curung turned up. They were in a little white car that was missing its front windscreen. On board were Reggie Nelson with his wife, Roslyn Egan, as well as Verena Friday and Jason Lane, all of them young people, at a guess in their mid to late twenties. In court as witnesses confirm their identity, their occupation is usually mentioned. In this case, the only person mentioned as having an occupation was Grace's mother, Lucy. It is possible, even likely, that none of the young people had a job. (Labour force statistics collected by the Australian Bureau of Statistics for the 2011 Census show that of seventy-three males at Ali Curung, aged between fifteen and thirty-four, only sixteen were in the labour force and they included five who were unemployed; of 105 females, only fifteen were in the labour force, including four who were unemployed.)

Jason had bought his companions grog at Wauchope, four six-packs, one each, and then topped up with two more 'sixes'. Verena and Roslyn had each had about ten beers by the time they got to the turn-off later that night. Verena said Reggie bought himself rum and Coke at Wycliffe Well though Reggie denied this. His wife, Roslyn, said they bought one 'Woodstock' (a bourbon mixer) and were trying to get some rum without success. The white car needed fuel and Reggie asked Grace's sister Gabrielle to help. She agreed in return for more grog.

It's easy to get lost with all this accounting for a day and night of seemingly prodigious drinking. The point in court, of course, is to cast doubt on the recall of the witnesses. A friend long familiar with remote Aboriginal communities suggested to me, as a general point, that a loose grasp of maths by Aboriginal witnesses means they overestimate the quantities being consumed. The sociolinguist Diana Eades also describes 'numeric specification' as uncharacteristic of Aboriginal ways of speaking English.[5] However, anthropologist Maggie Brady, who has worked primarily on alcohol misuse (as well as other substance abuse) since the 1970s, describes as 'enormous' and 'disastrously high' the quantities consumed by the two-thirds of Aboriginal drinkers who do so at harmful levels, with binge drinking – more than eight standard drinks per session – the distinguishing feature of Aboriginal drinking styles in rural and remote areas.[6]

Overestimation may be occurring with some witnesses in this case but not all. Some gave their evidence in very confident English and it was clear that they had significant experience of the so-called mainstream. The evidence on drinking was consistent; the day seemed to have started light-heartedly but by evening they were on a collective bender.

Gabrielle travelled with Reggie's group to Wauchope to get the fuel for his car; Lucy followed 'to make sure Gabby was all right'. Gabrielle bought more grog, eight six-packs, keeping four and giving four to Reggie's group. Then they all drove back to the Ali Curung turn-off. Gabrielle didn't know how many cans she'd had but she felt drunk.

At Wycliffe Well, meanwhile, Kumunjayi and Lance had had a sleep in a red Ford belonging to Lance's uncle. Now Uncle asked them to go back to Ali Curung to pick up other family to join the party. By Lance's account, they went back and forth a few times between Ali Curung and the roadhouses before ending up at the turn-off. The dangers of drink-driving seem not to have been given a second thought that day – by them or anyone else. Lance was a 'little bit' drunk, after eight or nine cans of VB. There was no sign yet of anything going badly wrong for Kumunjayi. She too was a 'little bit' drunk, he said, but she was still walking and talking.

The turn-off is a cleared area by the highway in a landscape of orange dirt and thin scrub, with a bus shelter, a solar light and two mailboxes. One, an old water tank, is decorated with Aboriginal motifs in now fading paint, a project by 'Senior Boys' years back. A sign across the highway says there's a police station at Ali Curung, twenty-two kilometres to the east, while another announces that the community is a restricted area under the *Liquor Act*. It is illegal to possess or consume liquor there without a permit (a small sticker adds 'No room for racism'). Fines, vehicle forfeiture, gaol terms apply. So people finish their sessions at the turn-off. Grog litter – cans and broken glass – is scattered on both sides of the highway. There are abandoned thongs, food wrappers, a dirty nappy. Nailed to a fallen burnt tree trunk is a small sign bearing a single word: 'Jesus'.

On the night of the trouble some people stayed in their cars, listening to music. Grace and Gabby were talking together outside their mother's grey car. Others gathered in or near the bus shelter. Reggie and Roslyn wanted to get going but discovered Reggie's car had a flat battery. Lance helped them try to push-start it. Tempers were getting frayed. The couple started arguing and Reggie smashed the rear window (the front windscreen having already gone).

Jason, who had been with them much of the day and had bought them grog, got into a fight with Reggie. 'He was jealousing me for his wife,' he said. That fight was finished when another broke out, between Grace and Kumunjayi. Grace had been Lance's girlfriend before Kumunjayi; now Grace was asking Kumunjayi for beer. Kumunjayi got angry with her, 'jealousing her for Lance', said Reggie. He saw Kumunjayi pull Grace's hair, but he didn't see Grace pull in return. Gabrielle and another woman locked Grace in Reggie's car – 'Finish.'

Jason saw the two women pulling each other's hair but he didn't see or hear anything else – he was busy, hungry (in court, he rubbed his stomach) and looking for more beer, which he got from Gabrielle. Some of the women were drunk and sleepy, others were off in the bushes going to the toilet, or they simply didn't see.

Gabrielle said Kumunjayi grabbed Grace by the hair only once, swearing at her – 'dirty cunt' was how the abuse was translated, to Gabrielle's embarrassment. Next thing Kumunjayi was lying on the ground. Gabrielle didn't know how she ended up there.

Lucy saw Lance run towards Kumunjayi. She thought he must have hit her, but someone was in her way, blocking her view. A couple of people were pulling Grace away.

Lance told Kumunjayi, 'I don't want to see you fighting,' and said he pulled her away. He did it 'gently' and took her to sit down. Reggie, though, said Kumunjayi fell and hit her head – a 'soft' impact. After that she lay still.

Lance then 'took off', said Gabrielle. When he got back, Kumunjayi was inside Reggie's car. She could no longer move by herself. The car wouldn't start and its rear doors couldn't open, so she had to be dragged through the front. Lance said he held her tight and asked a couple of the women to help.

Lucy's grey car by now also had a flat battery, so they moved Kumunjayi to the red car. It wasn't working either. Finally they tried a blue car, the women pulling her in from one side, Lance pushing from the other. Kumunjayi was still talking a bit, saying she wanted to go home and that she was feeling sick. According to Dr Sinton, as the bleed on her brain started she would have had a terrible headache, lethargy, changes in levels of consciousness and vision impairment.

Once Lance and the others got her inside the blue car, they realised she wasn't breathing. They drove straight to the clinic at Ali Curung. A subdural haemorrhage is not always fatal, but for Kumunjayi it was too late.

~

A drinking camp at a turn-off; inordinate distances driven and time spent to get grog; smashed and broken-down cars; a dying person in the hands of drunk and unfocussed countrymen: it all had echoes of another more notorious case in 2009, in which two men died, one of them slowly and not inevitably. Six men were sent to gaol for their manslaughter.

That turn-off was also on the Stuart Highway, some 120 kilometres north of Alice Springs. An unsealed road leads a further eighty or so kilometres west to the Anmatyerre community of Laramba, a restricted area under the *Liquor Act* like Ali Curung. The ban on drinking may well keep some trouble out of communities, but the drinking camps that spring up in response contribute trouble of their own. They are not always at turn-offs; they might be at boundary gates, for example. In Alice Springs they form on vacant lots, behind trees by the road, in the river, in the hills. Their essential feature is to be outside of community, out of sight and mind of the state, places brought into being by gatherings drenched in alcohol and, sometimes, by trouble that cannot be ignored.

The six men in the Laramba case pleaded guilty. I reported on the sentencing in the *Alice Springs News*, emphasising the role of alcohol. The article began: 'Five out of six were drunk on the night. One out of six is a reformed heavy drinker, sober on the night. Two out of six are alcoholics. Four out of six had parents who were alcoholics or heavy drinkers. Two out of six are married to alcoholics and these couples have had children. The two victims of the six were drunk at the time of their deaths.'[7]

Around a table with friends in Alice Springs I brought up Émile Durkheim's notion of 'anomie' in relation to these stories. Was this a way to describe what the stories seemed to be evidence of? Durkheim and sociologists after him use the term to describe the unruliness arising when normative checks on individual behaviour have broken down.[8] One context in which this happens is in the wake of serious upheaval in the social order. In his famous work on suicide Durkheim writes, about the absence of these checks, 'Those who have only empty space above them are almost inevitably lost in it, if no force restrains them.'[9]

Everyone at the table worked closely with Aboriginal people. One was a prominent figure in the substance misuse arena. He reacted to the word 'empty': 'I don't think the space is empty. People are hanging on strongly to their culture. It really hasn't broken down.' His work focus was centrally on reducing supply – of inhalants and alcohol – to give the culture a chance.

Also at the table was an Aboriginal man of broad bicultural experience, who worked in community development. He latched onto the idea of space, but rather than empty he saw it as 'not available, not free'. Ali Curung is on Kaytetye country, he pointed out, but people from other groups – Warlpiri, Warumungu, Alyawarre – had been moved off their country and been living at Ali Curung since the late 1950s. Kaytetye people no longer control it. The space is 'governed' by the groups avoiding one another.

Or the space is so highly contested, suggested an anthropologist at the table (a woman with long experience of working with Aboriginal-run night patrols in remote communities), that social relations readily descend into chaos, particularly for people not on their own country: 'The lid comes off.'

A man, a defence lawyer, saw this as the point. The root of

anomie is *nomos*, Greek for 'law'. An anomic space is literally 'without law'. People displaced from their own country are living outside the traditional boundaries of their law, while drinking camps, quintessential no-man's lands, are at an even greater remove.

Yet such spaces are not exclusive to Aboriginal people, argued the community development worker: 'It's just like Aussie teenagers going to Bali for Schoolies. Bali is outside the boundaries of their law.' He also wanted me to consider that a celebration may have been under way before things started to go wrong. Some people may have had a good week, for example, and had the capacity to shout the drinks and celebrate: 'We don't get a lot of chances to do that.'

The lawyer, who has seen more than his share of alcohol-driven devastation, countered that celebration is not the only explanation for heavy drinking: 'A lot of people want to drink because they want to shake off inhibitions and express things like the anger that is bubbling up inside them.'

The community development worker was shaken by the stories. He said they reminded him of the film *Once Were Warriors*. 'But is your book just going to show countrymen getting drunk and doing terrible things to one another?' he wanted to know.

No, I told him, there are some drunken white men too.

I felt properly challenged on where I was coming from. I know grog wreckage is not exclusive to Aboriginal people although it is easy to lose sight of that in Alice Springs. In a later conversation with this Aboriginal man, I told him about my heavy-drinking, likely alcoholic grandfather, my father's father, who turned to drink, as I've been told, when he couldn't get work in the Great Depression years. I told the man how hard the drinking made life for my grandmother and her children, how pitiable it made my grandfather, what a long shadow it left. He listened; he hadn't expected this.

'We don't hear enough of these stories,' he said.

He spoke about work among a small group of self-directed

men towards revitalising Arrernte ceremony as a way of return to reciprocal responsibility and civility. He was also interested in the civility of a different kind of drinking culture. There had been a gathering one afternoon at his workplace. A colleague, a woman, had gone out and bought delicious things to eat and drink. He enjoyed a crisp cold white wine and foods he had not tasted before.

'We need to learn more about these foods, about drinking like this,' he said.

It was the psychologist Craig San Roque's table that we had been sitting at, not for dinner, just for talk, some of us sharing a bottle of wine. That night San Roque said little, though more than any of us there he had turned his mind to the enchantment of drunkenness and the havoc it can wreak. In the mid-1990s he was asked by a Warlpiri man, the late A Japaljarri Spencer, about whether Europeans had a Dreaming story for drunkenness. Could such a story be passed to Aboriginal people to give them power over its destructiveness? This enquiry led San Roque to years of thinking, research and creative collaboration with Japaljarri and others including Barry Cook and Elva Abbott Cook Nangala who ran a unique rehabilitation setting at Injartnama Outstation near Hermannsburg. One culmination of this collaboration was the theatrical project *Sugarman*, a representation of the myth of Dionysus, revealing the seminal formulations of the ancient Greeks who had 'developed alcohol and observed its effects on the human being' – 'the delights of drunkenness and the destructions'. *Sugarman* was staged first at Injartnama and later in Alice Springs. San Roque describes the experience in an essay titled (after Nietzsche) 'A rebirth of tragedy'.[10]

'Seen, as if in Euripides' mirror,' he writes, 'was the repetition of the nightmare epic of Dionysus dismembering the state of mind of a community. Once it was ancient Thebes; now it is Hermannsburg, Kintore, Yuendumu or Alice Springs.'[11] And the list could go on.

He reports the reaction of three Aboriginal women who watched *Sugarman* at Injartnama: 'It makes us think. It opens our minds. We didn't realise that you whitefellas could cry, that you could feel sorry too …'[12]

The revelation for them was about white people; it seemed these women did not then see the story as relevant for Aboriginal people, for the possible 'evasive action' they could take. Yet many Aboriginal people do take such action. In his memoir *The Town Grew Up Dancing* Wenten Rubuntja describes his own epiphanic experience: 'I used to live in the pub … I was mad about drink. I was mad about beer garden. Take-away flagon. Down the creek and do the job in the creek, painting job. Nothing but drinking, drinking, drinking.' He brought it to a halt in the Stuart Arms one night in 1976, when his 'ideas collapsed'. (The image brings to mind San Roque's 'dismembering'.)

'I didn't know what to do. I didn't know what to think. My mind was exhausted,' continues Rubuntja. 'Only had *ngkwarle* [this Arrernte word for sweet foods is also used for grog]. I had three flagons with taxi … When I sat down, I saw the ground turning – coloured and spinning – like something had turned it around. Then I smashed this *ngkwarle* – I broke the three bottles … Then I been just give up. Just finish. Then land rights start … Then I been work for country.'[13]

Margaret Kemarre Turner has long held a strong line against grog. In early 2000, in a piece for the *Alice Springs News* looking at what the new millennium might offer, she made these comments:

It is killing whole families. I had a good family life destroyed by alcohol. I'm not a drinker and that's how I survived with my children. I had a bad breakdown, a lot of hurt, I fixed it myself. Aboriginal people were introduced to alcohol with no education in our lives about it. We are not made to be drinkers, that's what I tell my children. But if you're sixteen, seventeen, eighteen without many skills alcohol can seem the only way for making friends. Alcohol causes problems between Aboriginal and non-Aboriginal people. I've lived in many houses in Alice Springs and I've never had any problem with neighbours because I've kept an alcohol-free house. I never let anybody bring even one can of beer through the gate where I pay my rent. I even kept a grog-free house at Charles Creek camp. I was very strong, I fought it myself. I'd say no even to my family. I still loved them, I would say you can come and do your washing, do your cooking but I won't let you drink in my yard.[14]

These accounts of resolve by individuals are not as exceptional as might be assumed, although we don't often hear of them in the unending debates around alcohol policy (nor in the courts – as where there's trouble, more often than not there's grog). While thinking about this I reread Alexis Wright's *Grog War*, an account of the campaign in Tennant Creek in the decade 1986–96 to rein in the town's rampant grog trade. It was led by the Aboriginal-controlled organisation Julalikari Council, whose determined focus was on licensees' responsibilities. Their fight was ultimately victorious. It had a profound impact on Tennant's social and political dynamics and initially on the town's alcohol consumption (a 22.5 per cent decrease),[15] though this attenuated with time and the hard-won 'grog free day' is no longer.[16] What particularly struck me, however, were the reported statements of elders in the original 1986 Beat the Grog meeting:

'Wangangu [drink] can ruin your life ... Gotta think about your future ... Kids see you walking round [drunk] where future going to be ... Who is going to look after your children – 'cause you'll be finished. No way to treat your kids: "Here, twenty cents, go away!" No way.'

'I feel sorry for whole lot, wangangu can ruin your life. Finish up in hospital or coffin ... My kids bin see me change. I don't drink no more. Two years back I'm drinking all day all night. Three, four in morning start drinking. Think of your kids, your future. Wangangu can ruin your whole life.'

'Don't blame other people, blame that grog. Your body don't want to take that grog. You force it. Don't let that wangangu lead you; it's got a hook on your nose. Don't let it lead you, it'll lead you straight to the graveyard.'[17]

And so on for several more speakers, striking expressions of individual processes which have the powerful advantage of autonomy. It is notable that these elders all advocated abstinence. We too readily overlook that there are proportionately more abstainers (including ex-drinkers) among Indigenous people than in the general population; as many as one-quarter to one-third of the adult Indigenous population abstain, according to some surveys cited by anthropologist Maggie Brady.[18] She suggests that one reason people may choose abstinence, rather than moderation, is because 'it is easier not to drink at all than it is to moderate intake in an environment in which the sharing of alcohol and cash is expected, and in which there is continuous, brutal (psychologically and physically) and all-pervasive pressure to consume without restraint'.[19]

In interviews she conducted, one of the main reasons individuals gave her for why they drank heavily was angry resistance to discriminatory drinking laws (which certainly exist in effect if not explicitly in the Northern Territory). Reaction to personal trauma was another. And then there was one that is often overlooked – fun.[20] It's true that many of the gatherings described in witness evidence in this book, including in this chapter, seem to have started out convivially.

Writes Brady: 'Drinking is a valued part of the social world of Aboriginal, as well as other Australians, and has become enmeshed in Aboriginal cultural mores just as in Australian society as a whole.'[21] Gathering to drink and sharing supplies is used to express relatedness.

While getting 'full drunk' can also offend relatedness, leading to violence, anger and other abuses, it can be seen as a 'socially acceptable excuse' for such offences. She suggests that paralytic binge drinking may at times also be a way of escaping 'the persistent and crushing expectations of so many relations and the obligations that should be fulfilled'.[22]

In my question to friends around San Roque's table I was drawn to the idea of an 'empty' space in relation to the drinking with seeming abandon of Aboriginal groups in Alice and in the bush. Brady, however, offers a further explanation located within an 'occupied' Aboriginal social space, and that is 'non-interference' in another person's business, even if that business is doing harm. Further, 'the right to drink is considered incontrovertible, and it is not often subject to common sanction'.[23] Brady says this is the case in Central Australia and the Western Desert regions, where groups of drinkers, for example, are 'largely autonomous and not subject to any sanction or jurisdiction by others in the community'.[24]

~

A large group of drinkers had gathered at the Laramba turn-off just before Christmas in 2009. Headed that way from Alice Springs in the early evening were six men in a red Ford Falcon. Four of the men were armed: one with a hunting knife, another with a tyre iron, and two had nulla nullas (heavy hardwood hunting and fighting sticks). They were intent on confronting men in Laramba over a long-running feud between their family, the Gibsons, and another family, the Dixons/Staffords. In particular, they were going to look for the brothers Adrian and Watson Dixon and another man or men, whom they held responsible for an assault on Travis Gibson some months earlier, which had broken his jaw.

This injury had added to other recent afflictions suffered by the Gibson family. Two Gibsons had been killed in a car accident in 2008 in which a Dixon/Stafford family member was also seriously injured; another Gibson (formerly married to a Dixon) had not long before died from cancer. Why these sad events meant that the Gibsons had been forced to leave Laramba was never made clear to the court. The assault on Travis Gibson now seemed to have become the central grievance. Yet when he was in hospital after the assault he had been visited by the Dixon matriarch, Margaret Heffernan, in the company of his aunty, Beatrice Gibson.

In court Beatrice was asked why her family had left the community where she had lived 'forever': 'Them Dixon mob' had told them to go. Why? 'Because they enemy for us, because they hit Travis.' She hadn't seen the assault on Travis but said she knew the names of the culprits. They were the Dixon brothers – Adrian and Watson – and two Staffords.

Following the assault, Beatrice had left Laramba and gone to live at an outstation not far from the turn-off, but a 'mix of Mount Allen and Laramba' people came there and threatened her with nulla nullas. She and other Gibsons then fled to Alice Springs.

On the day of the trouble she was at Hoppy's Camp, a town camp in Alice on the banks of Charles Creek. She was playing cards when her brother Rodney Gibson turned up in the red Ford. It was their father and brother who had died in the 2008 car accident, and another brother who had recently died from cancer.

Rodney, a reformed drinker, was doing the rounds to gather up a party to avenge the assault on Travis. Beatrice didn't want him to go, taking 'all the drunks', but he ignored her. Travis had already agreed to go. Now Rodney found Travis's brother Luke drinking in the camp. Next he found Thomas McMillan, a member of their extended family, drinking in the creek. The three then went to a house in the suburbs to find Gilbert Dixon, Travis and Luke's uncle on their mother's side. As his name suggests, he is also related to the 'enemy' family, a 'cousin-brother' to Adrian and Watson.

Gilbert and his mother, the Dixon matriarch, Margaret Heffernan, had tried to settle the feud without success. Gilbert had also tried to take himself, his wife and children as far from it as possible, moving for a time to Adelaide, until both sides persuaded him to come back and help resolve it.

Such was the network of ties between the accused, the deceased and their families that the court had difficulty getting an interpreter for the committal hearing. Anmatyerre was the main language needed and its native speakers who worked for the interpreter service feared they might have a conflict of interest. So the court resorted when necessary to a non-Aboriginal interpreter specialised in a related language. When he found it hard to understand some Anmatyerre witnesses, the court fell back on English.

Benedict Stevens did not need an interpreter. He had previously worked as an Aboriginal Liaison Officer at the Alice Springs Hospital and gave his evidence in confident English. He said Gilbert (his cousin) had not wanted to join the revenge party. He'd been planning to go out to Hermannsburg to be with his kids for Christmas. As a present for them Benedict had given him the hunting knife, later used in the killings.

On the day of the trouble Benedict had gone to Margaret Heffernan's house to collect his laundry. It was still in the machine when he got there, so he hung it out to dry before sitting down to have some beers with Gilbert, Lawrence Rice (a Gibson relation), Margaret and her husband, and other family members. Then the men in the red Ford arrived. Thomas and Luke were singing out to Gilbert: they 'needed some hand with this trouble they had'. Rodney was 'peeping' around the corner of the house. Why he was reluctant to show his face was not explained, but he too was 'forcing' Gilbert to come along. They goaded him: 'You're afraid. Them boys out there reckon they can kill you. They're going to beat you up.' They kept on at him until Gilbert agreed to go. He'd had seven beers by this time.

Benedict tried to stop them. 'Hey, you're not a fighter,' he told Thomas. 'I've never seen you fight before.' Thomas turned on him with a boomerang in his hand: 'You want a piece of me as well?' Benedict was probably right though, because when it came down to it at the turn-off, Thomas did hang back from the fight.

Benedict told Gilbert: 'You'd better stay, brus. These guys don't help you out when you go to gaol.'

But Gilbert had already decided. He told Luke to get the sheathed hunting knife from his mother's bag. He put it on his right thigh, showing Benedict: 'How do I look, brus?'

'I said, "All right, you look all right" and then off they went, "Let's go." And that's when Lawrence followed them too.'

Benedict painted a sympathetic picture of Gilbert, but drinking brought out another side of his character. During sentencing it was revealed that he had an extensive criminal record, including fourteen convictions for aggravated assault, all of them occurring when he was drunk. He had been raised in a household of heavy drinkers – both parents as well as uncles and cousins. He became an alcoholic early and his wife was also an alcoholic; they had met through drinking. He had been through rehab twice and had relapsed after both programs.

When the six – Gilbert along with Rodney, Travis, Luke, Thomas and Lawrence – set out for Laramba they had a good supply of grog on board: on a trip that takes around two and a half hours they drank one and a half cartons of VB beer and a cask of moselle between them, all but the driver, the reformed drinker Rodney. This was on top of the grog they'd had during the day.

It was dark when they got to the turn-off and found the drinking camp in full swing. The spot is in fact beyond the turn-off, a couple of kilometres west of the junction with the Stuart Highway, down a dip, so not readily seen by passing traffic. Does the place have a name, a witness was asked. 'Just "the turn-off".' It's not the only place where a drinking camp will form along the Laramba road but it has the advantage of being closest to the Aileron roadhouse on the highway, where drinkers can go for limited resupply.

~

As Laramba is a mostly Anmatyerre community on Anmatyerre land, I wondered to what extent the idea of 'contested space' applies here. Every community has its own history and circumstances, of course. Those with a mix of displaced people, like Ali Curung and Papunya, can be particularly fraught, but contest or at least negotiation is the name of the Aboriginal social game. 'Australian law is codified while Aboriginal law is highly negotiable,'[25] says my anthropologist friend. Degrees of violence can be tools in the negotiations. Traditionally the violence was moderated by the group, by the right people within it, as defined by their relationship to the various actors.[26] Despite the drunken chaos on the night in question, this might help explain some of what would happen. And critically, some of what would not happen.

~

Adrian and Watson Dixon – the presumed assailants of Travis – were not at the turn-off, but that did not deter the Gibsons. Five of them got out of the red car, its high beams lighting up the scene. They were brandishing their weapons and swearing. 'Come on, we have that fight now,' Travis's brother Luke was saying in Anmatyerre. Most of the drinkers took off into the bush, but some were too far gone to move. One man was on the ground, 'just sitting, real drunk'. Travis punched him on the side of his head. Luke knew this man well from playing football with him and tried to pull Travis off. No such sentiment prevented him from taking after a young woman, not yet eighteen, with a nulla nulla in his hand. She managed to get away. S Glenn and D Tilmouth were easier targets.

Glenn, thirty-three years old, was 'full drunk' – out to it in the front seat of a blue Holden sedan. Travis and Luke began punching him with clenched fists and hitting him with nulla nullas. Gilbert, the knife in his right hand, stabbed him on the inside left thigh. The knife partially severed an artery.

(Gilbert turned himself in at the Alice Springs police station the next day, saying, according to police, 'I had an argument with my nephew at Laramba and I stabbed him.' Custody was likely now the safest place for him to be.)

The men turned to a white Mitsubishi, smashing its windows, slashing its tyres. It belonged to one of the Stafford men thought to have assaulted Travis. At some point Gilbert gave the knife to Lawrence Rice. Travis and Rodney found a woman hiding in the bush. She was a cousin to Glenn and Tilmouth and was Watson Dixon's niece. Rodney was yelling and threatening her with the tyre iron. 'You now,' said Travis and punched her in the mouth.

Tilmouth, forty-six, was next. He was 'charged up' but standing, supporting himself against the blue Holden. Travis, Rodney and Luke began punching him in the head and face and hitting him with the tyre iron and nulla nullas. He struggled with them. Then Lawrence stabbed him twice in the thigh. One strike fully severed an artery.

Tilmouth was Neil White's father-in-law. Neil was 'half-shot' but he had wanted to jump in and defend Tilmouth. Thomas McMillan – he whom Benedict had said was not a fighter – was Neil's uncle, and held him back. This was the only time Thomas actively involved himself. When he and the others drove off, Neil went to Tilmouth. He was no longer speaking. Neil tried to stop his bleeding with a rag.

One of the drinkers who had been hiding in the bush returned to the scene. He saw the 'old bloke [Tilmouth] stabbed and cars all smashed'. Kwementyaye Glenn was still moving and talking and bleeding, but Kwementyaye Tilmouth had 'already gone'.

When police caught up with Rodney Gibson in Alice Springs the next day, he was in the red Ford driving north along Charles Creek. Rodney pulled over, got out of the car and walked back towards them. The arresting officer made notes of their conversation. Rodney spoke of Benedict Stevens giving the hunting knife to Gilbert at his mother's place. The officer continued: 'I said, "Were you talking about payback for them blokes then?" He said, "Yeah, got the wrong ones. Wanted to pay back Watson Dixon." I said, "Those dead are the wrong ones?" He said, "Yeah, should be Watson."'

~

While the knifings were happening at the drinking camp, back at Laramba Peter Stafford was on duty for night patrol, a job he'd been doing for fifteen years. He'd started his shift around six and was due to finish at eleven, but all was quiet because people had gone to the turn-off to drink. He'd gone home and was asleep when a knock on the door woke him. It was Adrian Dixon, one of the brothers sought by the marauding Gibsons. He is a prominent man at Laramba, at the time a shire councillor and later elected council president. He told Peter that his son's car had been smashed up at the turn-off.

Peter jumped into the night patrol car, with Adrian and two other men. It was 'a little bit raining' but by the time they got to the turn-off the rain had stopped.

The smashed car was there of course, as was Kwementyaye Glenn, Peter's brother-in-law, with 'a big cut on his leg': 'He wouldn't talk. He was moving, not talk.' Kwementyaye Tilmouth, whom Peter described as a brother, was 'dead already, I think … I tried to wake him up'.

~

Stabbing to the thigh has an unusually high incidence in Central Australia. Some much-quoted research examined the 'epidemic' of stabbing admissions at the Alice Springs Hospital between July 1998 and June 2005. In that seven-year period the hospital had 1,500 stabbing admissions. This compared to 395 at the Royal Prince Alfred Hospital (RPAH) in Sydney over an eleven-year period. The research noted the high incidence in the Centre of stab injuries to the thigh (38 per cent of the total), in contrast to the RPAH injuries, which were most commonly to the head, chest and abdomen. The targeting of the thigh was put down to 'traditional punishment'. The authors of the research had even noted a 'particular pattern' of traditional stab injuries: 'medial thigh to kill, posterior thigh to permanently disable, and lateral thigh to punish'.[27] (In 2008 the head surgeon at the Alice Springs Hospital, one of the research authors, reported that the stabbing rate had declined dramatically, suggesting that this was due to tough new alcohol restrictions).[28]

Dr Sinton conducted the autopsy on the Laramba men. The fatal wound for Tilmouth had been just above and behind the left knee. Acute alcohol toxicity also contributed to his death. In the case of Glenn the same left popliteal artery was cut. Dr Sinton described the position of the wound as 'anteromedial' but the cut was only partial: 'One could easily surmise a lesser rate of flow from a less severe cut,' he said with typical caution. 'This wound was not inevitably fatal.' Medical treatment within the hour could have been life-saving. What about two hours later? asked the defence.

'If he was still alive, one would have to say on first principles that this man could still have been saved,' replied Dr Sinton.

How difficult would it have been for a layperson to treat him? asked the magistrate.

Dr Sinton's reply was unusually emphatic:

'Difficult, I mean this is quite terrifying. It's terrifying for medical people to see people bleeding to death in front of you ... First off, you have to make the diagnosis, that's a really important thing, to know what you are doing before you do it. So I imagine, I have to say, for lay people this would be one, terrifying, and two, quite mystifying.'

If the people around Kwementyaye Glenn felt terror, it did not galvanise them into action. For some, a countering fear might have been that if he died while in their care, and if they were in a particular relationship to him, they and their families might be held responsible for his fate, as payback practices could have it.

Peter Stafford said he tried to get Glenn into the night patrol car but couldn't. Peter suffers from back problems. What the other men might have been doing to help was not clear. They did, however, manage to get Kwementyaye Tilmouth into the car. Peter estimated that he was at the turn-off for about twenty minutes: 'We were trying to wake him up first.' But a man who had done some first aid training 'touched him for breathing and pulse, and no pulse'.

The drive from the turn-off to Laramba normally takes about an hour, but now Peter hurried. He drove straight to the house of one of the clinic sisters, but she told him she was not on duty. Whether he told her of the nature of Tilmouth's injuries was not spoken of in court. He then went to the other sister's house, about three kilometres from the community. She followed him to the clinic. It was getting on to midnight.

Back at the turn-off taking care of Glenn fell to Andrew Campbell. Earlier that day Andrew had driven to Alice Springs. He was still feeling a bit drunk after a session at the turn-off the night before, but wanted to get more grog. Kwementyaye Tilmouth had been with him, worried about his son who'd been fighting. Kwementyaye feared there would be more trouble. They went looking for his son at Hoppy's Camp, at Warlpiri Camp, around town – 'Nothing.

Couldn't find him.' So they got their four thirty-packs of VB and went back to the turn-off. Kwementyaye's last day – full of worry and grog.

When the carload of Gibsons arrived at the turn-off on their rampage Andrew had been in the scrub, settling a dispute with his wife. The first he knew of the trouble was when a couple of Stafford men fleeing the scene came running towards him. Then he saw his car being driven through the scrub. It was dark, no moon, 'a bit cloud'. Andrew held up a cigarette lighter to signal where he was. The injured Glenn was in the passenger seat. Andrew took over at the wheel and drove out of the scrub back to the turn-off. His blue Holden was not in great shape. 'Somebody killed that windscreen,' as Peter Stafford put it, and the back window too, but the car was still running.

The night patrol vehicle Peter was driving was a Hilux dual-cab with a cage on the back, similar to a police paddy wagon, and in reasonable condition. Why not put Kwementyaye Glenn in there too, Peter was asked. The back seat was taken up by two men holding Kwementyaye Tilmouth, he replied. The reason for not using the cage was lost in translation, but Andrew's blue Holden was a good option because it was 'a bit lower' – easier to lift Glenn into. Perhaps Glenn was a big man; this was never specified. When Andrew stopped at the turn-off Glenn managed to get out of the car: 'He had to crawl.' Andrew saw there was a lot of blood on his leg. He tried to put him back in but couldn't lift him. So he left Glenn on the side of the road, in the care of two women and a man, while he went to Laramba for help.

There were a lot of people at another drinking camp further west. Andrew stopped to let them know about the trouble. His passenger told them to run: 'Two person was stabbed.'

When they got to Laramba, Andrew went to see Glenn's wife, who told him to go get night patrol but they had already left. Before going back himself Andrew had to drain some fuel from another car. At the turn-off Glenn was finally lifted into Andrew's car. He was asking for water. 'So I gave him water,' Andrew recalled.

Halfway back to Laramba on this second trip Andrew stopped again. He could see Adrian Dixon driving towards him. Adrian put more fuel into Andrew's car, but Andrew's mind was on getting back to the highway: 'I had to follow those people [the attackers],' he said. So Adrian agreed to take Glenn in Andrew's car back to Laramba, while Andrew took Adrian's car and headed east. At the highway he joined five carloads of people waiting for the attackers to return – 'to do the revenge'. The attackers, though, had fled to Alice Springs.

If only Kwementyaye Glenn had been taken on Andrew's first trip back to Laramba. Why wasn't he? the defence asked. 'Feel like really heavy,' Andrew replied. The defence reeled off the names of people on the scene: 'There was enough people to lift somebody up, wasn't there?' Andrew's reply skirted the question: 'They was look after him.'

One of the men who finally helped get Glenn into the car had tried to stop the bleeding while he was still lying on the ground: 'I took my shirt off … wrap his leg.' Another man in the car said he kept talking to Glenn, asking if he was okay. Glenn was talking back, he could sense the urgency – he was telling Andrew to hurry up.

When Andrew stopped and swapped cars with Adrian, Glenn again opened the car door. This time he fell out. He 'was singing out … like in pain, you know'. There was a lot of blood. According to Dr Sinton, the fact that Glenn was still able to open the door could be read as a good sign for him at that stage.

Glenn was 'thirsty and sleepy', said one of the passengers, but 'we didn't have any water to give him so we let him sleep'. They had crossed the cattle grid just outside the community when they realised that he had stopped breathing.

The nurse on call was at the clinic with the body of Kwementyaye Tilmouth. Peter Stafford had told her there was 'another one coming in, the same'. When the blue Holden arrived she went out to check Glenn. She found him slumped on the floor between the back and front seats. His pupils were fixed; there was no apex beat, no respirations. He was dead. She went back inside to call police and ask whether to move his body. The next thing she knew the car had taken off, with Glenn still inside. He was not returned until some three hours later.

Questioned on 'that rather extraordinary sequence of events', the officer in charge of the investigation said most witnesses weren't sure how the car got to Andrew Campbell's place, but someone eventually noticed Glenn's body in the back seat and took the car back to the clinic.

~

It was Gilbert Dixon who bore primary responsibility for the death of Glenn, found to have caused it recklessly, while his five co–offenders contributed to it negligently. There was a similar finding against Lawrence Rice and his five co–offenders for the death of Tilmouth. All the offenders expressed remorse and signed a letter of apology written to the families of the dead men.

Around 250 people live in Laramba.[29] In two years the community had lost at least four of its men to unnatural causes; now six more were taken out of circulation for years to come. Gilbert Dixon was sent to gaol for thirteen years, Lawrence Rice and Rodney Gibson for eleven, Travis Gibson for ten, Luke Gibson for nine and Thomas McMillan for six. Their non-parole periods ranged from six and a half to three years.

The people who so ineffectually helped Kwementyaye Glenn but did not save him and then forgot they had his dead body in the back of their car committed no crime.

RACE IN THE DOCK I

The courthouse lobby was full of young white men, some of them with wives or girlfriends. I was used to seeing it full of Aboriginal people. There was chat and laughter, more like a pub after three on a Friday. They were all waiting for the first court appearance of five of their peers accused of murdering an Aboriginal man. It couldn't be more serious. And their intention was serious, I realised. This was a show of solidarity.

In the crowd I recognised the mother of one of the accused, talking with a man who might be his cousin or brother. I remembered this accused as a boy – about twelve or thirteen, whip-thin, sun-bleached hair curling on his neck, big dark eyes thickly lashed, black leatherette jacket, straddling his BMX bike, waiting for my son to come out and ride with him.

Court staff were taking extra chairs into the courtroom, but there wouldn't be enough. When the doors opened the white crowd surged in, me and other journalists with them. The public gallery benches rapidly filled from the front. By the time the Aboriginal crowd came in there was space only in the back rows. Many had to leave, but one woman was brought forward and given an office chair to sit on. She was dressed in black, hair peppered with silver

closely cropped in a sign of mourning, mouth shut tightly on the
urge to cry, eyes glistening. She was the dead man's mother, the
artist Therese Ryder. I had spoken to her at an exhibition years
earlier, about one of her paintings in Eastern Arrernte country – a
line of hills that seemed to dance.

At the edge of one of the benches was the mother of my son's old
friend, clutching her bag to her chest. The last time I had seen her was
about four years back, in a homewares store where she worked at the
time. We would have chatted about our boys. Her son's looks came
partly from her – the colouring, the cheekbones, but not the eyes.

Police had issued a comfit of a man believed to be 'linked to the
murder' six days after the body had been found. It was published the
next morning by the *Centralian Advocate*, taking up a good part of the
front page: 'WANTED', ran the headline, 'Do you know this man?'[1]
He was described as in his late teens or early twenties. That put him
in the age group of my son. I showed him the paper. 'He looks like
a Spears,' Rainer said after a while. 'Not necessarily Josh, but one of
them.' It was the eyes, large and very dark. For the rest he wasn't sure.

On the same day the police had also released, with permission
of the dead man's family, his name and a photograph of him. This
was unusual. First names and images of Aboriginal dead are often
avoided during mourning. 'He is Donny Ryder of Alice Springs,'
announced Detective Senior Sergeant Lauren Hill. She expressed
her 'deepest condolences' to his family and friends. The photograph
showed Ryder sitting outside a bistro with a schooner in his hand,
smiling broadly, flirtatiously, looking straight at the camera. He was
stylish – trimmed moustache and beard, black Akubra, black t-shirt
with 'Madrid' and a graphic printed across the chest, a digital watch
on his wrist. His upper arms were cicatrised, multiple horizontal
lines, 'sorry' cuts made for loved ones who had passed away. Most
of the published versions of this photograph would be cropped for

just his face, but the original shows a lot more about the man, his masculine aliveness, his ties to Arrernte traditions, his embrace of contemporary town life.

In the courtroom the five accused were told to stand. Their names were Scott Doody, Timothy Hird, Anton Kloeden, Joshua Spears and Glen Swain. Spears, indeed my son's old friend, was eighteen, the youngest of them; the oldest were Doody and Swain, both twenty-three. All five were charged with the murder of the thirty-three-year-old Ryder in Alice Springs on 25 July 2009. They also faced charges of unlawfully causing serious harm; possessing, using or carrying a prohibited weapon; and multiple counts of recklessly endangering life. What they might have been thinking or feeling was impossible to read: they were grave, impassive, as no doubt they had been instructed to be.

No applications for bail, remanded in custody: it was over sooner than expected. The packed courtroom emptied quickly. As she passed I touched Spears's mother's arm. 'I'm sorry for your trouble,' I said. She nodded, her chin and mouth trembling. I could imagine Therese Ryder's anguish to be more terrible – her son's life was over. The lives of the accused, if convicted, would drag out for decades in shame and behind bars. Cause too for a parent's torment.

This was Tuesday. Ryder had died in the early hours of Saturday the weekend before last. Even ahead of police confirmation that the five assailants were white and their victim black, there was widespread anxiety that this had been a racist attack. The victim, according to police, was seen to have had an exchange with 'some of the occupants' of a white dual-cab Toyota Hilux; earlier that car had been in the dry bed of the Todd River and had driven through 'two itinerant camps'.

~

The mostly dry river runs through the middle of the town. It was almost unimaginable without its circles of figures sitting in the sand around a thin line of rising smoke. The sight had its charm. Up close it could be different. The camps were often drinking circles, and when there was too much drink there could be real trouble.

Just three weeks before Ryder's death, on the night of 30 June, L Tilmouth had died in the river. She had been sitting around a fire with her husband and cousin-brother near a big tree not far from the Wills Terrace causeway, a stone's throw from the CBD. All three had been drinking. Her battered body was found in the river around midnight. Her husband, Joachim Golder, handed himself into police the next morning, spattered from head to toe in his wife's blood.

Golder had used a number of large rocks to deliver at least four blows to the back of his wife's head, two of them with severe force. All of them penetrated the scalp, two were down to the bone. She died of a sub-arachnoid haemorrhage to the brain caused by one of those blows. There were other injuries: a ragged wound to the right ankle and a very deep cut to her left foot exposing the cartilage; they had bled profusely, as had the head wounds. She had been punched in the mouth at least once and kicked in the torso, presumably while lying on the ground. She was dragged from the tree area, further into the riverbed, where Golder violently tore off her underpants, injuring her further. At some stage her cousin-brother had heard her crying, saying, 'Don't hit me, I'm your wife.'

The sentencing judge described the attack as 'a savage beating'. The only explanation for it, conveyed by Golder's lawyer during his jury trial, was that he was very drunk at the time. When he was not drunk he was said to have strong traditional values and a good work record as a stockman and station worker. He was found guilty of murder.

'You come from a respectable family from Santa Teresa,' the judge said to him. 'Your sisters have been in Court to support you throughout the course of your trial and are present today to hear you sentenced. It is a very sad matter for them. You have caused great sadness to your family from what you have done and the fact that you will now have to go to gaol until you are an old man.'[2]

Golder's sentence was mandatory life, with a non-parole period set at twenty-five years because he had been convicted previously of an unlawful homicide – of his brother. He had also been convicted of causing serious harm to a former wife, by stabbing her. Both crimes had been committed while he was drunk. 'It is readily apparent from your criminal history and the current offence, that when you abuse alcohol you are an extreme danger to those around you,' said the judge.

Drinking is banned in all public areas, so even without trouble, camps in the river were also regular sites of confrontation with police. Patrols would be seen heading for the camps as fast as the deep sand allowed, in their paddy wagons or on off-road bikes, and soon the officers would be pouring out the grog from opened cans or casks.

When the campers moved on, they often left things behind – food and drink packaging, but useful things too. Sometimes these were stowed in trees, a sign they would be collected later. Sometimes they were left where they'd been used – clothing, shoes, blankets, seemingly forgotten. If campers overnighted (which was banned but not necessarily detected) there was also little chance that they were not defecating in the open.

All this was the perennial subject of local conversation, private and public. We would hear a trace of its potential for heat and crude reductions in the Ryder case – Aboriginal witness accounts of insults yelled at them when the car was driven through their camps. 'You mob stink like this Todd River' was one. The smell of unwashed bodies and of hair and clothing permeated by the smoke of campfires and coal-roasted meat is not uncommon in the public spaces of

Alice Springs, and is particularly imposing in enclosed spaces like supermarkets or indeed the courthouse. It can be called upon as a matter for disdain and insult even when it is not present. An example: my daughter, Jacqueline, in her primary school years told me about an attempt by one of her peers to get all the white kids to sit at the back of the school bus and the black kids at the front because they were 'smelly black cunts'. The language, obviously, but the focus on smell too was something this child had learned elsewhere, because the black kids getting onto this school bus lived in residential care and there was no chance that they weren't as washed as the white kids. The word 'nigger' was also brought home from the school bus and it too was heard in the river, according to witnesses.

The campers' use of the river was not as simple as this being 'their' country where 'they' had always camped. The river rises in the hills north of the town, passes through the middle like a backbone and on southward through a gap in the ranges. This is Central Arrernte country; they call the river Lhere Mparntwe.[3] There are sacred sites all along its course, and the majestic river red gums that grow in the bed and on the banks are also revered. The campers were not necessarily, even mostly not Arrernte. Traditional owners could be upset by their presence, particularly if it led to trouble or to damage of trees. In 2006 the native title holder organisation Lhere Artepe issued a cultural protocol list of nine 'dos' and nine 'don'ts' and expressed its desire to work with the Town Council on the development of new and updated by-laws for managing public places. Its representatives had identified camping in the river, 'humbugging' tourists and begging as unacceptable, speaking explicitly of the problem of camping on sacred sites, of sacred trees being burned, of excessive drinking, its links to violence and its damage to the standing of all Aboriginal people in the eyes of others.[4]

In the very week following the incidents in the river and Ryder's death there was local and national uproar over the Town Council's proposed introduction of a by-law that would purportedly 'strip blankets from Alice homeless', as one ABC news headline had it.[5] In fact, the by-law was dealing with 'abandoned' items, such as blankets. The practice previously had been to 'impound' them: actually they were taken to Tangentyere Council, the service and advocacy organisation for town camps. Now the Town Council was wanting to add the words 'and dispose of'. In the blogosphere this soon became 'forcibly remove', with the spectre of heartless rangers wresting blankets from sleeping campers and leaving them exposed to the freezing mid-winter nights.[6] This never happened, though undoubtedly camping arrangements were disrupted.

The Town Council was also seeking to give its rangers the authority to move people on, to deal with public drinking and to put a stop to begging. These were measures that dealt with behaviour most associated with an Aboriginal 'them' in the white public mind and they received the most attention and heat. There was a lot of concern about the broad reach of other by-laws and their potential to limit individual freedoms, but particular outrage was reserved for claims and counter-claims around perceived targeting of Aboriginal people. Lhere Artepe's protocols from three years earlier had receded in the public memory.[7]

Layered onto these local developments, intensifying the 'them and us' atmospherics and some very real divisions, was the federal government's Northern Territory Emergency Response, more widely known as the Intervention. At the time of Ryder's death in 2009 it was two years old. The Intervention discourse was originally about 'normalising' the town camps, as going towards providing a safer environment for children. However, its measures in some ways (not all) entrenched their segregation. Drinking was now to be banned in the camps, not only in their communal areas but in people's homes. The infamous blue signs proclaiming the ban as well as the prohibition of pornography were erected at all town camp entrances.

In an attempt to curb spending on alcohol, tobacco and gambling, half of camp residents' welfare payments were 'quarantined' for things like food, rent and utility bills. These same provisions applied to the residents of 'prescribed' Aboriginal communities, seventy-three of them around the Territory.[8]

The many and complex arguments for and against these measures aside, I mention them here to outline some of the social divisions in the town and region, a high consciousness of which helps explain why, as soon as people heard of a car being driven at campers in the river, it was feared to have been a racist attack.

Another local event was also feeding the town's heightened awareness of racial division and tension. Just four months earlier, on 3 April, a white man had died in a street knifing, allegedly at the hands of two Aboriginal men. Grief and outrage over the killing were often expressed, overtly or by implication, in race-based terms. The prosecution of the accused assailants, the subject of the next chapter, would take much longer than the Ryder case to be settled in the courts, in part due to the accused men's fears that they would not get a fair trial.

~

Bail application hearings for four out of the five accused in the Ryder case were listed for the morning of 6 August. Family and friends on both sides were present, though not nearly as many as at the first mention two days earlier. This time the Aboriginal people attending did not hang back as the courtroom doors opened.

None of the defendants actually sought bail, though their lawyers did not rule out doing so later. Committal hearing dates were set. The slow legal process was moving.

The Ryder family left the courthouse and gathered on the lawns across the road. Therese Ryder, still in black, wore dark glasses and a black beanie over her cropped hair. Standing next to her was her son's fiancée, Jade Keil, a young white woman, her hair also closely cropped. I recognised prominent local older women, Ryder relatives from the Liddle and Turner families. There were others, women and men, whom I did not know. A prepared statement was read by Thomas Buzzacott, Ryder's cousin. A young woman held his arm to steady the trembling sheet of paper.

'On Saturday 25th July 2009 a young Arrernte man and beloved member of our family passed away as a result of a callous and random act of violence,' Buzzacott read. 'Arrernte families stand in unity and call for calm in the community over recent events and in the lead-up to the trial date of the perpetrators. We ask for the general public to disregard any form of intimidation.'

No such acts had become general knowledge. There was certainly anxiety that they might occur, that there could be retaliation on either side of the racial divide. And looking back, I suspect what I saw as a show of solidarity by friends of the accused on the first day in court was as much a show of white strength and numbers in anticipation of a black backlash.

The family had expected bail to be granted and were clearly opposed to such an eventuality, as reflected in their next comments. There had not been time to redraft the statement.

'We trust in truth for justice,' Buzzacott continued, 'regardless of bail sought by the defendants through the judicial system. A bail price is incomparable to the loss of a young life, to allow freedom for the perpetrators of a serious act of crime ... was wrong. Regardless of race this in itself was a cowardly and despicable act of violence.'

The statement referred back to the first mention of the case in court, when the courtroom had been packed out.

'On Tuesday 4th August 2009 the court mention drew support from Arrernte families during which time only parents of one of the defendants [the Hirds, I would learn] offered their condolence to our family, to a mother who lost her son, a wife who lost her fiancé and brothers and sisters who lost their brother. No-one could ever comprehend the pain and anguish they all must feel, to provide comfort for them to now live their lives without him.'

The statement then took a remarkable turn to address the 'big picture' of social division. I expect at the forefront of their minds here were the sweeping changes under the Intervention but perhaps also the proposed public places by-laws, and the then year-old overhaul of local government that had dissolved the old system of Aboriginal community councils.[9]

'We call on the whole community to support us in helping each other to make necessary changes to current laws and practices that are clearly not working. It is our belief that laws are there to help all people to build on better relationships and to live in peace and harmony. We need to allow for better understanding of the different cultures and work towards respecting our differences and beliefs. This will certainly reduce violence in the community which has been affecting each and every one of us. We are calling for healing of the people as it is human emotions influenced by drug and alcohol abuse that is impacting on our lives. Current laws are creating unnecessary conflict within the community.

'This is a vulnerable time when all young children and youth need our strength and courage to protect them. It is they who need our constant vigilance and guidance. Through our love and support as parents and families we must help them to live better lives, to allow for cultural exchange to broaden their learning in life and help them to achieve their dreams and aspirations. This is a crucial time for the whole community and governments to come together through compassion and understanding as human beings and as one community.'

Such breadth and generosity does not commonly mark the public discourse in Alice Springs and it was not yet two weeks since the death. It was moving to hear. In the private domain and smaller-scale contexts there can be great friendship, creative endeavour, goodwill and kindness between people and across cultures, but in contrast the public domain is often small-minded and begrudging, or embittered and full of complaint.

The family went on to thank the police for their 'quick response and action' and for conducting their investigation professionally and with 'cultural sensitivity'. They also thanked 'members of the community who willingly assisted the police'.

The final sentences were the hardest. Therese Ryder sank her face into her hands, Jade Keil and the other young women wept.

'As a family we remember a young man full of compassion and love with a vibrant energy for life and … one who always held a welcome smile with a "hello" for everyone he met. His working life was bound by his enthusiasm for life, connecting him with the spirituality of the land he loved whilst embracing friendship with all people within the community. He was a popular and proud young man who was loved by all his family and friends. He possessed a natural ability to share his love and in doing so maintained his personal characteristics as a true gentleman who was Arrernte, a Territorian and Australian and this is the image we share with the rest of the community.'

The statement did not use his name at all and from now on, in deference, I will refer to him as Kwementyaye. The *Alice Springs News* published the statement almost verbatim together with a photograph of the family.[10] My son, Rainer, who was working for the paper at the time, took this photograph and listened to what was said. The death and the way it was alleged to have happened, at the hands of five young white men some of whom he knew, had shaken him, as it had so many others. However, as the statement was being read there were shouted comments from a passing car. I didn't see the car and couldn't make out what was said, but Karen Liddle, who was in the Ryder family group that day and would become a spokesperson for the family during the legal proceedings, later spoke to the ABC about it: 'At the same time while we were doing that on the courthouse lawns, you know, we get groups of young ones … in cars going past swearing and sticking fingers up. That could have caused another sort of reaction, you know, but we managed to calm that down as well.'[11]

~

Kwementyaye was buried on 20 August. As I walked across town towards the Catholic Church Aboriginal people were coming from all directions, everyone dressed in black and white funeral clothes, even the small children, some of them solemnly holding single flowers wrapped in cellophane. The church was filled to overflowing. Bishop Eugene Hurley from Darwin was there to conduct the service. Every seat was taken and people were standing at the doors, in the forecourt, on the street. I stood for a while at the side, then decided not to stay. This was personal; conscious of the camera and notebook in my bag I felt I was intruding. The congregation was overwhelmingly Aboriginal, but some white people sat among them. Religion, school, football, politics, art, jobs, marriage – all could be the context for bonds across the cultures. There was tension though. An ABC TV cameraman was injured in a scuffle with a mourner and would spend the night in hospital.[12]

A memorial had grown at the spot where Kwementyaye had died. There are many such memorials on the streets of Alice Springs, most, though not all, for Aboriginal people, most for victims of traffic accidents, some for victims of violence. They start with flowers. For Kwementyaye, the family added a white cross after the funeral. The spot was on the verge of Schwarz Crescent, not far from the RSL clubhouse and grounds. The crescent curves around the base of Anzac Hill, becoming a causeway across the sandy bed of the Todd. Immediately north of the causeway Charles Creek enters the river.

On its opposite bank stands the Uniting Church's secondary college, St Philip's – first choice for many of the town's more affluent families. The college's immediate neighbour is the Charles Creek town camp, where Kwementyaye was headed that last morning, to his uncle's place. It was from the top of Anzac Hill that a local couple observed the attack on him.

The memorial cross by the road was decorated with motifs showing Kwementyaye's trademark black Akubra and his western-style boots. It bore the inscription 'In loving memory of a loving son, brother, partner, uncle and brother in law with an unforgettable smile.' On the night of Friday 25 September the cross was burned. This was immediately felt as an aggressive and likely racist act. It is how the family reacted, with Therese Ryder saying that Alice Springs – 'once a happy town where my kids grew up and went to school, made a lot of friends' – was now 'very sad ... full of racist thing'.[13] The family was frustrated, reported the ABC journalist, that more wasn't being done to promote understanding, that there was little discussion about ways to bring different groups together in Alice Springs.[14]

Two actions followed the cross-burning in quick succession. By Tuesday morning a new white cross, made from steel rather than wood, had been erected by a group of 'concerned Alice Springs men' – 'prominent business leaders, elected members [including the mayor] and general members of the community'.[15] On the following Friday a full-page advertisement ran in the *Centralian Advocate*. It showed a photograph of clasped black and white hands and bore the names of hundreds of locals who had chipped in the necessary $1,800. Their text read:

> We deplore all acts of violence, including those that have been perpetrated recently in this town. We offer our sympathy and sincere condolences to victims of violence and their families. We value the cross-cultural relationships we enjoy in Alice Springs and

reject all acts of racism. We advocate the promotion of harmony and improved understanding amongst all people in the town and a considered and thoughtful response to problems and difficult issues.[16]

Scott McConnell was the white man who spoke in the media about the replacement cross: '[We] thought we should take some responsibility and show some initiative and do something positive to show that Alice Springs has a heart and has compassion,' he told the ABC.

'We don't know who burnt this memorial, whoever did burn it is a bit of a scumbag, and it's reprehensible that we have people like that in the community, but I think it would be unfortunate for our community to jump to conclusions that it was done for a particular reason.

'Alice Springs is a very racially diverse town and like any town we have some issues around integration that could be argued are or aren't racist. As a community we need to acknowledge that there are issues on the periphery and we should never rest on our laurels that things are mainly good, but to think that there is some systemic problem that is very different is just untrue. There is only one community here, there's Aboriginal people, there's white people and there's lots of other different people, so let's all work together, one community one way.'[17]

Here was some kind of response to the Ryder family's appeal. McConnell's views didn't have the warmth or breadth of language, nor the focus on the young that the family's statement from the courthouse lawns had had, but they were backed by an action and projected a vision of community across the cultures. The situation had perhaps needed the burning of the cross, sufficiently close to the death of Kwementyaye Ryder but without implications for the legal action against his assailants, for sentiments like McConnell's and the advertisement's to be expressed.

Not so long before McConnell had had another occasion to make public statements about community relations, that time from a place of more personal grief. He was the boss and close friend of the white man who had died in the street knifing allegedly by two Aboriginal men, referred to earlier. McConnell said his friend's death was 'a wake-up call for the community … an appalling indictment on our town … When are we going to do something to deal with the issues that exist here? And when are we going to work together instead of telling the stories and looking for somebody else to blame?'[18] There was the same call for community action, but he assessed the issues to be dealt with as more central than he seemed to allow in his response to the cross-burning.

Almost a month after the burning, on 20 October, it was reported that the fire had in fact been accidental. A police examination of the scene revealed that a candle had been lit, most probably by somebody who loved Kwementyaye: 25 September was his birthday. The candle's flame had set fire to the flowers and tokens wrapped around the wooden cross, then the cross too caught fire. This information came from Detective Senior Sergeant Lauren Hill, who had been close to the investigation into the killing but was away on leave at the time of the cross-burning. 'If I was here and I certainly was aware of it, then yes we could have dealt with it in a more timely fashion,' she told the ABC.[19]

These events punctuated the waiting time. The committal hearing was listed for mid-December. There was private talk of course. What I remember are the many versions of the kind of violence supposed to have been visited on Kwementyaye.

'The police had to go to dental records to identify him,' a friend heard from her daughter who was in the attackers' age group and had heard it at a party. This was simply not the case. A white policeman responding to the 000 call recognised Kwementyaye; they had been friends at school. He knew the family, knew the relatives and made sure one of them was with him when he went to break the worst news to Kwementyaye's mother.

A friend of Rainer's told me Kwementyaye's face was 'all mushy – he was beaten to a pulp'. He had heard this from someone who worked at the hospital. This too was far from true, but people would hold onto these stories even after the forensic evidence was given in court and reported.

In many media accounts the attack became not a bashing but a 'brutal' bashing, Kwementyaye was 'beaten to death' – as if the facts we had learned were not bad enough. When I say this, though, more than one friend tells me that I allow adherence to the facts to break the story down into something small enough to be managed, when really it is huge. They say the facts of the legal case cannot accommodate this story. Yet surely it has to be accommodated short of the distortions, and the only way to do that is with reflection on as much as we can know of the facts, considered in the context of as much as we can know of the whole community. The Ryder family's own large vision of the task, expressed in their statement on 6 August, saw that.

~

A DVD was shown to the court. In it Glen Swain, in a police vehicle, re-enacted the attack on Kwementyaye.

The five were in Anton Kloeden's car, with Kloeden driving. Swain was sitting in the middle of the back seat. They passed Kwementyaye heading westwards along Schwarz Crescent, away from the river. He threw what Swain thought was a rock at the car (in fact it was a bottle, which smashed). Kloeden braked, did a U-turn and pulled up just in front of Kwementyaye, close enough for him to put his hands on the bullbar.

Hird was first out of the car. Kwementyaye started running. Hird fell over, Swain was behind him, in 'a light jog'. Then Kwementyaye stumbled and fell.

'I … got as close as what Tim was … [Kwementyaye] had his hands over his face. I then laid two boots in [and] shuffled around,' said Swain on the DVD.

The police gave him a mannequin to use. He placed it on the ground, the head towards Anzac Hill. He demonstrated two close-range kicks to the forehead. He also saw Hird make 'contact … with one foot' – speaking as if he'd already learned from police their disembodied way of talking.

Scott Doody was right by Hird's side; Swain didn't say more but there would never be any evidence that Doody struck Kwementyaye. Kloeden didn't get out of the car – he didn't have time to. Swain thought Spears also stayed in the car (not so) but said he wasn't noticing what anyone else was doing, he was just doing what he was doing – 'tunnel vision, like I said'.

Kwementyaye became limp – 'a rag doll type of effect … he appeared to be unconscious'. Swain saw a car approaching. Kloeden had turned the Hilux around, facing back towards the highway.

'Let's go, let's go, let's go!' said Swain.

It was all so matter of fact – impossible not to be chilled by it.

Swain was arrested on 1 August, was interviewed the next day, and the re-enactment followed the day after. At the start of the DVD he was asked if he agreed to the re-enactment. 'No problems,' he said. Did he understand who would see it and what a judge, for instance, would be capable of? 'Heck, imprisonment, home detention, that sort of thing.'

The re-enactment actually started with the lead-up to the car entering the river. We knew from the Crown facts that they had consumed by then a 'large amount of alcohol', leaving Lasseters Casino towards dawn on 25 July, all of them getting into Kloeden's Hilux.

Swain and the police set out, driving the route the five took, with Swain offering sporadic commentary. From the casino carpark, they went along Barrett Drive, turned into Tunks Road causeway, drove off it into the riverbed. The five were travelling 'a bit quicker' than the police vehicle, Swain said. It 'doesn't handle as good as the Hilux'.

Already the same strangely casual tone.

'I hit my head on the roof at that little bump there,' Swain said with a short laugh.

They passed under the Stott Terrace bridge. Swain's memory became less clear. They had had no particular destination, he said. He couldn't recall if they had had to stop for other cars. They drove along Sturt Terrace to the Schwarz Crescent causeway. At some point he and one of the others suggested they go to the Telegraph Station. They drove back into the river, heading north. 'This appears to be the track we took ... it veered off a bit'. There was a camp. 'The occupants' – that police talk again – got up and ran away: 'They obviously feared what could happen.'

His memory got a bit patchy. They kept going upstream towards the Telegraph Station but at some point a fence stopped them. He said Kloeden tried to push the fence down with his bullbar. The aerial snapped off. Swain threw it into the bush. They gave up and went back the way they had come.

They could see the camp again. Someone had a stick, it was thrown at the car. They turned, pulled up and jumped out to inspect the damage. A passer-by said something about a 'wakeup call for them'. They all agreed and had a chuckle.

Swain's recall was vague again. There were a few camps in the area. 'Nothing angry' was said – 'we were just being a bunch of pissed fellas carrying on'.

They left the river and headed back to Swain's house which he shared with Hird. He and Hird went in. Hird showed him a replica pistol. Swain had never seen it before, had a bit of a look, handed it back to him. They headed off again. As they were driving along they 'let off a round'. It made a sound 'like a real gun'.

They ran into a mate. Hird hid the gun, didn't want him to see it. It was jammed, and Hird was trying to unjam it. They ended up back at the river. Hird was still 'fumbling' with the gun. He let off another round. They could see the camp. Everyone jumped up and started running, they 'freaked out, as you would'.

The re-enactment of the attack on Kwementyaye followed.

Then Swain's memory hit a 'big blank patch'. He knew they ended up back at 'Josh Spears's mum's house'. He'd never been there before. He had a drink there, listened to some music, played some games. He couldn't remember how long for. Eventually he and the others left Spears and went back to Swain and Hird's place.

That was as much as the court heard about the events of the night from any of the five during the committal hearing.

The campers gave a different account. The car was going 'really fast', coming straight for them. The campers ran, all except one old man, Tony Cotchilli – he couldn't get up quickly enough. The car passed about a metre from him the first time. The second time, when he was on his feet with the others, it ran over his swag. Cotchilli said the five didn't say anything, but other witnesses said the five were swearing – 'black bastards', 'niggers'. The campers said they gave it back – 'white pricks'. Jeannie Bruno threw a firestick at the car – she stood up in court and showed hurling it with her right hand from shoulder height. She threatened the five with 'a big hiding'. She was thinking 'it might be triple K'. Others said they were frightened: 'too frightened' to be angry, said Donna Larry, 'shaking'. Bruno also said she was 'shaking'.

There were two camps, one to the north of the causeway – people from Balgo, Kiwirrkurra and Kintore, visiting town – the other to the south, said to be Warlpiri people, residents of Alice. Before the sun came up Kwementyaye had gone to the northern camp. Cotchilli said he 'went by'. Bruno said he stood for a while before moving on. 'We're not his family,' she said, 'we've got nothing to do with him.' But Donna Larry said Kwementyaye sat down by the fire before the sun came up, and shared a can of beer with Ashley Spencer. He was 'really drunk', 'asking for smoke', she said. He was there when the car drove through. There had been yelling from the southern camp where they could see the white Hilux coming. They were singing out, warning the people in the northern camp. Kwementyaye ran with the others, said Larry, he saw Cotchilli unable to get out of the way, he saw the firestick being thrown. It was daylight when he went on his way.

Was he drunk, staggering?

'Just a little bit,' said Larry, but Spencer didn't think so.

Was he angry?

'No,' said Larry. She saw him reach the causeway. He left his black hat and a coloured blanket behind.

There were other witnesses to the events in the river: people living on Sturt Terrace which runs along the eastern bank, with its houses mostly facing the river; and people out for early morning walks.

In her Sturt Terrace duplex Louise Dalton was woken before dawn by yelling. It sounded like Aboriginal people, angry, aggressive. She went back to sleep but was woken a second time. Light was starting to come through the curtains. Now the yelling sounded like an argument – people calling other people 'cunts'. She gave up on sleep, got up. A little while later she heard a bang, 'one sudden single sound'. She opened her front door, saw a white Toyota ute stationary on the gravelled area across the road, just before the turn-off to the causeway. Male voices were coming from inside – yelling, swearing, whooping, confrontational, sounded like whitefellas. She saw Aboriginal people in the river, they seemed upset, all standing, watching the car. After maybe thirty seconds the Toyota took off, wheels spinning in the gravel. She watched it speeding across the causeway towards the RSL. It was out of sight when she heard brakes squealing, gears changing.

Nearby Jared Ewin had just started breakfast. He heard a bang, went to the window, saw a white Hilux dual-cab cutting the corner to turn onto the causeway, an arm hanging out the window, driver's side, holding what looked like a gun – definitely chrome, looked like a revolver, the sun was shining on it. (Some doubt was established about whether he could have seen this.) A group of Aboriginal people were camped north of the causeway. Did they seem distressed? 'Not really, they moved a little bit.'

On the western bank Neil Bowey was out walking with his wife. He saw a white ute drive from Sturt Terrace into the river at what seemed to him a 'very unsafe speed'. He was quite amazed to see that it was a 'civilian vehicle'. He was used to seeing police or Tangentyere night patrol in the river, but this vehicle had no markings. He saw people in the river south of the causeway; there was an interaction between them and the people in the 'civilian' car. He couldn't tell if the exchange was 'irate', in fact he 'almost had the impression it was social', that perhaps the vehicle was from Tangentyere after all.

The people in this southern camp were confused too. When the car drove up, according to Maureen Walker, the men inside 'all said "say happy birthday to us". … Me and Trudy say "happy birthday" to them. We thought they was kind to us.' Did they say anything then? 'They swear at us … "You mob stink like this Todd River."' Trudy Wallace was asked about the exact words. 'Can I swear in here?' she checked. Yes, she was told. After the 'happy birthday', 'they said "you black cunts, fuck off out of this Todd River".'

On the eastern bank Matt Day was walking his girlfriend's dogs. He saw a Hilux driving in the river at high speed – fast for driving in sand, much faster than ranger vehicles. It was coming from the north. He was a couple of hundred metres away. He saw the car drive towards the northern camp, saw the campers forced to scatter. He went over to find out what was going on. 'He must have been worrying for us,' Jeannie Bruno recalled. 'He had a dog and he said, "Are you mob all right?" and then he went.'

Day said he saw empty VB cans lying around, a tyre track on a blue blanket the old man had been sitting on. The Hilux by now had driven off. Kwementyaye was there, Day had met him before at football games. Kwementyaye told him the Hilux had tried to run over a 'couple of old blokes'. He called the five 'white racist pricks'. He didn't seem drunk, he was holding a conversation quite well. Day was told in court that Kwementyaye's post-mortem blood alcohol reading was .220. Did he want to reassess his evidence? Day acknowledged that it was a 'very high reading', but Kwementyaye was talking fine, he said, not staggering, not slurring.

On top of Anzac Hill Deborah Clarke was sharing a take-away breakfast with her partner. They'd driven up there to enjoy the view as the sun lit up the range. Looking around, she noticed a man on Schwarz Crescent walking on the side of the road towards the highway. Then a vehicle came from the causeway and passed him. She heard a yell. The vehicle did a big U-ey, she heard the squeal of tyres. It was a white Hilux dual-cab with a big bullbar. It came back towards the fellow on the side of the road. 'I recall thinking it was aiming at him, either to scare him or do something.'

It stopped. People got out of the car. There was some yelling – she heard 'an Indigenous inflection'. The man who had been walking moved behind some bushes. There was an altercation. She could see half the man's body on the ground and some kicking motions from the attackers, two to three kicks. She presumed it was the prone man being kicked. 'In my mind they were in quite a tight cluster – must have been, to be behind the shrubbery.' They got back into the car, reversed back into the lane and drove off towards the highway. It all happened within a couple of minutes, but the kicking was over in a matter of seconds. Her partner, Matt Lemmens, gave the same time estimate: 'The fracas may not have been five seconds, it was so quick.' He saw three people moving from the car towards the RSL; one person made more than one kick. How far did the kick draw back? 'Half a step, I suppose.' This was in keeping with Swain's demonstration.

Clarke and Lemmens drove down to where Kwementyaye was lying by the side of the road, head towards the RSL. He was not moving. Clarke approached him, saw blood behind his head, in front of his mouth, on his head. A beer bottle and some coins were on the ground. His eyes were glazed, there was no rise and fall of his chest. She didn't touch him. Lemmens was already on the phone to 000. Police came very quickly.

~

Forensic pathologist Dr Sinton conducted the autopsy on the evening of the next day. His evidence was not heard in court until 24 February 2010, the final day of the committal hearing. His written report, as is usual, was tendered to the magistrate as his 'evidence in chief'. What we learned of it came through his responses to questions from defence lawyers in cross-examination.

He told the court that it was 'very likely' that Kwementyaye had a pre-existing aneurism. The rupture of such an aneurism was the 'most likely lesion' to produce the kind of haemorrhage that had killed him, 'one of the more extensive' he had seen. Although 'a relatively small amount', the blood had spread extensively through the sub-arachnoid space.

He could not isolate any single cause for the 'blunt force trauma' deemed to have caused the rupture. It was difficult to say whether it was caused by one blow or a number of blows: if injury occurs as a result of one blow, in terms of harm 'the rest becomes irrelevant':

aneurism rupture is an 'all or nothing' situation. He was 'not happy' to accept that the rupture could have occurred 'some hours before' the assault. This was 'most unlikely' as any form of sub-arachnoid haemorrhage is accompanied by 'an excruciating headache'. In any case, whether the bleed is slow or otherwise, there is a 'high risk of acute damage'.

All of this, the range of possibilities he was prepared to admit, was expressed with Dr Sinton's usual caution and contingency.

He did not reject the possibility that the rupture could have been a result of Kwementyaye running, falling and hitting his head on the ground. An aneurism can rupture spontaneously. If force is involved, the degree necessary to cause a rupture need not be great; it could be caused by 'any form of minor trauma to any part of the head'. He had not been able to isolate the exact site where the bleeding had started and in his experience it is possible to do so in only 50 per cent of cases. With such an extensive haemorrhage the blood vessels 'tear to shreds basically'.

There was a three-centimetre laceration to the back of Kwementyaye's head, through soft tissue, causing relatively minor damage and a small amount of bleeding. Bone was not visible. There was mild swelling around the site. Falling on a hard surface such as a bitumen road, or being kicked, or being struck by a bottle: all were possible causes for the injury.

There was an abrasion and swelling on the upper right side of the forehead, more likely the result of an abrasive blow but possibly consistent with a fall. There were abrasions to the area around the left ear, consistent with either a kick or a fall. There was a two-centimetre area of bruising to the left side of the forehead, but he was uncertain about its age. There were some lacerations on the right inner surface of the upper and lower lips, consistent with either a kick or a fall. There were a number of abrasions to the left and right forearms, the left shoulder, the right and left knees. These were consistent with falling onto a bitumen road. There was no skull fracture, no evidence of elevated blood pressure.

In the pathologist's opinion Kwementyaye's high blood alcohol reading would not have contributed to the sub-arachnoid haemorrhage, but it would have slowed down his mental and motor functions: 'He may not have been able to physically defend himself.'

Therese Ryder had been in the lobby before the hearing but hadn't come in. Other family members were in the front rows of the gallery. They listened to all this – the detail of the damage done to their relative, the likelihood of him having had a pre-existing aneurism, rendering him very vulnerable in the circumstances.

Dr Sinton's evidence seemed to me to significantly reduce the chances of a murder conviction, though it didn't absolve the five of responsibility: they had still assaulted Kwementyaye albeit without great force, the aneurism rupture was most likely to have occurred in the course of the assault, and he was dead at the end of it. 'You take your victim as you find him' – wasn't that the principle? But would a jury think it was murder?

The lawyers for Swain, Hird, Doody and Spears, who rode as passengers in the Hilux, now all made submissions that their clients should not be charged with the counts of 'recklessly endangering life' as there had been no evidence that any of them had been at the wheel. The Crown prosecutor argued against this: the four had been in the car for an extended time and had been in a position to get out if they'd wanted to. There had also been evidence of more than one voice coming from the car when it was driven at the two camps. The magistrate thought that a jury could consider that the four were involved on the basis of complicity. He decided that there was a sufficient case to put the men 'on their trial' on all counts. He asked them to stand and read them their rights. As they were being

led away Hird's mother approached the dock and raised her arms
towards her son: he bent down and hugged her tightly.

~

It was raining heavily as I drove home, always an event in this
desert town. People come from everywhere to the causeways and
bridges to watch the river rise. It was already flowing through the
Gap. Prisoners returning to the gaol would have to come this way. I
wondered if the five would see the river from their transport, if they
could or would even look, or would they keep their heads down, not
wanting to know what they'd forfeited. As I got out of the car the
woody, minted smell from wet bushland rose into my face. I breathed
it in deeply.

In the coming months, waiting for the trial, my thoughts would
sometimes go to the five – pacing or lying in their cells, as I imagined,
tormented by the impossibility of turning back the clock. I was
projecting more than usual. I had that memory of Spears as a boy, a
boy who had played with my son, and of the contact I'd had with his
mother. I ran into her once or twice during this time and we talked
about him, how he was coping. I also ran into Hird's mother, whom
I hadn't known before. We were both in a dress shop one day, she
recognised me from court and introduced herself; we talked about
her son too. His carpentry skills were being put to use in the gaol,
making things, teaching others.

All of this lapped onto my perception of the five. They seemed
recognisable to me. Ordinarily capable of doing harm. Ordinarily
capable of having remorse.

I didn't have that sense a year later when I followed the case of
three white men, two of them similarly young, accused of attempted
murder – a drug- and booze-addled random shooting of another
white man. One, Reuben Nadich, eventually pleaded guilty to
causing and intending to cause serious harm (for which he got six

years with a non-parole period of three years and three months). The shooting charges against the other two, Jason Corp and Benjamin Gaff, were dropped, but they each pleaded guilty to causing serious harm to another man on the same night – inflicting a beating on him with a shovel and steel-capped boots, after which he needed facial reconstruction. Once again in this small town, I had had contact with family members of two of the men, in particular with Gaff's grandmother, a smart, generous woman, active in community causes, who turned up faithfully in court to support him. Yet these men unnerved me. They were involved in an underworld of Alice Springs that I knew nothing of – illegal drug deals, standover violence, guns. Their base was an auto-wrecker's yard, vicious guard dogs behind the fence. It sounded like American television. On the night of the attack they were joy-riding, with gun and ammunition, when they came across their victim and his partner camping for the night in bushland north of town. In the confrontation one of the offenders infamously said, 'It's all right, mate, we thought you were blackfellas and we were going to shoot you.' This statement was widely reported and commented upon;[20] hardly any media attention was paid to what happened next. Nadich fired. That he'd been smoking methamphetamine was his only explanation.

The similarities – joy-riding with a gun, ready racist remarks, intoxication, random victim – don't escape me, though Hird's gun was a blank-firing replica, while Nadich's shattered a man's left shoulder and blew away a significant part of his underarm. My impression of the five was also untainted by them going into the witness box. They were serious in court, the least you could expect. They spent a lot of time staring at the floor. I saw it as a sense of shame. This was very different from the displays by Nadich and co. as they each took the stand. Nadich jittery and self-serving, Corp stunted, and Gaff gormless, immature.

~

There was still that chilling DVD re-enactment by Glen Swain – he who had kicked Kwementyaye twice in the head. His seemingly casual recall of events was put into a different perspective when the matter returned to court for what turned out to be not a trial but a plea hearing. We then saw part of Swain's interview with police, which took place the day before the re-enactment.

'Glen, were you provoked at all to do this attack?' he was asked.

'No, no way, I've got my own brain, make my own decisions.'

His tone was grave, this was serious. I don't know how long he had taken to get to this point. He had initially lied to police about where he had been on the Saturday morning (as did Kloeden, Hird and Spears), but now he was owning up. I looked over at Swain. He had his eyes on the floor.

'Were you forced by anyone to do this act?'

'No,' he answered almost inaudibly.

'Whose choice was it to approach [Kwementyaye]?'

'My own.'

...

'Why did you approach [Kwementyaye]?'

'He threw the rock at the car.'

'How did you feel when he threw the rock at the car?'

'I was a bit scared to start with. After it had hit, I was pissed off.'

'By approaching [Kwementyaye], when you kicked him to the head, twice in the forehead, what did you think might happen … ?'

'I didn't even think about what could happen to him. It was spur of the moment …'

He was asked if he had been intoxicated or under the influence of drugs.

'Just drink,' he whispered.

Had he seen Kwementyaye before or had Kwementyaye ever done anything previously to provoke this incident?

His answer was almost inaudible, but I thought he said 'no'.

'Did yourself or anyone try to stop what was happening?'

I heard only the words 'so fast'. Again I looked at Swain. He was watching now.

'Did you intend to kill [Kwementyaye]?'

On the tape he started crying. In the public gallery his mother was crying too.

'No way. I would never do that, intentionally do that to anyone.'

'Did you intend to cause harm to [Kwementyaye]?'

Through his sobbing I heard the words 'he was unconscious'. He was asked if he wanted to continue.

'Yeah.'

'Sure?'

'This is just the part that I knew was going to be hard.'

He kept sobbing.

'Let us know when you're right to continue, okay. Take your time.'

He blew his nose and cried more. After about a minute he said to keep going.

'What did you intend when you approached [Kwementyaye]?'

'I'd say nothing went through my head. I didn't think about what was going to happen, what I was going to do. Everything sort of fell into place, happened so quickly.'

'Have you ever kicked anyone in the head like that before?'

'No.' He was crying so much now that he could barely speak. 'It was such a dog act, to kick him on the ground.'

No-one would disagree with his judgment of himself. No-one who watched and listened would doubt his self-disgust, his remorse. What had sounded disturbingly casual in the re-enactment now took on a different inflection – the relief of having unburdened himself. The police had become in a strange way his confidants. They already knew the worst from his own mouth.

~

By 6 April 2010 the Director of Public Prosecutions had effectively offered to drop the charges of murder against the five in exchange for their guilty pleas to manslaughter. A plea bargain like this is a common enough occurrence. Other cases, involving far greater degrees of violence on defenceless victims have also been the subject of plea bargains. They are the decision of the Director of Public Prosecutions, based on an assessment of the likelihood of securing a conviction in a jury trial. The Northern Territory's mandatory penalty of 'life' for a murder conviction makes a guilty plea to the charge highly unlikely in any circumstance. For a manslaughter conviction, imprisonment for life is a maximum but not mandatory penalty.

As the terms of the plea were negotiated, the assault on Kwementyaye was separated from the events in the river. These were reduced to one count, to be faced only by the driver, Anton Kloeden. He was charged with having 'engaged in conduct that gave rise to a danger of death to Tony Cotchilli' in that he 'drove a motor vehicle through camps being reckless as to the danger of death'. A fresh indictment further removed the circumstance of aggravation – of having used 'an offensive weapon, namely a motor vehicle'. The maximum penalty for reckless endangerment is ten years, but for the same aggravated offence, it is fourteen years.

There is no outside access to the course of negotiations around a plea, but at the end of the committal the indication from lawyers for the four passengers in the Hilux was that they would contest the charges around the events in the river. The evidence from the campers, though widely reported and accepted by the public at face value, would likely have faced strong challenges in court as to its reliability, given that the witnesses had mostly been drinking, by their own admission, and it was inconsistent on a range of points. As well, the crime scenes in the river had not been safeguarded straightaway, which would have led to further challenges. However, there was strong evidence in relation to the endangerment of Tony Cotchilli – including tyre marks across his swag – and this evidence was tied specifically to Kloeden's conduct. As for the car being used as an offensive weapon, the charge was endangerment and not assault. In the committal hearing Kloeden's lawyer had argued that he had not even intended to harass, let alone cause harm. It would have been hard to prove otherwise.

Once the plea terms were settled the proceedings moved quickly, pushed along by Chief Justice Brian Martin. The hearing date was set for Friday 16 April. If he could not finish dealing with the matter then, it would have to wait until July, by which time the accused would have been on remand for almost a full year (although remand periods in other homicide cases have been longer). He would sit on the Saturday if necessary.

The five arrived in court uncomfortably self-conscious in suits and ties. Until then they had always worn open-necked shirts, casual pants. Now they looked like they were dressed for a wedding, especially Doody with his broad white tie, black shirt and dove-grey suit. They sat down in the jury box as the dock only has room for two. No glance to their families and friends in the gallery, eyes down or straight ahead, except when they stood, as their individual charges were read, to say one after the other, 'Guilty, Your Honour.' There were audible sorrowful sighs from the gallery – their parents, I expect.

The Crown prosecutor read the agreed facts onto the record. Essentially they were a distillation of what had been learned during the committal, although the court now heard that Spears had hit Kwementyaye with a bottle, and of a verbatim threat that one of the assailants, unnamed, had uttered during the attack – 'Don't fuck with us!' Verbatim exchanges from the incidents in the river were not included; we simply heard that there had been 'abuse'.

As his reading progressed the prosecutor's voice grew louder and more inflected. He had reached the point where Kwementyaye had been left lying on the road – and was being told by the judge to tone his reading down – when one of Kwementyaye's relatives, an elderly woman, became very upset. Weeping, she got up to leave the court, but at the door she turned and pointed at the accused: 'We're going to get you – see you, white bastards!'

The possible racist nature of the attack on Kwementyaye loomed large in the exchanges between bench and defence. Would these young men have reacted in the same way to a young white man who had thrown a bottle at their car? asked the chief justice, interrupting submissions being made on behalf of Hird. He accepted statements in Hird's references that he had worked alongside Aboriginal people and had had Aboriginal friends over the years. Yet racism takes all sorts of forms, he said, and the issue needed to be addressed. Hird had admitted kicking Kwementyaye – would he have had a different attitude towards a drunk young white man?

Hird's face was furrowed by anxiety. He seemed years older than his then twenty-two years. His lawyer said his actions were a sudden and quick response to a bottle being smashed on the car. There was nothing to suggest that his client was not 'indifferent to race, as he should be'. Indeed Hird's apology to the Ryder family had included acknowledgment of his friendship with some of them 'in his younger years'.

Doody's lawyer also contended that his client had had Aboriginal friends – childhood playmates from next door and later, members of his various sports clubs. He had never shown 'any indication whatsoever of any sort of racism'.

When it was Spears's lawyer's turn, he described a 'healing process' that had started. Spears had previously worked as a station hand at Pine Hill, where his father was employed. According to the station owner's reference, the Aboriginal staff there would be happy to have Spears back as a worker, which would be 'a good start for everyone'.

In all of these arguments a single Aboriginal person, or a few, are being made to stand in for Aboriginal people in general – you get on all right with these Aboriginal individuals, therefore you are not racist. The same strategy is used in the reverse argument – you treat an Aboriginal person or persons badly, therefore you are racist. Focussing his questions on what had actually happened in the river and on Schwarz Crescent, Chief Justice Martin tried to be more discerning.

He returned to the issue first thing as the hearing continued on the Saturday. Overnight he had been considering questions of motivation and of attitudes towards Aboriginal people on the night of the offences. Addressing the lawyer acting for Kloeden, he pointed out that, after initially driving close to the camp on the north side of the causeway, Kloeden had chosen to do so a second time when he returned from driving towards the Telegraph Station. At that time one of the campers had thrown a stick at his car. Then Kloeden drove close to the camp on the south side of the causeway, stopped and words were exchanged. Why should he not infer that 'at the very least' this displayed an attitude on that night of 'complete disrespect and lack of regard' for these people, because they were Aboriginal people camped in the riverbed.

The action did show a lack of regard and disrespect, agreed Kloeden's lawyer, but, even though it is 'notorious' that the majority of people in the riverbed are Aboriginal, he could not accept that there was specific intent to go out and look for Aboriginal people to annoy. His client had entered the riverbed for different reasons, he had travelled up it from Tunks Road causeway (well downstream from the events) and there had been no suggestion that any other group of people had attracted his attention. Chief Justice Martin accepted that the initial motivation for entering the riverbed was 'lairising, hooning and having fun', but once one camp had been targeted, a second camp was, when no-one had done anything in the second camp to provoke Kloeden's attention. That was concerning him.

Kloeden was more inscrutable than his co-offenders. His face gave nothing away, though once or twice, during private exchanges with his lawyer, I had glimpsed his youth in half-embarrassed, half-grateful smiles. Responding to the chief justice, his lawyer said Kloeden had told him that driving through people's camps is expected behaviour at the annual Finke Desert Race. Doing this is a 'feature of Alice Springs youth culture', he said. As for his client's role in the assault on Kwementyaye, he rejected that it was motivated by racism: Kloeden had wanted to retaliate for the bottle being smashed on the car. The lawyer illustrated the point with an anecdote from his own experience. After buying a gelato in Adelaide's Hindley Street he had been standing on the edge of the footpath when a flashy red car almost drove over his toes. He reacted by bringing down his hand on the roof of the car: instantly four men jumped out and began laying into him. They punched him a few times in the face and left him lying on the ground. It was an experience that hundreds if not thousands of men in Australia had had, he suggested: 'You touch someone's car, you place yourself at risk.' Reacting in this way to Kwementyaye's action was nonetheless wrong, which was why his client was pleading guilty, but it was not an example of racially motivated violence.

Chief Justice Martin also wanted to hear from Hird's lawyer about why his client had got the imitation pistol. Why had the five returned to the causeway? And why had they stopped on the corner before entering the causeway, while the pistol was unjammed?

It was because they had detoured via a nearby street where they had stopped to see a cousin of Spears, said the lawyer. From there the causeway was a logical route to the Stuart Highway and on to the west side of town, to Spears's mother's place. And they had stopped on the causeway corner because the pistol was jammed.

But there was no need to unjam the pistol, countered the chief justice – unless it was to let off a round and scare people in the camp from where the stick had been thrown. Why should he not infer that the pistol was deliberately pointed northwards to scare those people? He would be drawing that inference unless he heard evidence to the contrary.

If the intention had been to scare the campers, argued Kloeden's lawyer, the round would have been let off immediately opposite the camp. However, the round was let off at the far end of the causeway and none of the witnesses from the northern camp had made a statement about having seen or heard the gun. He said the gun had also been discharged earlier at some distance from the river. The motivation on both occasions was to annoy the general population, not specifically the campers, he argued.

Spears's lawyer added that the position of people in the car – with Hird sitting behind the driver and the car driving west – was what led to the pistol being pointed northwards.

The chief justice was unconvinced. He said he would draw the inference that the intention was to frighten, to say 'here you are and basically "up yours"' – not uncommon, he said, in this type of situation of drunks hooning around.

But Hird had the replica pistol at all times, said Swain's lawyer, and there was nothing to suggest that the gun had been passed around the group. Chief Justice Martin expressed impatience with the contention of all counsel that their clients did not know what was going on. Were they trying to tell him that when Hird let off the first round that the others were not all cheering, that they were not part of it? 'I didn't come down in the last shower,' he said.

~

Journalists and commentators looking at these events from afar have been entirely focussed on, even obsessed by, their racial dynamics. This has also been the case for many in Alice Springs. The town has a reputation for racism, despite the strong presence of many who see themselves as anti-racist. Among them, many see matters of racial division and racism in the community as primary, as viscerally overriding whatever else might be going on. Others can see these matters as occurring in everyday life along a spectrum of seriousness; and, as obnoxious, corrosive, vile as they can be, they do not obliterate everything else in considering a given situation – such as, in this case, the coexisting stupidity and aggression of young, very drunk men.

'You couldn't write about a spectrum if you were black,' challenges a friend.

I know I live completely outside the black experience of inter-racial tension. Indigenous writer Alexis Wright describes it as 'like being in hell'.[21] Nonetheless I want to present what two other Aboriginal people here have told me about the racism they've experienced. This is not to provide some kind of 'last word' but they are examples of broad-ranging reflections on the experience of being black in Alice Springs, which includes but is not totally defined by racism.

As a child Damien Armstrong lived in New Ilparpa, a town camp on the Stuart Highway south of the Gap. In high school if he stayed behind for band practice he would miss the bus to take him home; it was a long trudge back carrying his guitar. He'd see schoolmates, who lived in the rural area close to the airport (where I live), being driven home in big 4WDs. They'd tell him the next day that they'd seen him on the highway: 'Gee, thanks for the offer of a lift,' he'd think. It was one of the experiences of adolescence that made him realise that race mattered. I might see it as towards the 'softer' end of the spectrum, but it was still cuttingly fresh in his mind when he spoke of it years later.

It had also gone towards hardening his resolve to achieve, though not everyone reacts like that. He spoke of the deteriorating conditions at the camp, as welfare dependency and grog made their inroads, and some young people around him, including his sister, took their own lives. He had thought of suicide too, but his passion for music saw him through: 'I watched footage of big concerts, in stadiums with thousands of fans and saw that it didn't matter what ethnic background you had. Musicians like Jimi Hendrix, he was a good-looking half-caste bloke. He was making money from his art, he had adoring fans, the world appreciated his talent. I was more determined than ever to learn how to play, to see the world and what it had to offer.' He went on to establish the band NoKTuRNL, which allowed him to do just that.[22]

I interviewed Armstrong in November 2010. More recently I sat down with the actor, writer, producer Trisha Morton-Thomas.[23] She was doing pre-publicity for the comedy series *8MMM Aboriginal Radio*, set in Alice Springs, which aired on ABC television in 2015. She too spoke of realising in adolescence that race mattered: coming from an Aboriginal family in Central Australia she 'didn't have the same freedom as [her] non-Aboriginal counterparts'. 'I don't know if it's racism,' she said, 'but more like ignorance from other Australians that try to keep you down all the time.' She didn't see that it was her job to educate people: 'If you're not being taught the truth about this country at school, it's up to you to pick yourself up and go away and study it, or learn something about it on your own. If you're constantly swallowing what the media and anyone in control is giving you, then you're never going to be free, as an individual or as a society. You have to be thinking.'

But there was a threshold beyond which she felt obliged to act. We were speaking at a time when there was an outbreak of vile racist commentary on the Facebook sites of certain groups in Alice Springs. Morton-Thomas was angry and thought it was high time to involve the Anti-Discrimination Commission: 'I believe in freedom of speech,' she said, 'but there are certain words you don't use. These words are meant to hurt people, that's why they say them, they are meant to downgrade and make people feel small, worthless and useless, words like boong and coon and nigger and black "c"'s.' She said she loves Alice Springs, she spoke of the humour, the generosity of many, of the times when the 'whole town will come out in support of an Aboriginal cause', of other times when the attitude is 'those bloody Aborigines whingeing again'. But she was not prepared to put up with abuse: in such cases 'pulling out the race card is our only defence'.

For neither Armstrong nor Morton-Thomas was racism all-encompassing, as sharp and deep and varied as their experiences of it had been. It was one of the things to consider when thinking about the town or telling their own stories. Morton-Thomas had more reason than many to resent police, for instance, to suspect them of racism. Her nephew Kwementyaye Briscoe had died in police custody. The coronial inquest found staff who had been 'utterly derelict' in their duties and an extensive 'catalogue of errors' in the way Briscoe had been treated, suggesting 'mismanagement for a period of time by Police Command at a level higher than just "local"', but it did not identify any criminal offences.[24] Morton-Thomas felt a deep rage with police over the death (as well as with the town's drinking culture and the government's alcohol policies).[25] Yet when it came to portraying police in *8MMM Aboriginal Radio*, she believed she had been 'very fair': 'I could have portrayed them as just hostile, but there's a mixture, and I think it is a pretty balanced mixture in the police and in the community.' Armstrong spoke about his experience of class as well as racism: 'In primary school, children don't see the world in terms of class, your mates are your mates. In high school, your clothes aren't good enough, where you live starts to affect you socially, affect what opportunities you can have in life.

These things start to matter even between Aboriginal people. There's a class division between people who live in town and town campers.' And for him too the grog loomed large as a social issue: 'In the camp people had stopped looking after their houses and their own health. What was once a nice place had changed.' He recalled the turning point: he was in his first year of high school when he started to see people living in camp whom he didn't know, and the space on the camp that had been used for an after-school program, as an art room and playroom, became a drinking spot.

At the time of Kwementyaye Ryder's death, excessive drinking and what to do about it had dominated the town's political debate and field of social action for more than a decade (from well before the Intervention's attempts to stem 'the rivers of grog'). Drunkenness in the Ryder case would be the focus of the *Centralian Advocate*'s commentator, a local journalist who had followed the court proceedings from the outset. Drunkenness had 'clouded [the] judgment' of the offenders; drunkenness and rage at their actions had led Kwementyaye to 'lash out and throw a bottle at the side of the car'; drunkenness had 'confused his motor functions' – 'he might have escaped had he not been drunk'. Noting the chief justice's 'pinpointing' of the case's 'racist overtones', he wrote: 'But the township of Alice Springs often shows it has made pockets of peace in the racial divide. Making peace with alcohol could be a much longer wait.'[26]

My own comment at the end of the case took on the race debate, albeit at a tangent. I argued that there was some collective responsibility for what had happened, arising from 'the complacent society that produces such a gulf of experience between black and white'. My focus was on employment and lack of it, and the way that this situation was feeding attitudes of contempt on one side, resentment on the other, anger on both. There was no great contrast between Kwementyaye and his attackers in this regard. He was employed as a trainee ranger at the time of his death and had a history of fencing and stock work, while the five also had full-time jobs or apprenticeships. But that similarity was not (and is not) typical of those coming before the courts, and high unemployment was and is strongly associated with high levels of violence and other ills in Aboriginal communities. Pertinent to my argument was one of the key recommendations to come from a meeting at the time of some 150 local Aboriginal men concerned to 'Stop the Violence' (their activity had begun a year before Kwementyaye's death and was ongoing): 'We need real jobs,' they said. 'When males are unemployed we are disempowered, bored, angry and frustrated. This leads to substance misuse and violence. In a job we are happier, healthier and better members of our communities and leaders of our families. Put us to work so we can take personal responsibility for our lives.'[27]

Another local perspective had come from a medical doctor in a letter to the *Centralian Advocate* following the burning of Kwementyaye's memorial cross, written when that was still assumed to have been a deliberate act. He noted the greater segregation between black and white that had developed in his quarter of a century in the town, 'to the detriment of all'. One 'unintended' cause, he suggested, was the development of alternative private high schools to the one public high school where everyone mixed. 'Increasing affluence' was another, leading to greater use of cars to get around town and thus less time spent in public places, with less casual interaction between people. The 'fencing off' of school grounds and sporting facilities, controversially under way as he was writing, was another factor – 'part of what drives fear of "the other", which exacerbates the antisocial behaviour of the "have-nots".' He had seen the development of 'antagonistic attitudes and fear' even within his own family. He deplored the lack of significant initiatives by the then Labor government 'to create social harmony between

Aboriginal and non-Aboriginal people, and to decrease the gap between the haves and the have-nots'.

'We all live here,' he wrote. 'More Territory residents than ever before were born here, and, black or white, feel part of this landscape. Our politicians have failed to provide leadership on this, the fundamental issue of NT politics ... It is time for all of us to let our leaders know where their responsibility lies.'[28]

There were echoes in his letter of the statements made to date by Kwementyaye's family (and that would be made later by Kwementyaye's aunty, Karen Liddle). After the case was finalised some of the family would become less conciliatory, more critical of the legal process and more inclined to see it as discriminating against Aboriginal people. Margie Lynch Kngwarraye, another of Kwementyaye's aunties, was among them. She is well known in Alice Springs for her forthright views on Aboriginal issues. In a letter to the *Centralian Advocate* following what she saw as the 'lenient' sentencing, she described the crime as 'a vicious act of violence' which had been 'excused' by lawyers as part of a youth culture of 'hooning and lairising'. (In fact, the terms 'hooning and lairising' had been applied to the events in the river, not to the assault on Kwementyaye.) Kngwarraye saw 'bias' in the chief justice's hastening of the plea hearing, which had been overly concerned with the welfare of the defendants, she argued; and the court had also ignored the victim impact statements attesting to Kwementyaye's good character, while it had taken the defendants' character references into account.[29]

Sometimes, during sentencing submissions, victim impact statements are read onto the record by the Crown prosecutor, particularly if a victim, such as a relative of the deceased, asks for it to be done. Relatives seem to find this goes some way towards vindicating the value of the life lost and they take a measure of comfort from it. Their statements are sometimes also incorporated in judges' sentencing remarks. We see instances of both in other cases in this book. I don't know why it wasn't done by the Crown prosecutor in this case. Perhaps the haste of preparing for the plea hearing did have something to do with it. At sentencing Chief Justice Martin commented that 'it is unnecessary and inappropriate to detail publicly the personal and intimate information provided in the victim impact statements'. Yet it seems that the family would have appreciated that at least their accounts of Kwementyaye's life be read onto the record. They were hurt by the failure to do so and were not comforted, or not sufficiently, by the chief justice's summarised acknowledgment, respectful though it was. It was an opportunity missed, in contrast to many other aspects of his judgment, in which he showed an acute awareness of the exceptional community interest in this case and of the need for its adjudication to be well understood.

Kngwarraye saw that failure and other points she identified, including statements by the chief justice in another matter, as making a case for reform of the judicial system: its sentencing was 'impacting the stability of the whole community', she said, and it was contributing to ongoing racial discrimination towards Aboriginal people. On the matter of character references, however, Kngwarraye overlooked the fact that Kwementyaye's good character was not being contested, unlike that of the defendants. The point of defendants' character references – which in my experience are always accepted more or less at face value – is to assess potential for rehabilitation.

The most sober of the 'outside' examinations of the case would be by *Four Corners*, but it framed a simplistic 'yes or no' assessment of the crime as a racially motivated attack.[30] *The Drum*'s commentator would have the attack as 'an overtly racist act of violence' in which Kwementyaye was 'beaten to death'.[31] *Overland*'s commentator felt a comparison to the American deep south was begging, and went on to discuss 'the *rise* of racism in Alice Springs' (my emphasis). This he based on the Ryder case – including 'the shocking views' of many of

Four Corners' interviewees – and on one other reported incident of racial harassment. He also took *Four Corners* to task for even seeking to interview the families of the perpetrators, which he saw as 'a terrible moral failure'.[32]

Calm analysis in the public domain of whether or not particular statements or conduct are racist and of the damage flowing from them is rare enough in Alice Springs and, judging by these moralising certainties, in the national arena too. These commentators would have their supporters in Alice Springs. Six years later the fatal attack on Kwementyaye is still being described by some here as a 'vigilante' crime. That implies a level of ideology, intent and organisation behind the actions of the five for which the court heard no evidence and a lot of not implausible counter-arguments. Racism was 'the elephant in the room' of the case, as Kloeden's lawyer had acknowledged. In the plea hearing the chief justice's questions and comments addressing that elephant sounded forthright and insistent to me. His judgment would weigh his reasoning carefully with the arguments put on behalf of the defendants.

~

We did not hear from the defendants themselves on the racism issue, but from two of them there was an assessment of their actions in their own words. There had been Swain's police interview – his naming of the attack on Kwementyaye as 'a dog act' – and now a statement came from Anton Kloeden. It was written by hand and read aloud by his lawyer. Kloeden later agreed for a typed verbatim copy to be released to me:

> In the heat of the moment it never crossed my mind an assault would cause death.
>
> I am sincerely sorry it has taken the death of Mr Ryder to realise violence is not the answer to resolving problems.

The hurt and trouble this has caused the Ryder family & my family I can guarantee it will always be on [my] mind & I will never put myself in a situation like it again.

I may not have got out of the car but I completely understand my decision to turn the car around to resolve the issue was not the right choice & unfortunately the death of Mr Ryder was the result. Something never intended but happened none the less.

Without knowing someone its easy to judge them. Young, dumb got caught by police he must be guilty & assault people often which is not the case at all.

I didn't know Mr Ryder at all & judged him from one act – throwing a bottle at my car & as the driver took it upon myself to confront him.

The speed of which it all happened, the actions of the others & being in the wrong lane meant I stayed in the car.

After 8 months in jail the worst punishment has been done – Caused pain & trouble for the Ryder family, my family (the innocent victims who don't deserve any of it), have on my mind for the rest of my life that a person is dead because of my actions & having a criminal record – manslaughter at that & the implications of it (work, travel …).

These are all lifelong punishments.

It had taken Kloeden that time in gaol to accept responsibility for his role in Kwementyaye's death, said his lawyer. He did not have this self-critical awareness initially. Having stayed in the car, he had struggled to see his conduct as legally liable for the death. He accepted now that it was circumstance, not moral courage, that had meant he avoided more direct involvement in the assault. He was even 'quite glad' – his words, said the lawyer – to have been sent to gaol, recognising it as 'a wake-up call' and the 'correct punishment'. This was despite being on G Block, where remand and maximum security prisoners are held, and seeing each day 'a person drag their fingers across their throat in a signal to him, an unmistakeable signal to him and his co-offenders'. The lawyer continued: 'There's one bloke in the gaol who says, "We're going to chop off your head. We know where you live, we'll kill your family, rape your grandma, rape your sister, cook you like a kangaroo. When you get out you're going to get fucked. There's a price on your head. The family's waiting for you ... We're going to kill your father, Selwyn Kloeden." For him hearing those last words is the worst thing.'

The vengeful threats stood in strong contrast to the restrained public statements by the Ryder family, although Therese Ryder confirmed to *Four Corners* that they were real: not coming from her quiet Catholic family but from other family members in other communities 'where we would be shoved aside'.[33] At the time of writing there has been no retribution of this kind, but all Kloeden knew then was that his parents had been working for years in the Aboriginal community of Hermannsburg, west of Alice Springs, and he too was known there. He had finished high school interstate but used to go to Hermannsburg during the holidays. After Kwementyaye's death, there had been a meeting with community elders where they confirmed that the Kloedens were welcome to stay. His mother was a school teacher, though, and the Department of Education was not going to risk it. They would only offer her a job in town, so for some time his parents had to live apart.

The consequence of the threats for Kloeden and his co-offenders was that they were kept away from the general prison population, which was at least 80 per cent Aboriginal, and confined to their cells for twenty-two hours a day. These harsh conditions were likely to endure, Kloeden's lawyer submitted, for the term of their sentence. (Soon after sentencing, however, the lockdown decreased to eighteen hours a day.)[34]

At the plea hearing Joshua Spears made a new admission through his lawyer that the blow from the bottle he used to strike Kwementyaye had been to the back of the head. A stubby-size Strongbow cider bottle had been found at the scene with both his and Kwementyaye's DNA on it; it hadn't broken. His lawyer described the admission as 'life-changing' – over-cooking it perhaps, but as with Kloeden it showed Spears taking increasing responsibility for what he had done. Initially – out of 'sheer fear', said his lawyer – he had denied even getting out of the car. Now he wanted the Ryder family to know that he saw his attack on Kwementyaye as a 'cowardly act' that he 'deeply regretted'. He had not foreseen its consequences: he had thought it would be a 'quick dust-up and off, over and done with'. He didn't intend to seriously harm Kwementyaye, but he didn't have the life experience or maturity to make a proper decision at the time.

'Informed decisions are not made by people when they are blind drunk,' observed the chief justice.

No-one was surprised to learn just how heavily they had been drinking, all except Kloeden. He told his lawyer he had had nothing to drink after sundown the night before, as he knew he would be driving.

Spears had started the Friday night at a friend's place, downing six cans of rum, presumably mixed with Coke. He went on to Bo's – Bojangles Saloon, a nightclub, now defunct, styling itself as a bar from the Wild West (and where, we would later learn, Kwementyaye had first met his fiancée). At Bo's Spears had four, maybe six, vodka and oranges. Sometime after midnight he made his way to the 24 Hour Store on the next block, no doubt to get something to eat, a hot pie maybe, part of many a Friday night drinking routine. From there he got a lift across the river to the casino, but he was refused entry – he was too drunk. The other four had been inside and now came out. It was between two and three in the morning. A couple they knew had rented a room in the casino hotel; they went there and drank some more, leaving at around six. Then they headed off up the river in Kloeden's car, with Spears in the front passenger seat. His recall of the trip was not strong, said his lawyer, but he did know that he had more to drink – some Strongbow cider picked up at Swain and Hird's place.

Hird had a beer with his father late on Friday afternoon. On the way home he bought a carton of Strongbow cider. He drank steadily through the evening with a friend who had his own supply, until going to the casino in the early hours where he drank some more. It was a night 'punctuated by drinking', said his lawyer, with no meal that his client could recall.

Swain was likely to have been Hird's drinking companion as they lived in the same house. He began on a 700-ml bottle of Bundaberg Rum around 5.30 pm. He drank the hard liquor, without sharing, into the early hours, when he topped up with a schooner at the casino. His lawyer calculated he'd had the equivalent of twenty standard drinks, about as prodigious a total as any heard of in the cases described in this book.

Doody's lawyer didn't specify the liquor consumed but suggested that his client was probably the 'worst off' of them all. Doody had been working out bush and it was his 'pattern' to come into town on Fridays and let his hair down with his mates – 'the gentlemen seated in the dock'. His recall of events after leaving the casino was vague as he was 'happily affected by alcohol'. He did remember going to Swain and Hird's place to get more grog but he doesn't drink cider and still had his own supplies.

Evidence at the committal hearing from various of their friends had suggested that Swain and Hird at least continued drinking through the day after the attack on Kwementyaye. What had happened was weighing on Swain's mind; he talked about it to more than one friend: he was 'very drunk', 'sick and pale', an Aboriginal man had thrown a rock at the car and 'they bashed him and left him there', he thought he'd 'fucked up', 'they may have killed a fellow', 'maybe a jogger had seen it'.

A by-product of the evidence was more detail, if any was needed, of the drinking culture in their circle. On the Friday, at the end of his working week, Spears's brother Nathan had a rum with his grandfather and turned in after dinner, but he started drinking at a friend's place mid-morning on the Saturday, a six-pack of Bundaberg Rum mixers. Later that day he bought a ten-pack of the same and went to another friend's place. That night he went to Bo's. On the Sunday, he was 'pretty hungover'. A friend of Spears, Andrew Kerr – very reluctant to give evidence – spoke of having had 'drinks' the weekend before when he had 'tried to smash a bottle' on his own head – 'a bit of a game we had going'. Another friend, Zac Eckermann, speaking of 25 July, said of himself he had had 'a lot to drink that day and night'.

~

Three of the five offenders were in trades, and the other two were likely headed that way. Swain had tried his hand at several: tiling, mechanics, spray-painting and finally pest control, with various labouring jobs in between. He was now well into a two-year traineeship as a pest controller. Hird was a qualified cabinet-maker, having started his apprenticeship at age sixteen. Kloeden had Year Twelve under his belt and was an apprentice boiler-maker. Doody had started Year Twelve but withdrew and began an apprenticeship as a refrigeration mechanic. When his employer went out of business he turned to bush work in property maintenance. Spears had completed Year Eleven 'but only just'. He had a flair for drawing and began a sign-writing apprenticeship though he didn't keep it up. After an eighteen-month stint at Pine Hill Station, where his father worked, he had come back to town, taking a job at an equipment hire firm.

This background explains no doubt the presence of several men in hi-vis vests and work boots who were in the packed public gallery for the sentencing one week later. Unusually, room had been made in the witness box for a television camera (to be focussed only on the chief justice), and extra chairs were brought in for the large media contingent, including some journalists from national outlets. I chose to sit among the families: Swain's mother and sister were on my left, and on my right were members of Kwementyaye's family – Karen Liddle, her three daughters, and Therese Ryder further along. Tears were already running down her face.

Chief Justice Martin began his 'unenviable task', looking directly at the five. They all met his gaze, at least to start with: 'What began as an unremarkable night in Alice Springs when the group of you set out to have a social night and, elsewhere, the deceased did likewise, ended the next morning with a tragedy from which there are no winners. First and most importantly, a life has been taken needlessly. The unlawful killing of the thirty-three-year-old male victim is a great tragedy and leaves a legacy of grief, anger and distress among family and friends. In addition, a violent death through the commission of a crime diminishes our wider community. Imprisonment of the offenders cannot change these consequences. Imprisonment will punish and express the strong disapproval of the community, but it cannot compensate for the loss of a life.'

If Kwementyaye had not died, the offenders 'would have been guilty of an assault that caused relatively minor harm', said the chief justice: 'It needs to be understood clearly that although cowardly and violent, your joint physical attack upon the deceased did not cause any fractures and did not cause any major external injury. In particular, the deceased's skull was not fractured … Ordinarily, it is not expected that a victim of an assault causing such relatively minor injuries will die. But the deceased did die.'

The cause of death, as we had heard at the committal, was bleeding from a blood vessel at the base of the brain, and this was most likely the result of a pre-existing aneurism bursting. What caused it to burst had not been precisely determined, but it was accepted that the conduct of the five was responsible:

'The group of you threatened [him] and chased him with the intention of assaulting him. In fear he ran away and fell over. The aneurism might have burst when he ran and fell and, therefore, you are responsible because your threatening conduct caused him to run and fall. Alternatively, the aneurism might have burst when blows were struck to his head. If the blows were the cause, your physical attack upon the deceased directly caused his death, but it is impossible to know whether it was the blows or the fall.

'In one way or another, all of you were involved in the threat, chase and violence inflicted upon the deceased. In this way you are all responsible for the dreadful consequences of your unlawful conduct, notwithstanding that the victim was susceptible to suffering dire consequences as a result of relatively minor trauma.'

Many people in Alice Springs and most reporters and commentators have struggled to acknowledge the facts of the limited violence of the attack on Kwementyaye. *Four Corners* nowhere mentioned the assessment of the injuries as 'relatively minor'.[35] *The Australian* swept the chief justice's remarks aside, describing instead a 'brutal assault', in which Swain – the 'trainee pest exterminator', 'consumed by hate' – had 'lined up Ryder' for his 'vicious' kicks; and Spears had 'crashed' a cider bottle on Ryder's head in a 'savage' blow that had 'probably triggered the brain aneurism that caused his death' – most of this was wild hyperbole, and the last suggestion entirely inaccurate (the chief justice had said the blow from the bottle had likely caused the laceration to the back of Kwementyaye's head).[36] A British journalist, in a feature article published in *The*

Guardian, preferred his own opinion of the forensic evidence to the pathologist's. For him the forensics seemed 'clear and devastating' and things 'looked grim' for the offenders until 'in almost every moment that matters' the chief justice 'excuse[d] the "relatively minor violence" he found took place'.[37]

For *Overland* and *The Drum*, both commentators rejected that the violence could be considered negligent. 'I'm no lawyer,' said *The Drum*'s commentator, 'but last time I checked, repeatedly kicking a defenceless man in the head and smashing him over the back of his skull with a bottle was quite a bit more than "negligent".'[38] The *Overland* commentator expressed himself in similar terms. Neither felt the need to reflect upon the chief justice's clearly outlined explanations and reasoning; and both showed themselves to be unfamiliar with, or uninterested in, the legal process involved: the guilty plea had been made without specifying whether the offence was negligent or reckless (practices have changed since, and indictments now expressly state what element applies, as we saw in the Sebastian Kunoth plea). The chief justice was thus in a position of having to satisfy himself that recklessness – in effect, an aggravating circumstance – had been proven beyond reasonable doubt.

Both commentators were also ignoring the frequency and nature of casual male violence, the sometimes lethal consequences of which are notorious. Another local example is found in the events leading to the death of Scott McConnell's friend, the subject of the next chapter. That killing also had racial dynamics, although they attracted virtually no outside attention. More interesting, though, is the parallel violent behaviour of the men involved, some of them significantly older than Ryder's attackers. It defies a simplistic black versus white analysis: the alleged killers may have been black, but so were two of the five men in the McConnell group, all of them intent on pursuing the fight until just before its fatal conclusion.

~

In the killing of Kwementyaye Ryder, Chief Justice Martin found that none of the five offenders 'thought about the possibility of death occurring' and none 'intended to cause serious harm'. Thus the manslaughter of which they were guilty was not reckless, which would have involved 'an awareness of a substantial risk that death would result'. It was negligent, involving 'a great falling short of the standard of care that a reasonable person would exercise in the circumstances'.

Each offender admitted responsibility for the death in the sense of aiding and abetting the others in the attack, but their physical roles and moral culpability were not identical, which is why they would receive varying sentences.

The chief justice accepted that Doody had not touched Kwementyaye, but, he said, 'You are responsible for the consequences because, although you did not say anything, you encouraged the others by your presence and you knew there would be a physical assault. In your drunken state, however, the possibility of serious harm or death did not occur to you. Like all the others, in the space of those few seconds you simply did not give any thought to the consequences.'

He accepted that Hird had initially got the replica pistol to have fun: 'However, somewhere in the journey you decided to fire it off in the vicinity of the Schwarz Crescent causeway for the purpose of scaring the people in the camp to the north of the causeway. In your drunken state, you started behaving like a lout and you were displaying a degree of aggression which was uncharacteristic for you.

'When you became aware that a bottle had been thrown at the car, according to your counsel you have a memory of saying "Let it go", but Mr Kloeden did the quick U-turn. I am far from persuaded that you took such a benign attitude. If you did, your attitude changed very quickly after Mr Kloeden pulled the vehicle to a halt and the deceased ran away. You were the first out of the vehicle.'

Hird had reacted 'spontaneously and instinctively', without 'rational thought', 'with anger and with an intention of physically attacking the victim'. He was the first to reach him, and rather than confront him verbally, notwithstanding that Kwementyaye had fallen to the ground, he kicked him in the head. The fact that he was wearing soft shoes was 'purely fortuitous'.

'Subsequently, when you learnt of the consequences, like the others you were sick with worry about the implications for your own life and you were so unwell that you were unable to go to work. Eventually when you were arrested you found it to be a relief.'

Only Kloeden was held responsible for deciding to enter the river and for what had happened there. The chief justice accepted that he had not initially had in mind to harass anyone, but as he was driving he made 'the offensive and stupid decision to harass the Aboriginal people camped in the riverbed'. His conduct was also 'highly dangerous'. It was 'highly likely' that he knew some of the people in the camps would have been asleep and some affected by alcohol. While he 'aimed to miss', he did so with an awareness that he was creating 'a substantial risk to the life of those in the camp and you decided to take that risk'. It was 'pure good luck' that he had not injured or killed people in the northern camp and, in particular, the old man Tony Cotchilli, who'd been unable to get out of the way.

He had 'displayed aggression' even though he was sober. This was his 'underlying state of mind' when he heard the bottle (thrown by Kwementyaye) smash on the side of his car. 'In a spontaneous moment of anger, and with confrontation and retribution flashing through your mind, you did the quick U-turn. Your action in executing the U-turn and driving up to the deceased amounted to an aggressive threat to the deceased and was carried out in the expectation that the deceased would be attacked physically in some way. In this way you encouraged a physical assault, which you anticipated would occur, but I accept that you did so without giving any thought to the nature of the physical attack or the possible consequences of it.'

There had been evidence that Kloeden had driven away 'at a leisurely, normal pace'.

'I accept,' said the chief justice, 'that when you drove away you did not realise that the deceased had been killed or seriously injured, but it was obvious that an attack had taken place leaving the deceased lying on the ground not moving. Your actions in driving away in this manner disclose a lack of concern for the wellbeing of the victim.

'Subsequently, when you found out that the deceased had died, like the others you were terrified about your own predicament, but you were also appalled at the consequences of your conduct. Although you knew that you would inevitably be caught, you agreed with Mr Swain to tell a false story. In the week following the killing, you were in such a state of extreme anxiety that you lost six kilograms in weight.'

Spears, 'heavily intoxicated', was the last out of the car and was carrying the stubby bottle of cider. The chief justice found Spears's admission, that he had struck Kwementyaye on the back of the head with the bottle, 'very much to [his] credit'. The blow, as we have learned, was likely the cause of the laceration to the back of Kwementyaye's head.

As with the others, he found that Spears had not given any thought to the consequences of the attack: 'You followed along with the actions of the others in a spontaneous response to the smashing of the bottle [on the car]. You are not a violent person by nature and, not only were you younger than the other offenders, but in my assessment you lacked the maturity to make decisions independent of the collective response to the smashing of the bottle.'

Swain too was given credit for his 'full and frank confession' and other assistance to police. He had been the only one of the five to confess. He was very drunk at the time of the attack and the chief justice found that he had followed Hird out of the car 'in a spontaneous reaction ... not knowing what to expect or what might occur'. When he kicked Kwementyaye twice in the head, it was out of anger and as part of the group attack, but like the others he was not thinking rationally and gave no thought to the consequences.

'After you had delivered your two kicks, you realised something was wrong because the deceased was lying motionless on the shoulder of the road. You stopped and, when you became aware of a vehicle approaching, it was then that you called out "Let's go". You called out because you realised the deceased had stopped moving and was unable to defend himself and because there was a vehicle coming.'

As the long judgment wore on, the Ryder family to my right became more and more distressed, crying and with heads in their hands. Tears were also streaming down the faces of Swain's mother and sister on my left. The chief justice spoke of the Ryders' 'devastation', of Therese Ryder's eloquent and sorrowful victim impact statement in which she had said that her son's death felt like 'the end of the world'. She wanted the offenders sentenced to life because they had taken a life. He saw this as 'perfectly understandable' but it was not the way the law of the Northern Territory worked. A sentence of life imprisonment is reserved for cases in the worst category of manslaughter and this crime 'does not fit into that category', he said. As with all crimes, there is 'a scale of seriousness'.

The relativising of a son's death, the detail of each offender's role in it – essential as this is to the court process – would be a torment for any mother to hear. On top of it Therese Ryder had had to listen to the outline of the offenders' past lives, one after the other, and their prospects for rehabilitation, all deemed 'excellent'.

The chief justice based this assessment on submissions from the offenders' lawyers, as is standard. The same kind of submissions are made on behalf of Aboriginal offenders, looking at family background (including hardship, physical and emotional, if present), education, training, employment, as well as acknowledging, where relevant, kinship and traditional responsibilities (we have seen examples in earlier chapters). The prosecution provides information about the offenders' criminal histories, if any.

Overland's commentator found the chief justice's summaries 'the most appalling part of his decision … He notes character references in [the offenders'] favour, proving that many of them have friends and employers who think nice things about them. This hardly balances out what they did.'[39] The writer seems to be labouring under a misapprehension: the offenders' backgrounds were not being considered as mitigating factors in assessing their culpability, but rather as a way of assessing their prospects for rehabilitation. The flipside of their advantage, which his outrage ignores, is that there was nothing in their backgrounds that could mitigate their culpability – no disadvantage, like that considered frequently by the courts and given weight to, especially when offenders are young.

For each of the five the chief justice accepted that their actions in the killing were 'totally out of character'. Various acts of kindness or generosity on their part in other contexts were acknowledged: Doody had given up his plans to race in The Finke in order to help a paraplegic friend do so; Hird was living with a young woman who had a child from a previous relationship and was said by his partner to be 'very kind-hearted and respectful' and to be playing an important role 'as a father figure for her son'; Swain was the sponsor of 'an underprivileged child from a foreign country' with whom he corresponded.

I watched the five as the chief justice spoke of each of them individually, their faces either flaming or drained of colour; Hird and Spears both cried. I expect it was from a mixture of excruciating shame and anxiety.

Doody and Spears had never come into contact with the criminal justice system; the other three had, for minor offences: Hird for a cannabis offence, no conviction recorded; Kloeden for assault, no conviction recorded, and some road traffic offences; Swain for two dishonesty offences seven years earlier, and one conviction for driving dangerously.

There was a strong emphasis on the work records of all five and on the fact that their employers were all willing to have them back at the end of their term in prison. More than once Chief Justice Martin commended the attitude of these employers. While he referred to difficulties some of the five had experienced as they grew up, all of them had the support of their families – described variously as stable, loving, supportive, hard-working, well known – and each had positive references from a range of referees.

It was more than Therese Ryder could bear. She got up to leave but through her tears she cried out – the offenders might look 'good on the outside, inside there is racism straight out!'

The chief justice had already spoken at some length about what he termed the 'racial overtones' of the case. He accepted that the offenders had each grown up in circumstances that had brought them into 'close contact' with Aboriginal people and that they had always 'gotten on well' with them. However, on this occasion their 'normal attitude and standards of behaviour were pushed into the background'.

'I am satisfied that as the Hilux crossed the causeway, within the vehicle there was a negative attitude towards, and an atmosphere of antagonism towards, Aboriginal people. This group of young men was then confronted by an Aboriginal person, the deceased, standing on the roadway holding a bottle. It is relevant that it was an Aboriginal person who threw the bottle which smashed against the side of the vehicle.

'If a drunk white man had done likewise, I am satisfied that as a group, the offenders would have reacted angrily and sought to confront him. However, it is difficult to avoid the conclusion that the nature and rapidity of the reaction, and the actions of some offenders in kicking and striking the deceased while he was on the ground were influenced, at least to some degree, by the fact that the deceased was an Aboriginal person. Ultimately it remains unknown whether the attack would have gone as far as it did if the deceased had been a drunk white person. I doubt that any of the offenders now know the answer to that question.'

The chief justice was drawing the inferences that he had warned the defence he would. It seemed to me a meaningful teasing-out of what was known to have taken place, stopping short of what could not be known with certainty. He came back to the issue when he analysed the features of the crime. Out of seven elements he identified, the first three concerned the abuse of, and aggression and antagonism towards Aboriginal people and Kwementyaye Ryder. He then came to aggravating circumstances, which have to be proven beyond reasonable doubt. He identified four: that the attack was carried out jointly; that Kwementyaye was lying on the ground, defenceless and incapable of posing any threat; that the kicks and blow with the bottle were delivered to the head; and that a weapon (the bottle) was used. The primary motive, he found, was to 'exact retribution' for the bottle being smashed on the car. Then he returned to the race issue: 'The responses and actions of Mr Kloeden, Mr Hird, Mr Spears and Mr Swain were influenced to some degree by the fact that the deceased was an Aboriginal person. However,' he reiterated, 'it remains unknown whether the attack would have gone as far as it did if the deceased had been a drunk white person.'

Four Corners described the chief justice's approach as 'cautious',[40] although caution is surely what should be deployed in any judgment of a serious criminal matter. *The Guardian*'s journalist saw the remarks as 'a masterpiece of stuttering reticence'.[41] Missing for the *Overland* commentator was a proper 'sense of revulsion' – 'the five young men engaged in recreational activities that wouldn't be out of place in a gathering of Klansmen'. Their attack on Ryder 'was an attack on Aboriginal people in Australia' and the judgment 'was an attack on our decency as a people'.[42]

To consider these comments it is worth digressing to another Alice Springs case where race hate was found to be proven.[43] In early 2006 a defenceless Aboriginal man was attacked by two white men. They had come across their victim lying on the floor in an abandoned house known to be frequented by Aboriginal drinkers. Their attack was premeditated (they had gone looking for a fight), entirely unprovoked, and it involved two courses of action: after a first assault the attackers went away, then returned for a second go. None of the injuries were life-threatening. The assailants each pleaded guilty to two counts of aggravated assault.

In an appeal in 2008 against the severity of their sentences, Chief Justice Brian Martin was on the bench with two other judges. The original sentencing judge had found that one of the offenders, Shaun Mackley, was motivated by racism and that his race hate was an aggravating feature. The chief justice (and his fellow judges) agreed.

The evidence came from a psychologist whom Mackley had told that 'he noticed becoming prejudiced towards Aboriginal persons at around the age of seventeen. At this age he regularly verbally abused Aboriginal persons in Alice Springs, sometimes initiating the abuse and other times responding to abusive comments. At around the age of seventeen to eighteen years, on at least six occasions Mackley briefly exchanged minor punches or kicks with Aboriginal male persons. He listened to racist music. Mackley told the psychologist that he had been well known for his racist attitudes.'

Mackley's lawyer had put to the original sentencing judge that 'Mackley had reached an understanding of his former racist attitude and was ashamed of his behaviour, but the Judge remained "somewhat sceptical".' He thought there was a continuing risk of reoffending and that was a conclusion open to him, said the chief justice.

On the other hand, the sentencing judge had found that Mackley's co-offender, Dion Grivell, was not racially motivated. The aggravation of his offence was that he had used an offensive weapon – his security officer's baton. On the question of racism it was accepted – as it was for the offenders in the Ryder case – that Grivell had 'worked amongst Aboriginal persons and had Aboriginal friends'. His motivation was 'personal anger directed at no-one in particular'. The chief justice again thought that finding was open to the sentencing judge.

When it came to re-sentencing, the chief justice had this to say on the racial motivation issue: 'In my opinion Mackley's culpability and the gravity of his conduct was significantly greater because he was motivated by racial hatred. In addition, the element of general deterrence looms larger in Mackley's offending by reason of that motivation. Men like the appellant who perpetrate acts of violence by reason of racial hatred must understand that their violence is reprehensible and completely unacceptable to the reasonable members of our community. Victims of such violence are deserving of such protection the law can provide and a clear message must be sent that this type of violence, even when committed by young persons, will be met with significant terms of imprisonment.'

Mackley's racism was judged a proven (beyond reasonable doubt) aggravating feature of his crime and earned him nine months longer in gaol than would be served by his co-offender Grivell. In the Ryder case, racial motivation was strongly rejected by the defence, and they put forward not implausible alternative motivations. The chief justice's finding of attitudes and an atmosphere of racial antagonism underlying the crimes neither fully accepted the defence's arguments nor rejected them, but weighed them against the inferences he could draw from what had happened and found balance in the middle.

~

A collective dread seemed to settle on the court as the chief justice drew closer to the actual sentencing of Kwementyaye's assailants. I have come to recognise this feeling, almost physical in its transmission. However expected and deserved a term of imprisonment may be, it is chilling to watch and listen as it is meted out.

The chief justice first went into the way penalties for manslaughter are approached by the court. He did so specifically 'to explain to the family and friends of the victim, and to the community, why the offending is not in the more serious category for crimes of manslaughter'.

A sentence is not determined solely by 'the fact that a life has been unlawfully taken'. While every crime of manslaughter is serious, this crime was 'toward the lower end of the scale': 'For example, if a greater degree of violence had been inflicted, or if the attack had been prolonged, or if the offenders had been aware of a substantial risk of causing the deceased's death, the crime would have been in the more serious category. None of these types of aggravating features existed.'

He continued: 'As the crime of Manslaughter is committed in an infinite variety of circumstances, and by a wide range of offenders, necessarily the penalties for the crime of Manslaughter vary considerably. Over the last ten years, sentences in the Northern Territory for the crime of Manslaughter have ranged from a two-year sentence, suspended after service of six months, to fifteen years with lengthy non-parole periods. A significant number of cases resulted in head sentences in the approximate range of four to six years. None of the individual cases are of particular assistance to me because none of them involved circumstances close or similar to the circumstances of the crime with which I am concerned.'

Now came the calculus. Scott Doody, who had not struck a blow, was sentenced to four years from the date of his arrest, suspended after twelve months. Having already served almost nine, Doody would be released in just over three months' time. He would be banned from drinking alcohol for two years from the date of his release and from using or consuming any illicit drug for three years. (If he breached those conditions he would be returned to gaol to serve the full sentence.) The chief justice accepted Doody's lesser moral culpability given his lesser role in the physical assault.

The chief justice found that there was no significant difference in moral culpability between Hird, Spears and Swain, who had each struck Kwementyaye, and Kloeden, who had 'set the events in train'. Hird, Spears and Kloeden all got six years, backdated to their arrest, with non-parole periods of four years. Swain benefitted from a six-month discount for his cooperation with police. His sentence was five years and six months, with a non-parole period of three years and six months. Kloeden also got five months for recklessly endangering the life of Tony Cotchilli, but it was to be served concurrently. Had the offence stood alone it would have been fully suspended, said the chief justice, for dangerous as the conduct was, it had not caused any actual harm. Kloeden was also disqualified from driving for three years from the date of his release.

As is standard – notwithstanding the protests of the commentariat, for the practice is written into the *Sentencing Act* – all five had received reductions in their sentences because of their guilty pleas and 'genuine remorse'. The head sentences for Hird, Kloeden, Spears and Swain would otherwise have been seven years and six months.

From the gallery there was sobbing as the chief justice rose and the five were led away. Outside in the lobby friends and families on both sides held one another and wept; others stood stunned by the sheer misery of it all. The young ABC journalist, who like me had followed the proceedings from the start, cried in my arms. Kwementyaye's aunty, Karen Liddle, cried in the arms of Hird's parents.

Therese Ryder, Jade Keil and other members of the Ryder family gathered on the lawns opposite the courthouse, not far from where they had made their memorable call for calm some eight months earlier. They too were crying and holding one another. The media contingent watched and waited. Soon Karen Liddle was seen leaving the court, together with Del Hird, mother of Timothy, and Merryl Spears, mother of Joshua. They made their way over to the Ryders. There, the mothers of the two gaoled sons spoke with and embraced the mother of the dead son.

After a while the Ryder family were ready to speak to reporters. It continued to be extraordinary, the way they summoned the strength to do this.

'I appreciate them' for apologising, Therese Ryder said of the two women. 'It sort of makes me feel satisfied. I've been waiting for that time, for the mothers, parents and that to come up and apologise and say sorry to me. Because I never ever blamed the families. They were at home not knowing what was happening, like me.'

She was asked why she had left the courtroom. She said she 'couldn't stand' being in there any longer – 'hearing about what happened, the story being read out about my son lying on the ground and being kicked'. About her angry comment accusing the offenders of racism, she said: 'For a mother like me, the feeling inside me, I'd say anything.'

She also spoke of Kwementyaye: 'There was no story read out about my son. He was a local himself, he was born here in Alice Springs, went to school here, made friends with a lot of white kids. There's still a lot of friends out there that miss my son as a good mate. And he also was a hard-working man. He was a good young bloke, he never got in trouble with the police in his life before. That's why

I miss him so much, he was the happiest in the family, he brightened up everything for the family … the pain will go on in me for as long as I live.'

Karen Liddle was standing closely at Therese Ryder's side and now she also spoke: 'Myself personally I feel sad for everybody, for us, for our loss, and also for those families too, for how foolish those boys were in what they did. They ruined their lives, their families' lives, our lives, and [now they should] just stand up and be men and do their time, for their sake and their families' sake.[44] We've got a lot of family support and we're just happy with the outcome today.'[45]

The community can learn from these events, she said: 'We all live in this community as Aboriginal and non-Aboriginal people and long-term residents must stick together. We're satisfied with what has happened. They are only young men and their sentences – they are going to spend a long time in there.'

I caught up with the two women as they walked away. I didn't expect them to know who I was. I told them that I had lived in town for a long time and how terribly sorry I was for their loss.

Then I went home to my own son, preciously alive.

RACE IN THE DOCK II

It was the fourteenth day of the trial. In the dock, charged with murder, were two young Aboriginal men; the dead man was white. If found guilty the accused would go to gaol for 'life', serving at least twenty years before the possibility of parole. Both were pleading not guilty.[1]

Their parents had been in court throughout the trial. Filling the public gallery that day were aunties, uncles, brothers, sisters, cousins, nephews, nieces, some of them small children, and at least one grandmother. The jury retired to consider its verdict just before one o'clock. The wait began.

The family of the dead man left the courthouse. The family of the accused men settled in on the narrow benches that line the walls of the lobby, children playing under their parents' feet. Now and then, the judge's associate would emerge to talk to the lawyers and prosecutors; conversations stopped and everyone watched until he disappeared again. He was the person the jury attendant would tell when the jurors were ready with their verdict.

The hours wore on, the children became fractious. The anxious adults were preoccupied, so the security guard, a white man, suggested the children play hide-and-seek with him. He was the kind of person who just can't help being friendly. The court had installed a metal detector in the entrance, like the ones at airports, and he would chat to each person passing through it, ask about their day, comment on their shirt, their smile. Now he had the children running all over the lobby, hiding behind the pot plants or around corners, whooping with delight when he found them. The adults watched and smiled.

By five o'clock most of the court staff had gone home. Who knew how much longer this would go on? The kids were getting hungry, so the guard suggested that everyone chip in for pizza. Out came the change and the five-dollar notes. He was just figuring out how many family-size to order when the judge's associate appeared. This time the lawyers and prosecutors followed him back into the courtroom.

The jury had sent word that they weren't close to a verdict. They wanted to stop for the day and come back tomorrow. It was 6.20 pm. The anti-climax settled on the families like a heavy blanket. They trailed out into the night. The guard watched them leave with disappointment; he'd been looking forward to the picnic with them.

~

The town was accustomed to news of alcohol-fuelled violence afflicting Aboriginal individuals and families. This time it was a much rarer event, the killing of a white man. The lines separating the races would be sharply drawn in the trial of his accused killers – or at least it initially appeared that way.

The dead man's name was Edward Hargrave. He died on the night of 3 April 2009 in a suburban street from a single stab wound. The photo released by police at the time showed a handsome man with light brown hair in a short fringe across his forehead, warm blue eyes and a wry smile. He'd come to Alice from country Victoria in the early nineties as a competitive boxer, loved the place and stayed. In this town mad for motor sports he switched from boxing to motocross and then to racing quads. He started a family with Sarah Woodberry, whose father owned a successful motorbike dealership. They had three little girls and, although he and Sarah hadn't known it when he died at the age of thirty-seven, a fourth child was on the way. His memorial service began with a long cavalcade of cars, bikes and trucks driving through the town; it was attended by hundreds of people.[2]

The two young Aboriginal men accused of his death fled but were soon arrested. They were Graham Woods, twenty-five, and Julian Williams, twenty-two. On remand, they complained of being threatened and abused by guards, and for a while they were moved to Berrimah gaol in Darwin. Woods became convinced that he would not get a fair trial in Alice Springs, so in mid-2010, with the backing of his family, he applied through his lawyers to have the case heard in Darwin. Williams joined the application. It was supported by an affidavit from Woods's father, Graham Senior, who said that following Hargrave's death he had had difficulty getting work in Alice Springs for the first time in his life. Threatening and offensive remarks had been made to him and his family; he believed they were being blamed for the killing.[3]

Woods's lawyer, Russell Goldflam of the Northern Territory Legal Aid Commission, also made an affidavit about his personal and professional experience of local antagonism towards Aboriginal people on the basis of race. He had lived in Alice Springs since 1981. The antagonism was, he said, 'common, widespread and deeply felt'. He had observed 'countless examples of petty acts of discriminatory conduct or speech directed against Aboriginal people'; had noticed that 'at unguarded moments, many Alice Springs people casually use derogatory terms for Aboriginal people such as "nigger" or "coon" in ordinary conversation'; as a lawyer he had 'frequently acted for, advised and taken instructions from Alice Springs residents with frankly hostile attitudes towards Aboriginal people'; and, on occasion, he and colleagues had 'acted for clients who have committed offences motivated or influenced by racial antagonism against Aboriginal people'. He noted the 'intense and continuing discussion and debate within the Alice Springs community about the issue of local race relations' sparked by both Hargrave's death and that of Aboriginal man Kwementyaye Ryder who had died three months later. Goldflam had acted on behalf of one of the five convicted of Ryder's manslaughter. At the time of Woods's application they had already been sentenced, their guilty plea having expedited the process.[4]

Many locals viewed the Hargrave killing as a black on white attack, the inverse of Ryder's, seen as white on black. In the coverage of the Ryder death and legal proceedings, the race element was highlighted; it prompted and framed, virtually to the exclusion of all else, much of the national and international media interest. As Goldflam noted, having been in discussion with the producer of *Four Corners*, the ABC was about to broadcast the program 'A Dog Act', entirely focussed on whether or not Ryder's killing had been racially motivated. There would be no national media coverage, beyond some brief news reports, of the trial of Hargrave's attackers.

Goldflam attached to the affidavit examples of the local media coverage of Hargrave's death, which he argued revealed an implied bias.

The biweekly *Centralian Advocate*'s front-page coverage of the death was headed 'Good Guy Who Could Do Anything'. The story spilled onto page two. Alongside details of the killing and of Hargrave's life, there was a vox pop survey of locals' views on 'gang-related street crime'.[5]

A fortnight later the paper led with a plea from Hargrave's parents, headlined 'Don't Let This Happen Again'. Their comments linked the tragic death of their son to the town's 'real issues': 'I see grown men in their late twenties walking aimlessly in the streets with no direction or pride in themselves,' said Richard Hargrave. 'There are young children roaming the streets with nothing better to do and no guidance from their parents. I see people living for their next government cheques, so they can afford to buy grog.' Trish Hargrave recalled the 'gentle and clean' Alice of the past. Now the town had become a 'violent and dirty place that has attracted trouble makers and criminals of the worst kind'. The word Aboriginal wasn't mentioned – it didn't need to be.[6]

Comments, partly in a similar vein, were aired on local ABC radio following Hargrave's funeral. One report quoted Scott McConnell, Hargrave's boss and friend, who was with him on the night of his death and would be a witness at the trial. 'A person of Ed's stature, to be picked out like this and to have this happen to him, is an appalling indictment on our town,' he said. 'When are we going to do something to deal with the issues that exist here? And when are we going to work together instead of telling the stories and looking for somebody else to blame?'[7] The 'issues' weren't specified – they didn't need to be. 'Social problems' is the other catch-all term. The people and situations on the problem side of the ledger, if not youth, are always seen to be Aboriginal.

In June, in the lead-up to The Finke, the ABC reported that a paraplegic competitor would be doing his best to honour Hargrave, who had helped him modify his bike. The report, in words not chosen carefully, went on to say that Hargrave had been 'murdered during a disturbance in April'.[8]

In December a report on the committal hearing, leading the *Centralian Advocate*, was headlined 'DNA found on knife'. Readers had to go to page three to learn that the DNA was the victim's. It was not clear if any of the DNA belonged to the accused.[9]

Clippings from the weekly *Alice Springs News* were also included with Woods's application. Two were articles I had written, in which Hargrave's death was briefly referred to in the context of discussing racial tension and division. One article spoke of 'two Aboriginal men' accused of Hargrave's murder; the other named them. Both articles were prompted by the Ryder case.[10]

Neither this material nor Goldflam's oral submissions were enough to persuade Justice Jenny Blokland, who heard the application in July. The alleged treatment of the applicants by prison guards, if true, was serious but it had since changed, she said. Local 'intensity of feeling' had also diminished in the year or more since the death. She noted submissions from the Crown reporting that no antagonism had been evident in and around the court at the committal. In her view, any residual concern could be dealt with by the trial judge. In the interests of the community, trials are usually conducted where the offence has been committed and in front of juries from the same area. This trial would go ahead in Alice Springs.[11]

~

Apart from what they saw as evidence of local racial prejudice towards their clients, the defence team had presented Justice Blokland with a further concern: that the jury selection process in Alice Springs was racially skewed. In response to this Justice Blokland thought the trial judge could properly direct the jury and, no matter what its racial makeup, there was no reason to believe the jury would not comply.

Then in September 2010, just ahead of the trial's scheduled start, the defence team, headed by prominent Territory Queen's Counsel Jon Tippett with Goldflam as junior counsel, tried again. This time their challenge to the jury array was considered by the Full Court. The central argument was that juries in Alice Springs could never be representative given the way they were selected. Aboriginal people make up around 21 per cent of the town's population, but never comprise a similar proportion of jury members. Aboriginal people also make up the overwhelming majority of inmates in the Alice Springs gaol. The point was not that juries should be made up of a proportionate number of Aboriginal people, as true random selection would not necessarily achieve this; but selection procedures should provide for that *possibility*.

Various factors precluded it, they argued. These included the broad disqualification provisions in the NT's *Juries Act*. To qualify as a juror anyone having been sentenced to a prison term had to have completed their entire sentence at least seven years before. In the initial jury list for *The Queen v Woods and Williams*, one in four people were disqualified, most likely on the basis of having a criminal record.

In the Full Court, the trial judge, Justice John Reeves, described this as a 'startling figure'. Acting Chief Justice Dean Mildren was less surprised in view of the 'very extensive mandatory sentencing provisions we've had in the Northern Territory over a very long period of time'.[12]

Goldflam pointed out that the disqualification provisions did not distinguish between short and longer sentences and hence the degree of seriousness of the offence. He also provided comparisons with other jurisdictions: 0.3 per cent of potential jurors in Victoria were disqualified or exempted; 0.5 per cent of the general population over the age of twenty-one in New South Wales had received a prison sentence. There was a 'gross' disparity between these figures and the disqualification of 25.4 per cent of the array in Alice Springs.

The defence team also put its finger on some of the ways that bias against Aboriginal people had come to be taken for granted in the town's day-to-day administration and services. Potential jurors are summonsed by mail, with addresses gleaned from the electoral roll. But the roll does not record house numbers for addresses in town camps, where a substantial minority of the town's Aboriginal people live. As well, at the time there was no direct postal service to town camps (this began to change in 2011).

Part of the challenge succeeded. The Full Court found that the jurors had not been summonsed in strict accordance with the law, and that the checks for disqualification had been carried out by SAFE NT, a division of Police, Fire and Emergency Services, which 'is not indifferent to the prosecution'. The court quashed the jury array and processes were tidied up. It would now be up to potential jurors to declare their criminal record; court staff would check only after empanelment.

However, the disproportionately low participation by Aboriginal people on juries is not entirely caused by these processes, as we shall see. Nor was it, in the trial of Woods and Williams, the only race issue that judge and jury would have to contend with. The spectre of racial bias would dog the conduct of the trial to its penultimate day.

~

The trial finally got under way on 7 March 2011. Almost two years had passed since Hargrave's death and the arrests of Woods and Williams – a limbo of grief and anger over the legal manoeuvres for Hargrave's family, of anxiety for the accused men and their families.

It was standing room only for the jury selection even though only a quarter of the 300 people summonsed were in attendance. (Another quarter had already been exempted or had deferred, and in any case, according to Goldflam, this is not an unusually low proportion.)[13] Crown prosecutor Ron Noble read out the list of witnesses who would be appearing. A potential juror could yet be exempted if they knew any of the witnesses, or were acquainted with any of the lawyers. One by one, thirty-four people sought to be excused, or said they might need to be; twenty-nine of them were. Justice Reeves erred on the side of caution: even the 'perception of the possibility of bias' was of concern, he said.

Justice Reeves was on the bench in this case as an 'additional judge' of the NT Supreme Court. He had been appointed to the Federal Court in November 2007, the first NT-based judge to be so. He brought to the trial local experience of Alice Springs, where he had practised as a solicitor in his early career and served as an elected member of the Town Council. Later he moved to Darwin, became a Labor MP for the Northern Territory during the first Hawke government, before subsequently returning to the bar.[14]

Of the twenty-nine people he excused from jury service, a number were Aboriginal – at least four, judging by their appearance, though that is not always a definitive guide. (It is family and culture that identify them, Aboriginal people insist, not skin colour or other physical features.) One of the four was a plumber who had been working with Hargrave before he died; another, a ranger, had worked with one of the witnesses and was 'affiliated' with the Woods and Williams families. A woman who worked as a researcher with an Aboriginal organisation was related to the Woods family – 'my full family', as she put it; and a woman who worked as an electorate officer had, by coincidence, been at the scene of the crime on the night and had also had dealings with one of the witnesses.

A ballot was then conducted, using numbered marbles drawn from a barrel. The numbers matched those on the remaining list of potential jurors. The defence lawyers – the local junior counsel, not the QCs – stood next to their clients. This was their chance to vet the selection. They appeared anxious to eliminate white men and women who looked to be of Hargrave's age group and social milieu. Although they sometimes hastily conferred with their clients, mostly it was the lawyers' call. They issued twenty-four challenges, the permitted twelve for each of the accused. No reasons needed to be given. Only one person was eliminated by the Crown. I was surprised that she had not sought to be excused as I immediately recognised her as the mother of one of the men convicted of the manslaughter of Kwementyaye Ryder. Her name wasn't lost on prosecutor Noble. She looked relieved when she heard him call out, without even turning round, 'Stand aside!'

There were only eight marbles left in the barrel when a jury was finally assembled. Goldflam later commented that the process 'was not so much one of randomness as one of attrition'.[15] The six men and six women ranged across ages, ethnicities and backgrounds. They seemed to include two women of Aboriginal descent (again, I say this on the basis of physical appearance – there may have been others). They were joined by two reserve jurors, both women. Woods and Williams, they were told, were now in their charge as the sole 'arbiters of the facts'.

From the outset, Crown prosecutor Noble tried to head off the race angle. In his opening address to the jury he referred to the 'racist taunts' on both sides. But he pointed out that while Woods and Williams were 'part-Indigenous', so were some of Hargrave's friends present on the night. He also said that Scott McConnell, Hargrave's friend and boss, would give evidence that he had tried to explain to the accused men that he worked for an Aboriginal corporation. Noble thus rejected any suggestion that the case was about violence based on race. The 'bottom line', he said, was simply violence: the Crown case was that Graham Woods had inflicted a fatal stab wound on Ed Hargrave and that Julian Williams, acting with 'unlawful common purpose', had struck a blow with a pole immediately after.

The defence lawyers were initially restrained on the race issue. Tippett QC for Woods (brought in from Darwin by NT Legal Aid) mentioned the 'prejudice' that 'we all suffer from in one way or another'; he asked that the jurors be 'objective' about the things that 'humans do in circumstances of great pressure'. John Dickinson QC had been brought in from Melbourne by Aboriginal Legal Aid to represent Williams. He echoed Tippett – 'we're all human' – and urged the jurors to put aside 'emotion and prejudice'.

~

Apart from racing quads, Ed Hargrave had been an expert welder and worked for Ingkerreke Outstations Resource Services, an Aboriginal organisation whose enterprise arm, Ingkerreke Commercial, specialised in construction and metal fabrication. Hargrave trained its apprentices – young Aboriginal men – in welding. 'Ed was proud of the boys,' his brother George wrote in his victim impact statement, 'for their skills and the quality of the work done. He would tell me on the phone how the boys in the workshop were, not only at work but in their family lives too because they were mates.' George thanked these men and their families for 'their support at Ed's funeral'. He made this point before describing those he held responsible for his brother's death as 'the fucking scum of the earth'.

On the night of the death, Ingkerreke staff were out on the town to farewell a colleague. He was Faron Peckham, a middle-aged local Aboriginal man. A qualified tradie, he was leaving Alice to take up a job in Queensland. Hargrave was at the farewell, as was his young brother-in-law, Luke Woodberry, also employed at Ingkerreke at the time. They were joined by another workmate, Greg Smith, and his wife, Rosina Ross, who are both Aboriginal.

Smith and Ross had been having a social drink at the suburban Gillen Club before meeting up with the others at the Town & Country, a pub (now defunct) on Todd Mall, at about three in the afternoon. The boss, Scott McConnell, arrived a little later. McConnell had become CEO of Ingkerreke in 2005, taking it in a new direction with a focus on full trade apprenticeships and commercial activity to generate 'real jobs' for Aboriginal people.

From the Town & Country the Ingkerreke group moved along Todd Street, where there was a karaoke bar at the Memorial Club, known as the Memo. (It too later closed its doors but has reopened under Aboriginal ownership.) It was a Friday and drinking sessions would have been going on all over town. There was nothing unusual about that, except that Alice locals, black and white, do their drinking extra seriously, downing 1.34 times the national average.[16] Faron Peckham, whose farewell it was, told police later that night that his group was 'intoxicated'.

In their trial evidence the Ingkerreke group all admitted to drinking but not, they said, excessively. The boss McConnell had been drinking Fourex Gold and Jack Daniels but said he was 'well and truly in control of his faculties'. Peckham had likewise been on beer and spirits; he said they all had. He described the group as 'happy and in a celebration mood'. Smith had had a couple of drinks at the Gillen Club, then drank steadily from 3 pm, Carlton mid-strengths; he'd had about eleven by the time he left the Memo. Young Woodberry had also been drinking Fourex but insisted he was 'never drunk'.

The accused men had been doing their bit, sharing two cartons of beer between five. In the afternoon Graham and his brother Corey had been to Musicworld. Corey shouted Graham a CD and bought one for himself by the American rapper 2Pac. They went back to Graham's flat on Northside. Graham's very pregnant wife, Coralie Neil, was over at his sister's place with their son. The brothers listened to their new music while having a few drinks with their cousin Julian Williams and a couple of friends. After sundown their friends went home, and Graham, Corey and Julian walked into town, finishing their last cans on Anzac Hill. They were 'happy' and 'pretty charged', Woods later told police.

From Anzac Hill they wandered down the mall and along Todd Street to the 24 Hour Store, where Corey bought them each a cheese and bacon pie. It was here that they came into contact with the Ingkerreke group.

It started with what the prosecutor described as a 'taunt' aimed at McConnell. He'd left the Memo, a few doors down, to go to an ATM. He said he was called a 'fat white cunt', twice.

'White cunt' is a common enough term of abuse in Alice – I have been called a 'white cunt' for irritating a fellow user of the roads. 'Black cunt' would be just as common, if not more so. Also common, as Goldflam said in his affidavit, are those more racially specific terms of abuse, terms like 'boong' and 'coon', that have no equivalent for non-Aboriginal people. In this trial evidence we don't hear them though. Race on both sides is invoked as an adjective.

In his police interview Woods denied using this term of abuse (and others, such as 'fucking white cunts, this is our land') but he said it sounded 'pretty much like' what Williams had said. It was Williams, according to Woods, who had started teasing 'the chubby bloke' and who kept it up. From the start, Williams maintained his right to silence, so we never heard his account of events.

McConnell said he was told he needed to go on a diet and was also squirted in the face. Initially he'd feared it was acid but in fact it was only water (Woods said Williams did this). McConnell's verbal retort, he admitted under cross-examination, was that his abusers were 'softcocks'. There was some argy-bargy, and McConnell, by now 'extremely annoyed', used his mobile to call his friends who were still inside the Memo.

Hargrave was the first to respond, with young Woodberry not far behind. They found McConnell and his tormentors in the carpark opposite the club. Smith and Peckham soon followed. Punches were thrown, with five men on the Ingkerreke side and four on the other – the Woods brothers Graham and Corey, Julian Williams and another cousin who had turned up, Jermain Woods.

Hargrave was a big man – 188 centimetres tall, weighing 110 kilograms. The forensic pathologist provided the court with this precision, and Hargrave's size was repeatedly stressed by the defence. We could see his companions for ourselves, as one by one they gave their evidence. Peckham was older than the rest but tall and well built; Smith, probably in his thirties, was tall, lean, tough-looking but edgy; Woodberry was relatively short, stockily built, young and strong; McConnell, probably in his forties, was of average height but with a large frame and carrying a lot of weight. The contrast with the other side was sharp. Graham Woods, in particular, was of slim build, although he looked fit; Williams was a little bulkier, as were

Corey and Jermain Woods. Each was in his early to mid twenties and of only average height.

Jermain, Graham told police, had the 'pissed horrors'. He was knocked out cold in the fight. He said he was hit on the left side of his face and was 'asleep for a while'. Who hit him? 'The bloke who's dead.'

The altercation escalated. Jermain got to his feet and took off towards Bloomfield Street. Corey, Graham and Julian were behind him. The Ingkerreke group followed. Passing the Flying Doctor base, Corey jumped the hedge and hid. From there, Graham and Julian were on their own. As they ran, Hargrave, Woodberry and Smith were closest to them. Smith said he was 'sprinting'; later, Hargrave overtook him. McConnell and Peckham were walking and soon lost sight of the others.

Tippett QC described it as 'a hunt'; Ingkerreke boss McConnell preferred to see it as 'responding' but admitted that, in one of his six phone calls to police to get help, he had spoken of wanting to 'break some fucking skulls'. He had also declined to accept the advice of the operator to return to the Memo or come to the police station. At the end of the fifth call he told the operator, 'All right, we'll deal with it, thank you.'

The problem police had in responding was that the groups were on the move. It was a busy night, but not unusually so for Alice. Between 6 pm Friday and 6 am the next day police attended ninety-one 'jobs', including three assaults, eight domestic disturbances and thirty-six general disturbances. A patrol was despatched immediately to the Memo following the first call from McConnell but the men couldn't be found.

Woods and Williams were headed for the home of Woods's sister, Lindy, in the Keith Lawrie public housing flats on the corner of Bloomfield and Musgrave streets, about one and a half kilometres from the Memo. They stopped at the railway track to get their breath.

In his police interview Woods admitted that he threw rocks at his pursuers from there, but they kept coming: They 'chase us right up to Keith Lawrie'; he was 'puffed out', 'that exhausted from running' when he got there.

~

The interview was conducted on the evening of 6 April, three days after Hargrave's death. Woods had been arrested the day before at Sixteen Mile, an outstation just north of town. His 'prisoner's friend' was his grandmother, Agnes Woods. She'd been a prisoner's friend once before, for another grandson. In that role, as Graham relayed back to the interviewing officers, she couldn't answer questions, she was there to make sure he 'got treated fair'.

Detective Senior Constable Vanessa Barton asked most of the questions. She had a steady, not unfriendly manner and, in the circumstances, Woods seemed quite comfortable with her. He told her that he was known as 'Junior' in the family; he had two brothers and four sisters; English was his only language. He'd been to the local Catholic school till Year Nine and could read and write, though 'not very good'. He had been in work, but not over the last five weeks.

Woods came across as an ordinary guy with a pleasant appearance and demeanour. He also seemed somewhat immature given that, like Hargrave, he was a father of three with a fourth on the way (the child would be born the following week). He spoke fondly of the children who were in his sister Lindy's flat on the night, including 'my little boy, Latrell'. Detective Barton commented on the unusual name, and he told her that it came from a movie, 'a good movie'. At this stage the three-hour interview had been going for over two hours, with one short break. Barton kept taking him back over the events, working her way slowly towards getting from him an increasingly detailed and candid account. He spoke quietly and from the start became upset when describing the critical moments.

He admitted that he was not in danger when he ran out from Lindy's flat to meet Hargrave, but he qualified this by saying, 'I was in danger when they was chasing me.' In his first account of the clash he said Hargrave 'came running towards me' and Julian Williams had 'a little pipe or something': 'I'm pretty sure Julian must have hit him.' (This, like all of his comments about Williams, could not be used as evidence either for or against his co-accused, as Justice Reeves made clear to the jury.) Woods said he went outside because Williams was his cousin and also because he thought the men who had chased them 'were going to come inside my sister's flat'. He was frightened because 'they may come closer to where the kids was'; and they were singing out, 'We're going to kill youse cunts.'

'Julian was the one who wanted to keep fighting,' Woods continued to insist. 'Julian walked out first with a bottle and a little pole.'

Woods initially admitted to picking up a stick from the ground outside. It took him some time to admit to anything else. Barton asked him if he'd taken anything with him from the unit. At first he said 'I'm not sure', then 'I think I did, a stick from inside'.

Barton went back, asking him to describe the layout of the flat, who was there, what they were doing, where he went inside the flat. He described going into the kitchen to grab a glass of water, but still he didn't think he'd taken anything with him. Then greater uncertainty crept into his account: 'Everything happened so fast.'

She took him to the encounter with Hargrave: 'You've raised your arm, this fella has grabbed it, the same arm as the stick is in …'

'I don't even know what happened,' said Woods, but again he said, 'Julian hit him with the pole.'

After the break Barton started with the moment where Woods said he was pushing Hargrave.

Why do you describe your action as self-defence?

Woods said Hargrave grabbed him, punched him in the stomach, he grabbed Hargrave on the shoulder: 'I thought I was bleeding, that's when I let go ... I don't know if I had an object in my hand or not.'

Again Barton retraced the steps towards the critical moment.

'I thought I was stabbed or bleeding,' said Woods, 'that's why I panicked and I ran as soon as he let go.'

Back over it, calmly, steadily.

'Something sharp stabbed me,' said Woods. He lifted his shirt to show a scratch on his stomach.

'Might there have been a knife in your hand?' asked Barton finally.

'Might have been,' Woods conceded.

And if so, where do you think you would have got it from?

'Probably inside the flat ... when I was getting a drink of water.'

'You said you were trying to defend yourself – what was that fella doing?'

'He was swearing and all that.'

She talked about Williams and what he was doing.

Again Woods said, 'He was the one who wanted to keep going.'

And why did you go back out there, with a stick and maybe a knife?

'Because he's my cousin.'

What did you think the men were going to do?

'Thought they were going to come inside my sister's flat.'

'You went out to fight, you say you wanted to frighten them ...'

'I hoped they would go home ...'

After a few more questions Barton came back to what Woods was holding in his left hand.

'Probably a knife,' he said at last.

Where did you get it from?

His voice was very low as he answered: 'My sister's kitchen ... the sink ...'

He described panicking afterwards, trying to calm himself; he showered twice in quick succession, once in Lindy's flat, once in Corey's, in the same complex.

Barton asked again about Williams.

Woods was crying as he answered. He said he turned on Julian, telling him: 'If you would've stopped fighting, none of this would've happened.' To Barton he said: 'It was all a big game for him, he just laughed and smiled, "We're all right."'

Why were you panicking? asked Barton.

'First time I seen someone else's blood.'

What did you think had happened?

'That I hurt him pretty bad.'

Barton asked him whether his life had been in danger.

'I tell you the truth, if they would've caught me they would've beat the shit out of me.'

Asked again how he had felt, he answered, 'Felt like upset.'

Upset how? Angry way?

'Because they kept on coming, they just kept on coming.'

Woods ran out towards Hargrave in the middle of the street. Hargrave 'stood his ground', as the prosecution described it, or went to meet him, as the defence had it. They grappled. One on one, according to Faron Peckham who had a clear view of them. Hargrave grabbed Woods's right arm, apparently in an effort to get the stick: his back was exposed. Woods stabbed him.

'Do you think he made you do that?' asked Barton.

'No,' said Woods, 'I forgot all about a knife in my left hand, I thought I pushed him, at the last minute I realised I had a knife in my hand.'

In one movement the knife cut Hargrave's scalp through to the skull, then penetrated the back of his right shoulder towards the neck. (That it was done in a single movement was a key plank of the defence and not excluded by the forensic pathologist. Ultimately this must have been accepted as reasonably possible by the jury.) The eighteen-centimetre blade went through muscles, downwards and forwards; it fractured one rib, cut another, cut a major artery, and completely severed a smaller one.

Hargrave took a few staggering steps. He tried to say something to Luke Woodberry, his young brother-in-law: 'He couldn't get the words out, I knew something was wrong.' From across the road Peckham saw 'a dead man walking'. 'Ed, are you okay?' he called. He saw him crash into a fence and hit the ground. By the time Peckham got there, Woodberry was on top of Ed, 'to make sure they didn't come back for him'. There was a lot of blood coming from the back of his head. Woodberry put his hand there to try to stop the bleeding: 'I was just trying to keep him alive really.'

~

In court, the families of the accused and the family of the dead man never looked at each other. The parents of Woods and Williams would sit as close as possible to the dock, close enough to touch their sons, to speak to them in whispers at the end of each trial day. Hargrave's family – his parents daily, his siblings and in-laws some of the time, his widow on the final day – would sit as close as possible to the entrance and as far as possible from the accused and their relatives.

Luke Woodberry, just twenty years old at the time of Hargrave's death, was still emotionally wrought by the events two years later. He reluctantly admitted under cross-examination that the pursuit across town was 'a chase' and that he had wanted to 'fight'.

Greg Smith didn't need pushing. He said the accused men were 'egging us on' and he was ready to 'give it back to them'. He still seemed ready to, in the witness box. Tippett QC, a short man with a big voice and combative manner, went in hard. Smith came back just as hard: 'I don't think so, mate', he would say, 'I don't know, mate', angry and scornful. Tippett put to him that he had told police that his intention was to chase Woods and Williams and beat them up. 'Exactly,' Smith replied. The way he saw it, Woods and Williams had challenged the Ingkerreke group to fight. 'They were baiting us all the way,' he said. 'We was invited back there.' En route he hid in the saltbush along the railway line; from there he saw Woods and Williams 'throw rocks at the boss' – McConnell – and 'hunt him down like a dog'.

McConnell described the scene when he arrived in Musgrave Street as 'pandemonium'. Tippett suggested that the Aboriginal women in Lindy Woods's flat were 'defending their home': they were 'yelling and screaming', telling the Ingkerreke group to 'fuck off' and 'banging sticks on the ground'. McConnell couldn't say, but Peckham gave evidence that the women were brandishing sticks, hitting the ground and swearing. Asked if he had threatened to punch and kill women, Smith said, 'I might have.' Asked if he had threatened to harm children, he said, 'No, who knows, yeah.'

The diminutive Lindy Woods, well advanced in pregnancy when she gave her evidence, said she was watching TV with her sister Samantha and Coralie Neil, Graham's then pregnant wife. Three children were with them in the flat. Lindy heard banging on bins and yelling. When she let Graham in she could see 'two fellas' – one 'white … big built, tall', one 'dark … a big fella as well'. They were coming up the street towards her flat and 'another fella' was on the opposite side of the street. The two near her were swearing: 'You black cunts', 'Get them pricks out.' She said they were throwing rocks and dirt at her and Coralie.

The 'dark' one was Faron Peckham. He was an impressive witness. Justice Reeves later remarked that Peckham was in the 'unusual position' of having all counsel – the prosecutor and both defence lawyers – rely on him. He was 'fairly even-tempered, controlled', said Justice Reeves; he seemed 'fairly definite about what he saw and not willing to adopt positions he didn't agree with'.

Asked to describe Hargrave's attacker, Peckham said the man was 'roughly my colour, skin tone that is, a bit dark'. He described an exchange of words with the women. They asked who he was and he replied, 'This is my grandfather's country. Who are youse?' The prosecutor asked whether he had said this in English or 'language', meaning an Aboriginal language. Peckham said he had spoken in 'plain English'.

While many local Aboriginal people are related (by blood or 'skin') or know one another, it is not always the case. Peckham and Smith did not appear to have a connection to Woods and Williams or to know them; their loyalty on the night was to their non-Aboriginal workmates, and their antipathy was to their boss's Aboriginal tormentors.

As for generalisations about the aimlessness of young Aboriginal men and the trouble this causes, they too were tested by what the court learned of Graham Woods. He had worked full-time for two years as a labourer in a gardening business and, before his arrest, had been about to take up a permanent position as a truck driver at the Granites Gold Mine, in the Tanami Desert north-west of Alice Springs. The court also heard that he had no alcohol or substance abuse problems – 'unusual for a person in your position', Justice Reeves told him.

~

If a murder trial is always a heavy responsibility for a jury, the trial of Woods and Williams piled on extra pressure. To start with, at least some of the jurors would have been aware, from the media coverage, of the legal challenge to the jury array on the grounds of its built-in bias. This awareness may have accounted for some of the sensitivities that were revealed as the trial went along, and some jurors may have been more self-consciously determined to scrutinise themselves and what was put before them for bias or prejudice. But before the trial got even that far, the small-town web of connections evident during the jury empanelment – particularly among Aboriginal people with their large extended family networks – resurfaced on the very first afternoon.

Justice Reeves received a note from a juror wondering whether he or she had a conflict of interest. A work colleague had told the juror she was an aunty of both Woods and Williams, suggesting that the juror could use this as an excuse for not serving. The note explained that the juror was not on close terms with this colleague and had never met the accused men, but felt uneasy about the perception of bias. Justice Reeves didn't see a problem, and neither did counsel. A message was sent back that there was no cause for concern.

The next day was Tuesday, publication day for the biweekly *Centralian Advocate*. After lunch a copy of the paper was being passed between counsel at the bar table. The headline on page one was innocuous enough – 'Court told of fatal stabbing' – but inside, on page two, the juror's note was completely misrepresented. According to the article, the *juror* was 'related to the accused but had never met the two men and their family ties would not affect the juror's decision'. After 'a brief deliberation', the article said, Justice Reeves had 'allowed the juror to remain'.[17]

Tippett for Woods was first to his feet, wanting time to seek instructions. Prosecutor Noble was sanguine, feeling the situation could be dealt with by directions to the jury, but Dickinson for Williams could hear 'alarm bells' ringing.

After a brief pause, Tippett applied to have the entire jury discharged. Even if a substantial retraction were printed, it would not appear until Friday. The jury would feel 'compromised' by their perceived lack of impartiality, and this could 'infect' their capacity to deliberate fairly. Better to discharge them now before a lot of evidence had been given (there had been only one witness so far).

The concern was not limited to the jury, said Tippett; it extended to the town of Alice Springs.

Dickinson backed his call: even if His Honour set the record straight in court and a retraction were published, there was no way of ensuring that the jurors would not still have to deal with a lingering perception in the community that they were compromised. This would play on their minds, and they might feel more reluctant to accept evidence in favour of his client.

Prosecutor Noble promoted a minimalist approach: discharge the juror, though it was no fault of that person, and continue without a taint on the other members.

The upshot was that the erring young journalist and his editor were carpeted. They were at risk of being found in contempt of court, but of greater concern to Justice Reeves was what they could do to correct their inaccuracy. Their next edition was not due out until Friday, explained the editor. But perhaps their sister paper, the *Northern Territory News*, a daily, could do something.

Tippett did not think the *NT News* was widely read in Central Australia and believed that the problem remained. He linked the situation to Woods's past application to have the trial removed to Darwin because of a perception of bias against him. Dickinson picked up on this point: given its history, the trial didn't need another reason to tip the balance towards 'unfair'.

Noble reliably took a sober view: properly directed jurors would be true to their individual oaths, they would all know that they were not tainted, and with the retraction published, anyone who had been misinformed would soon be disabused.

The jury had been released for the day and now the court adjourned. Justice Reeves had rejected the application to discharge the whole jury and he would be reflecting overnight on his course of action, then leaning towards discharge of the single juror.

By the next morning he had decided that would be wrong. It

would not only reinforce the effect of the *Advocate*'s inaccuracy, it would also set an unfortunate precedent: a juror, or jury, could be targeted by publishing inaccurate information about them.

The *Advocate*'s editor appeared with the *NT News*'s detailed correction. With the *Advocate*'s own correction following on the Friday – a double column on the front page – Justice Reeves was satisfied. (The *Advocate* would not return to report from the trial, except for a brief account of the verdict.) Drama averted, Justice Reeves explained the decision at some length to the jury and then urged them to put it aside.

Day four was drawing to a close when the jury again struck a snag, this time in relation to one of the very matters the defence team had raised in their challenge to the original array. Court staff in Darwin had discovered that one of the sworn jurors was actually disqualified from serving because she had been sentenced to a term in prison on the wrong side by some months of seven years ago. The one-month sentence had been wholly suspended, but it was still a term of imprisonment within the definition of the *Juries Act*.

Tippett, backed by Dickinson, wanted time to consider and asked for an adjournment, but Noble said it was clear, the juror should be discharged. By the next morning Tippett and Dickinson agreed. The juror concerned was called: she was one of the two who appeared to be of Aboriginal background. Ironically, this whole scenario would have been avoided had SAFE NT continued to do the background checks of everyone on the list before selection and empanelment.[18] The juror was discharged, and one of the two reserves was chosen by ballot to replace her.

There was still at least one Aboriginal woman on the jury. We cannot know what difference that may have made, but we do know that one other juror was conscious of her presence. In his summing up, Dickinson QC for Williams had told the jury the case was 'ripe for sympathy and prejudice', that it had 'racial overtones', and he referred to 'a debate going on' in this town 'that we all know about'. He obviously did not feel the need to be more specific but went on to urge the jury not to allow 'sympathy' for the Hargrave family to 'colour' their analysis of the evidence.

One juror objected to this message strongly enough to send Justice Reeves a note on the matter. Dickinson's comments had been 'offensive and insulting' and 'at no time in any breaks have the racial backgrounds been discussed prejudicially amongst jurors'. 'I expect I do not speak only for myself,' wrote the juror, adding, 'There is at least one Indigenous member of this jury who may also have found the comments insulting.'

In his or her umbrage, the juror also wrote: 'Quite frankly it would seem that his [Dickinson's] client was the initiator of any racial issues, so it was disappointing to have this raised as a theme which may influence the jury.' The lid had again been taken off.

Dickinson QC was not in court to hear all this, he had left for Melbourne where he had commitments in the Victorian Supreme Court, leaving junior counsel Ted Sinoch to represent Williams. Sinoch now applied for the jury to be discharged and the trial vacated, on this its thirteenth day. The juror had concluded, said Sinoch, that 'the racial dimension' to the offending had been initiated by his client and it appeared that the juror's views had been relayed to others. (The juror had written on the back of the envelope that brief discussions with others had shown 'that several jurors felt the same' and that the note was submitted 'on their behalf'.) The jury was now 'tainted' with a view that was 'prejudicial' towards his client, said Sinoch. Dickinson's comments were 'nothing out of the ordinary' and were the sort that would be made on any matter that had 'an inter-racial element'. It was the juror's sensitivity that suggested 'a prejudicial mind'.

Justice Reeves wanted to know what the 'inter-racial element' was.

Sinoch's answer began simply: 'The person or persons at whose hands the deceased died were Aboriginal; the deceased was a non-Aboriginal or Caucasian man.' He then referred to, without explicitly naming it, Kwementyaye Ryder's death: 'Your Honour may be aware that this matter follows or rather is attended in general community consciousness with another matter where the reverse was the case.' In this context, Dickinson's exhortation was 'appropriate', said Sinoch, it was the juror's 'apparent offence' that was 'remarkable'.

Justice Reeves thought the note showed that the juror, and the others he or she had spoken to, seemed to be rejecting 'any racial element' and was saying that the matter would be dealt with impartially. But Sinoch saw danger in the juror having canvassed the views of others, rather than simply expressing his or her own view. Had the juror started a 'groundswell' of a view prejudicial to his client? If His Honour would not discharge the jury and vacate the trial, could he at least explain to the jury 'in the strongest possible terms' that Dickinson 'was not seeking in his comments to create a racial divide', he was 'merely seeking to ensure that racial prejudice or bias was expunged' from the jurors' minds?

Justice Reeves was reluctant to justify Dickinson's comments to the jury: Dickinson had been the 'only person' in the trial to raise the issue of race, apart from the evidence given of various slurs on both sides. If Dickinson had had 'a greater knowledge of the local situation', he would not have embarked on that particular reference. 'In a sense' Dickinson had created the problem for his client, while he, Justice Reeves, had been at pains to avoid making any allusion to any 'background' to this matter.

The implication was that Dickinson, the outsider, had said what was locally unsayable, best left alone.

Tippett for Woods did not back Sinoch's application; he felt the issue could be dealt with by a direction to the jury. Prosecutor Noble agreed, though he commented that the words 'ripe for prejudice' were 'unfortunate'. What was more unfortunate in Justice Reeves's view was Dickinson's reference to 'the debate that's going on, that we all know about'. What debate, he asked rhetorically, before answering himself, almost to the point of being disingenuous: 'The political debate about policing in the town? The federal opposition leader has called for more police. What? The debate in the newspapers? All those matters are entirely irrelevant and why he referred to them I don't know.'

Justice Reeves said he would speak to the jury, but in a way that he hoped would not cause further offence. Sinoch was left with his 'nagging concern' that there would be fallout for his client, from the notion that he was the 'initiator' of the events. Justice Reeves felt that was taken care of: 'I've already told them, the issue for them to decide is what happened in Musgrave Street, not what happened out the front of the 24 Hour Store.' This direction in part, he said, was to 'avoid any prejudicial issues'.

The argument was not quite over. There was discussion between Sinoch and Justice Reeves about his summary of evidence to the jury that allowed for the possibility of Williams having struck Hargrave a blow. In his summing up, Dickinson had argued the Crown had abandoned its case in this regard. Justice Reeves, however, said he was being careful to draw the distinction between something being possible and something being 'reasonably possible' in the view of the forensic pathologist. (The pathologist had said the wound to Hargrave's head could have been caused by a sharp edge, such as a knife or a broken bottle. However, he agreed, under cross-examination from Dickinson, that there was no evidence that a bottle had been broken over Hargrave's head. He also ruled out that this wound could have been inflicted by an iron bar or similar.) It would be a matter for the jury to look at the whole of the evidence, said Justice Reeves.

Tippett, returning to Sinoch's application, raised the possibility of vacating only one trial, that of Williams. It had crossed Justice

Reeves's mind. At this point Williams, who had sat impassively in the witness box for two weeks, became agitated. I heard his whispered plea, to 'Ted!' (Sinoch); they conferred briefly. Williams's head was in his hands; then he began hitting it, repeated blows to the forehead, as though what he was hearing was unbearable. Was it fear that the jury might accept that he had struck a blow? Was he worried, given the consequences for him that Sinoch foresaw, that the application looked set to fail? Or did he dread its succeeding and having to go through the whole trial again, at some undetermined date in the future?

The application did fail. Justice Reeves spoke to the jury, invoking his personal experience of the local situation. He understood, he said, having been a member of the Alice Springs community 'in the dim distant past', and of the broader Northern Territory community, that they might take offence, but the case needed to be tried on the evidence. The central issue was what happened in Musgrave Street, where Hargrave died. What happened outside the 24 Hour Store and the Memo, but more particularly the chase, were relevant to 'the state of mind of the accused' but most other aspects were 'completely irrelevant'.

~

Williams need not have been so worried: he was acquitted. The jury must have determined there was no evidence beyond reasonable doubt that he had struck Hargrave, nor evidence to support a finding of 'aiding and abetting', for which he would have had to have known that Woods had a knife. He looked stunned as he stepped out of the dock. He kept his eyes on the floor as he walked behind the bar table and past the family of the dead man in the gallery, not even looking around for his own family. His mother, whom he resembles strongly, stood up, tears running down her face, and followed, with his father and others behind her. After two years in custody, Williams was free.

Woods too was acquitted of murder, but was found guilty of manslaughter. Although the court never hears a jury's reasoning, Justice Reeves, in sentencing Woods, spent an hour outlining his own reasoning based on the jury's verdict. He considered the events outside the Memo and the subsequent chase to be 'too removed in time and place' to have bearing on the sentence. Woods's defence team had argued that these events provided the context for Woods's action, leading him to act out of fear for himself and his family – 'even if it was a classic case of excessive self-defence'. Justice Reeves rejected this, saying that the jury must have found that he did not act in self-defence or defence of others, or they would have acquitted him both of murder and manslaughter.

Woods had always maintained that he was not aware, until the knife went in, that he had it in his hand, but in Justice Reeves's view the jury must also have rejected this and the argument put by his defence team that the blow had been struck 'independently of his will'. Woods's 'high degree of culpability' for his crime was ameliorated, however, by it not having been part of a sustained attack and not having had a murderous intention.

Woods became angry in the dock during an exchange between Justice Reeves and Goldflam over the interview he had given to police. Goldflam argued that Woods was entitled to credit for conceding crucial facts in the interview, albeit slowly. Justice Reeves thought differently: Woods had lied and prevaricated and had even attempted to blame his co-accused for the fatal blow. Woods would have sensed then what was coming. He appeared resigned when the detail was finally announced: a head sentence of nine and a half years with a fixed non-parole period of four years and nine months.[19] My hand was shaking as I noted the term. Woods's tearful mother muttered, 'Bunch of bloody liars.' She was able to hug her son before he was taken away: 'Don't you worry, son, don't you worry.'

Jade Keil, fiancée of Kwementyaye Ryder, had sat in court for most of this trial, obviously feeling, like so many others, that there was a link between the two cases. She too was angry about the sentence, seeing it as a case of a black man treated more harshly than white men.[20] Ryder's five assailants had pleaded guilty to manslaughter and the judge had determined that the manslaughter was negligent rather than reckless. One relevant factor was that Ryder's injuries were minor and would not normally have resulted in death; the offenders had thus not been aware of a substantial risk of death. Ryder's attackers were sentenced, as we have seen, to terms ranging from four to six years. The four-year sentence for the one who had struck no blows was to be suspended after twelve months; the remaining four had non-parole periods of three and a half to four years. I said something to Keil about the difference in the type of attack, in particular about Woods's use of a knife. I didn't press the point with her, but the sentence, or at least the non-parole period, was not much harsher even though Woods's culpability was deemed greater – he was judged to have been 'reckless' rather than 'negligent'.

Two narratives, even three given the differing emphases from the two defence cases, had been constructed for the jurors. Their verdict showed that they had gone about extracting the threads from each that they thought were supported beyond reasonable doubt by evidence and plausibility. It confounded simplistic views, if any were still held, that this was a 'black and white' case. Predominantly not black, though more ethnically diverse than the term 'white' allows, the jury set a black man free, and while sending the other to gaol, it was for a lesser offence.

The events that ended with Hargrave's killing had initially appeared to have strong inter-racial dynamics. The trial revealed a social picture of Alice Springs where, in contrast to much of the rest of Australia, there are frequent and complex interactions between

Aboriginal and non-Aboriginal people. In this picture, as with the Ryder case, when it comes to thinking about what is going on in the community, racial division and tension are part of the mix not necessarily overshadowing all else – such as a male propensity to violence, fuelled by a drinking culture.

~

It would be glib to say that 'justice had been done'. Julian Williams, after two years on remand, may have felt he had paid dearly enough for his acquittal.

Graham Woods, it emerged at sentencing, had made two offers in writing to plead guilty to manslaughter the year before. They had not saved him the trial and its anguishing possibility of a murder conviction and 'life' sentence, but they gained him at sentencing a two-and-a-half-year discount. More might have been allowed if a guilty plea had been made at the earliest opportunity, said Justice Reeves, and if the letters had contained expressions of remorse. Goldflam for Woods was surprised by this expectation – he had written many plea offers and they did not usually deal with remorse. Woods had shown remorse in his police interview when he said he was 'disgusted' with himself; and he had expressed his 'deepest sorrow' in his letter of apology to Hargrave's family, read out in court following the verdict. 'As a family man with young children,' he had written, he could begin to imagine their 'heartache'. He asked for their 'understanding and forgiveness'. Not a day went by when he didn't wish he could 'turn back the clock', but now he and his family had to live with what he had done 'for the rest of our lives'.

The words of remorse echoed the words of grief and anger expressed by Ed Hargrave's young widow, Sarah Woodberry, who asked to read her own victim impact statement to the court. 'We have been given a life sentence. There will never ever be justice for us, for those of us that are left behind. What we will continue to endure is greater than any punishment this court could possibly hand out.' She had left Alice Springs as she no longer felt safe in the town where she had grown up. 'If it can happen to Ed, it can happen to anybody. No one is safe here.' She was now raising four children by herself, including the last-born, Ed's only son, whom he had never known.

WARLPIRI VERSUS THE QUEEN

Outside the courthouse there was cheering and shouting: the verdict was 'not guilty' and Liam Jurrah, this favourite Warlpiri son, was telling reporters that his dream was to return to elite football 'to make my families happy again'. He'd been accused of causing serious harm to his cousin, Basil Jurrah; it was behind him now. He set off down the street, surrounded by the adoring young boys of his large extended family. Cecily Granites, his grandmother, brought up a joyful rear with aunties, uncles, cousins and countrymen. Their joy would be short-lived: one week later Liam was again arrested, this time charged over a drunken assault on a woman. It earned him a six-month gaol sentence, suspended after three. More violent offences would follow.[1]

Inside, in the courtroom where Jurrah had spent most of the previous two weeks, a little-known Warlpiri man sat alone, looking down the barrel of years behind bars. Just ten minutes earlier the room had been full of Jurrah family and friends, a large media contingent and the usual gathering of lawyers and court staff for an expected interesting verdict. Now it was deserted. No relative or friend stood behind Peter Delano Hudson as he was sentenced to four years and nine months for a cruel assault on his wife, Daphne White.

Hudson's non-parole period was set at three years. He heard Chief Justice Trevor Riley express the view that his prospects of rehabilitation were poor. His fourteen-year marriage was now finished: he accepted that, said his lawyer. His plans were focussed on regaining access to his three children. By the time of his earliest release the eldest would be almost an adult, sixteen – as old as Hudson was when he began living with her mother.

All of this had been a long time coming. Hudson had first been convicted of failing to comply with a restraining order eight years earlier and since then, a further seven times. He had six prior convictions for assaulting his wife and one for causing her serious harm, earning him two years in gaol. He had been drunk in every one of the attacks.

After the last assault he had fled, surrendering to police ten days later. He had been in gaol ever since. His early guilty plea meant that his wife was spared coming to court to give evidence against him. So I would never have known anything about her and probably would not have lingered to hear Hudson's sentence if it hadn't been for the Jurrah trial. Coincidence doesn't seem the right word to describe her appearance in that trial as a witness.

I recalled Daphne White from the Jurrah committal hearing, held in late July 2012. She wore her hair afro-style, her light-coloured printed skirt and top flattering on her full figure and dark skin. She projected a sense of herself as an attractive woman, even though she looked toughened by drink.

Eight months later at the trial she was very much altered. Her hair was pulled back in a little knot, she was heavier, her face looked puffy; her tough, rather defiant air was gone. Throughout her evidence she held a tissue to her right eye, wiping it. She looked uncomfortable, miserable even, and spoke in a low monotone, mostly through a Warlpiri interpreter. What had happened in those intervening months, I wondered. On the day of Jurrah's verdict I found out.

Although a domestic violence order (DVO) required Peter Hudson to keep away from his wife if he was drinking, they had been on the grog together on the day of the assault. It was late September and the couple were at Nyirripi, a small Warlpiri community about 150 kilometres south-west of Yuendumu. Daphne worked there in the store; Hudson had sporadic work with a Community Development Employment Program. Their younger children were aged seven and five. The first-born, then thirteen, had been boarding at Kormilda College in Darwin, but she had become homesick and returned. Her father was disappointed as he too had been sent to Kormilda, completing Year Ten and gaining a good level of literacy and numeracy.

The court did not hear anything of the whereabouts of the children on the day of the assault. It was a Friday, and their parents got steadily drunker until supplies ran out. An argument blew up about where more grog was going to come from, as it is banned in Nyirripi like in most Aboriginal communities in the NT. Hudson got into a rage and punched Daphne with enough force to knock her to the ground. She hit her head and passed out. He kicked and punched her repeatedly to her head, face and body. He was wearing pointy-toed cowboy boots. She suffered multiple lacerations, swelling, bruising, grazing, a puncture wound to her left leg which would leave it lame, and a number of facial and other fractures. She lost a tooth and the sight in her right eye. It needed ongoing treatment, but she was having trouble keeping appointments.

That explained it then, at least in part, the changed demeanour, the air of misery, the swabbing of her eye.

In her evidence at the Jurrah committal Daphne had agreed that she'd been drunk on the night of the events that had led to Liam's arrest. The serious harm to Basil had happened at Little Sisters town

camp, where Daphne was staying with her sister. The camp sits just
south of Heavitree Gap. The range rises steeply behind it. The sky
above can be thick with birds hovering off the range and over the
neighbouring rubbish dump. Ilparpa Valley rolls out to the west. To
the east, though, the camp is hemmed in by the railway, then the
Stuart Highway. Residents have to cross both on their way to the
river or to the small supermarket and bottle shop on its far bank.
There are two roadside memorials to pedestrians who have been run
over here. The camp's English name reflects its past history as the site
of a novitiate house for Catholic nuns, the Little Sisters of the Poor.
Its Arrernte name is Inarlenge. Many of the stories told of it, like
this one, are about drunken violence, and long-term residents have
complained bitterly about the heavy drinking and the pressure on
them from outside visitors. But there are other stories too. The artist
Margaret Boko has lived there for a long time and the camp features
in many of her paintings. She shows the way the houses are grouped
allowing family to live close to one another. She shows children
playing outside and she dots the ground with flowers. The birds are
playing too, some of them with plastic bags blown off the dump into
the updraft. Cars and roads are part of the picture; so too the telecom
towers on top of the range as well as its secluded waterholes.

Daphne had started drinking in the afternoon, in the river, rum
mixed with Coke, and sharing some VB beer from two cartons
bought by a relative at the Todd Tavern drive-through. Later with
family she bought another bottle of rum and some food at the
Heavitree Gap store and went back to the camp. Her evidence about
drinking at the trial was less detailed, but one thing stood out: she'd
been with family when she was drinking in the river, but back at
Little Sisters she was drinking rum alone.

It was 7 March 2012, a Wednesday. Almost all of the civilian
witnesses were drinking that night and so was Liam Jurrah. In the

interview he gave to police the next day, he told of drinking with four companions, in the river under the bridge at the back of Old Timers, an aged care village, which lends its name to another town camp on its southern border. Both are within easy walking distance of Little Sisters. Jurrah's companions were Christopher Walker, Josiah Fry, Dennis Nelson and Elton Granites. The five men started drinking at about 4 pm, VB, a bottle of rum and a bottle of Smirnoff vodka. After they finished they had 'a feed', then bought more grog, 'the same thing', said Jurrah, from the bottle shop at Heavitree Gap. This session they finished around 10 pm. Describing his state by this time, Jurrah said: 'I knew what I was doing.' The interviewing officers didn't ask him just how much he personally had drunk.

There were quite a few visiting reporters covering this trial: Jurrah had played a thrilling style of football for the Melbourne Demons, and his star had not yet faded. Local reporters covering court are normally left to improvise a working area as best they can, but for Jurrah's trial the court set up a temporary media room with a few desks and power points. The chat about the case changed after the evidence of heavy drinking on the night. Even though Jurrah's account of his innocence seemed plausible, the heavy drinking introduced doubt.

Most of the witnesses agreed they were a 'bit drunk' or more so, 'half-shot'. Daphne White was pressed on this. Wasn't she 'full drunk'? No, 'just a little bit', she insisted through the interpreter: the bottle was 'still half full'. Besides 'when I'm full drunk I go to sleep'.

Her sister Ingrid White said she was 'half-shot'. Her brother Samuel White just said he was 'drinking grog'. He may even have been under the influence when he was giving his evidence at the trial. The only male witness who'd not been drinking was the oldest of them, Murray Woods; he suffered from diabetes and kidney disease.

Basil Jurrah, the victim in the case, agreed at the committal that he was 'half-shot', having been drinking all day, starting before lunch at the Todd Tavern. At the trial there was a new detail: his take-away grog purchases included 'a four corner', a two-litre bottle of Jim Beam. Basil claimed to have had it, part finished, in his pocket when he got to Little Sisters that night.

Philomena White, twenty-two years old, had not been drinking. It was she who called the police when the fighting erupted, she who took the young children inside; until then they'd been sitting with their mostly drunken relatives. She watched through a window as the fighting continued. Asked whether Basil Jurrah had been trying to hit people, she said no, 'he was too drunk'.

Freda Jurrah is the mother of Daphne, Ingrid and Samuel, grandmother of Philomena. She is also Liam Jurrah's aunty. She normally lives in Nyirripi but was with her children at Little Sisters on the night of 7 March. She told the court she had 'never tasted grog in [her] life'. I felt like cheering.

I thought of Freda again when her son-in-law Peter Hudson was sentenced. After the assault, he had dragged Daphne into the shower to try and clean her up. Then he left the house, apparently to get a towel. When he got back he found Freda and her present husband attending to her battered daughter. It was they who sought medical help. Hudson took off.

~

I've never known personally anyone to arm themselves. Some men close to me have gotten caught up in fistfights, but that's it. I was on an errand in the centre of town one weekday, at around 3 pm, passing through the grounds between Adelaide House and Flynn Church. An Aboriginal man was walking ahead of me with an air of purpose. Suddenly he bent down and picked up a stout stick and without a glance in any direction, reached behind him and tucked it into his jeans, pulling his jacket over it. I was struck by his lack of hesitation or inhibition in arming himself – in a public place, in broad daylight.

Where do he and multiple others like him fit in the definition of the 'ordinary person similarly circumstanced' against which the jury was told to judge Liam Jurrah if they found him responsible for the attack on Basil Jurrah? Chief Justice Riley provided the jury with a definition, close to standard, of such an 'ordinary person': he would be a male of similar age 'living today in the environment and culture of a community such as Alice Springs'. He wouldn't be drunk or affected by drugs, not particularly bad tempered, or excitable or pugnacious. 'He possesses such power of self-control as everyone is entitled to expect an ordinary person of that culture and environment to have.' This assumes a degree of homogeneity in the culture and environment of Alice Springs that might be desirable from the judicial point of view but which does not currently exist.

By most witness accounts Little Sisters camp on the night of 7 March was bristling with weapons. People were picking them up, sometimes using them with devastating effect and throwing them down again. The police, however, found only a nulla nulla and a metal pole. They disposed of both without any forensic testing. The officer in charge of the investigation, Senior Constable Sean Aila, described their search as a 'quick look around'. The chief justice was incredulous. Basil Jurrah had been severely beaten, suffering multiple lacerations 'down to the skull' and six fractures to the head and face. And he was not the only victim. The agreed facts revealed that a fourteen-year-old had also suffered severe head injuries. This was Liam Jurrah's 'little nephew', who joined the fighting on his famous uncle's side. Some forensics might have helped the jury decide who had had what in their hand, said the chief justice. Senior Constable Aila was left squirming in the witness box.

Freda Jurrah had tried to stop the fighting. When Christopher Walker, one of Liam's drinking companions, arrived at the camp, Freda and her family could hear him singing out in the darkness, 'Anybody there who wants to fight with me?' This was the polite version.

Freda's granddaughter Philomena also left out the swear words but suggested he was more provocative: 'I'm here, come and try me. I'm the murderer, come and fight.'

Freda told him nobody wanted to fight, to go away.

'You wait till I go get my family,' he said.

Can we see here vestiges of fighting as a 'dispute processing device', as described by anthropologist and geographer Marcia Langton in a well-known essay, 'Medicine Square'? These are the generalised rules:

- The aggrieved calls a fight by swearing and accusing.
- The event must occur in a public place.
- No-one but particular kin and close friends may interfere.
- Kin must call off the fight if it goes too far.
- Individuals tend not to become extremely violent (unless extremely intoxicated) and finish the fight with threats and boasts about what they could have done.

So Walker arrives at Little Sisters calling for a fight, swearing and provoking. This happens in a public place, in the communal area of the camp, where kin are gathered. Freda Jurrah, the non-drinker and a senior woman, tries to prevent it going further but, under the influence of heavy drinking by almost everyone else on the scene, fighting erupts and soon does go too far, with nobody effectively interfering except for young Philomena when she calls the police. In her essay, published in 1988, Langton argued that dispute processing by swearing and fighting was 'misperceived by the Anglo-Australian legal system and its enforcers as drunken anarchy'.[2] Twenty years later in another well-known essay, 'The end of "big men" politics', her emphasis had changed. In light of the 'lateral violence' resulting in intentional and unintentional injuries being 'the third leading broad cause of Indigenous Australian disease burden', we could no longer afford, she argued, 'to ignore the much-weakened hold of cultural values and norms of social behaviour, and the descent into anarchy and lawlessness in many Aboriginal communities from time to time … the evidence has been mounting for three decades that even the most stalwart upholders of Aboriginal laws feel powerless to deal with new plagues of alcohol and drug abuse.'[3]

As the police arrived, for the first time that night, Walker took off. Later he did return with family, including Liam Jurrah. Freda told Liam, 'You can't fight.' He told her to 'stay away'.

During the fight Freda's daughter Ingrid, thirty-seven years old, was hit on the forehead with an axe by Josiah Fry, another of the men who'd been drinking with Liam. She was 'bleeding all over' from the laceration. She also received a small cut to the head from Liam but she said this was an accident. It happened when she got between him and the young man he was arguing with, Lemiah Woods. Ingrid's evidence put a nulla nulla in Liam Jurrah's hands and that was not contested by his counsel. She also got into a fight with another woman who hit her on the arm with a nulla nulla. Ingrid just pushed her away.

Lemiah, 'half-shot', got into a fistfight with Dennis Nelson, another of Liam's drinking companions. Lemiah had been sitting around a campfire with his parents and Freda and her children. He said Liam, Walker, Fry and Nelson, together with a woman, had come running towards them, all armed, with axes, crowbars, sticks and rocks. He had a crowbar too but threw it down in favour of fists. He gave as good as he got, 'fifty/fifty'. While he was fighting, he was struck from behind, possibly with an axe. He showed the court a scar on his left arm.

Daphne White armed herself with an 'iron picket' and was fighting with the fourteen-year-old, Liam Jurrah's 'little nephew'. She said he had a nulla nulla, and so did his aunt, who joined in. It was not clear from evidence at the trial if the fourteen-year-old's head injuries resulted from this contest.

Reinforcements arrived from Hidden Valley town camp to stand with the Woods and White families against Liam Jurrah and his companions. Among them was Basil Jurrah. He denied that his group brought weapons with them from Hidden Valley and he mostly insisted that he only went to Little Sisters to drink, not to fight. Essau Marshall was with him. Essau agreed when it was put to him that the Hidden Valley group was 'fired up' because they'd heard their family members were 'threatened'. He picked up a rock when he got to Little Sisters and put it in his pocket, ready to use 'in self-defence'. Then one of his family gave him a nulla nulla. There was no evidence that he used it. When the fighting got too hot, he took off into the scrub.

Allan Collins was also with the Hidden Valley party. His evidence put a nulla nulla in Basil Jurrah's hands during the fighting. Another witness, Douglas Watson, had the Hidden Valley group all picking up weapons before leaving for Little Sisters. He had a nulla nulla, he said, and Basil Jurrah had a machete. At the committal Watson said the armoury had included iron bars and boomerangs, but he hadn't seen anyone with machetes.

Liam Jurrah told police that when he and his companions were advancing into Little Sisters, the Woods and White families, supported by the Hidden Valley reinforcements, were throwing weapons at Christopher Walker – axes, machetes, wheel-spanners. He said people in his party, including women, had armed themselves with branches, ripping them from trees. He said Walker may have had an axe, and many other witnesses also put an axe in Walker's hands. Josiah Fry, according to Liam, had found an axe near the railway line and he, Liam, tried to take it off him at Little Sisters. When it was put to Liam that witnesses said he was carrying a small axe and a crowbar, he admitted to carrying a machine part in the shape of a number seven which might look like an axe. Later he said he picked up a crowbar 'to pretend' he was going to fight, and he broke a piece of wood from a couch, to use in 'self-defence'.

It was put to him that another witness had seen him with a knife and an axe.

'I didn't have any knife.'

That he chased Basil Jurrah with an axe and hit him with a machete.

'I had a crowbar, something I told [you] before.'

He consistently denied striking Basil Jurrah and the jury believed him – or at least could not find otherwise beyond reasonable doubt.

It was known during the trial that two men had been before the courts in relation to the same events, but no detail of the charges was given. A few days after Liam was acquitted, the men were sentenced. They were Christopher Walker and Josiah Fry – two of Liam's drinking companions on the night. Every account of the serious assault on Basil – those implicating Liam Jurrah and those not – had indicated more than one assailant. It was chilling to learn from Chief Justice Riley as he sentenced Walker that the second assailant had not been identified. The agreed facts were that this unknown person had struck Basil Jurrah on the head with a machete and then dealt other blows. The jury's verdict in Liam Jurrah's trial may have been right, as 'beyond reasonable doubt' is the high standard that evidence must meet, but clearly the court did not get to the bottom of what happened at Little Sisters. Walker pleaded guilty to his part in causing serious harm to Basil Jurrah – with the blunt head of a small axe – but Fry's guilty plea was to lesser charges of unlawful assault on Ingrid and Samuel White. His weapon was a nulla nulla.

~

If the challenge to 'ordinariness' is stark in the town camps, it can also be evident in the streets of downtown Alice Springs. During both the committal and trial of Liam Jurrah, there were outbreaks of physical fighting and angry shouting outside the courthouse. At the committal the unrest was reported on *Ten Network News* as 'rival factions square-off' while 'inside a story of tribal feuding and warring factions emerged'.[4]

Much the same media treatment was given to a briefer incident during the trial but this time it emerged that the crowd was swelled and emotions fuelled by a separate incident of violence on another town camp. The trial had broken for lunch when a few punches started flying. Shouting reached a crescendo as police came pouring out of the adjacent station. Most of the crowd was on the lawns opposite the courthouse. Some police took up position at the edges, making their presence felt; others went up to people and started talking, to calm them down. The young men who'd engaged in fisticuffs melted away. I approached a group of women who'd withdrawn from the crowd to sit under a tree. Did they know what it was all about? I asked. They said a young man 'from the Granites family' had said things to upset people. Yes, it was part of the feud that had been going on 'for the last four years'. There were sighs and exasperated looks.

'But I'm also upset for my daughter,' one woman said.

I looked at her. Her hair was cropped short – a sign of mourning – and she was dressed in black.

'She died on New Year's Eve. We're here to see the man who killed her. It's his first time in court.'

This was Sebastian Kunoth; the woman's daughter was his wife. The hearing was due to start after lunch. Not much happened and the case was adjourned; all was quiet by the time the Jurrah trial was over for the day. A couple of mounted police were stationed photogenically on the corner and were there again the next morning.

By then anyone covering the Liam Jurrah case was familiar with the Granites name. In tandem with Walker, it designated one side of an infamous Warlpiri feud,[5] said to be at the root of the fighting at Little Sisters; Watson designated the other side. Although it seems to have had its roots in the sad death of a young man on the Walker/ Granites side from cancer, believed to have been caused by sorcery, both prosecution and defence dated the feud from the stabbing death of a young Watson man in September 2010.[6] His assailants were from the Walker/Granites side. The feud had festered ever since, with greatest impact at Yuendumu, some 300 kilometres north-west of Alice, home community to the families of both sides. There had been numerous sanctions by the courts for offences along the way and more would come,[7] as well as extensive government-sponsored efforts at mediation. The dispute was finally put to bed, symbolically buried in the sand, at a ceremony in August 2013.[8]

At the time of Liam Jurrah's trial a man on the Walker/Granites side was serving time for the manslaughter of the young Watson man. Two other men, Dennis Nelson and Christopher Walker, had served prison terms for their actions on the same occasion. Both were drinking in the creek with Liam Jurrah on the night of 7 March and were with him again during the first incursion at Little Sisters. Dennis Nelson might have been saved from getting into more serious trouble then by being extremely drunk; he was carted off by police. Christopher Walker went on, as we know, to attack Basil Jurrah.

During both committal and trial, defence counsel for Liam Jurrah, Jon Tippett QC, tried to open up the running sore of the feud but he met with strong resistance. His logic no doubt was to create an impression of prejudice and antipathy tainting the evidence against his client.

Basil Jurrah is a big man, tall and heavy-set. At the committal he was led into court in prison garb. (We would learn at the trial, in the absence of the jury, that he had multiple convictions including riotous behaviour, going armed in public and assault.) Scars on his head were visible through his close-cropped hair. Though he appeared to understand much of what was put to him, he spoke mostly through an interpreter.

He went to Little Sisters for 'smoke and grog', he insisted at the committal. He denied getting weapons before he went, denied obtaining a weapon later and repeatedly denied that he and his companions were intending to fight. The crack came when Tippett raised 'the trouble at Yuendumu' that involved 'Kumunjayi Watson'. Tippett suggested Basil Jurrah was angry about the trouble. There was a long pause. Tippett repeated the proposition that he was angry, and it was translated by the interpreter.

'Yes,' said Basil finally, but again he denied that he wanted to fight the enemy.

Tippett named 'the enemy' as the Walker/Granites family.

Basil Jurrah agreed but repeated that he had gone to Little Sisters for grog.

'You hated Liam Jurrah' because of the problem with Kumunjayi Watson, said Tippett.

No, said Basil.

'Rubbish!' said Tippett, suggesting that he was 'blaming this man' – indicating Liam in the dock – 'for nothing'.

Objection by the prosecutor; mutterings and apparently gestures in the public gallery. The magistrate asked people to sit still and make no comment. Tippett resumed: Kumunjayi Watson's family were blaming the Walker/Granites families for his death.

It was as if a blind came down on Basil Jurrah's face. Tippett had crossed the line. Again a long pause, then Basil spoke to the interpreter, who explained the difficulty the witness was having with the questions, related to 'his obligation'.

Indeed, it was his 'obligation' that had taken him to Little Sisters, Tippett proposed.

Basil agreed.

And because of those obligations he intended to fight and hurt the Walker/Granites mob.

Yes, said Basil.

He intended to blame people in that mob for the fight that happened, said Tippett.

Pause. The interpreter translated and Basil replied: 'I seen Liam Jurrah and Christopher Walker with my own eyes.' He denied that people had told him that they were there. 'I know his face,' said Basil.

They went through it all again at the committal and again eight months later at the trial. There was trouble taken then to keep the jury from knowing that Basil Jurrah and the witness Douglas Watson were prisoners. They were already in the witness box, in civilian clothes, before the jury entered. This time Tippett didn't go in as hard on the feud. He spent a long time trying to discredit Basil Jurrah's evidence in relation to how much he had been drinking. On his reasons for going to Little Sisters, Tippett got him to admit that he was 'a member of the Watson family' and that there was 'trouble' between them and the Walker/Granites families. He wouldn't 'press' him on what the trouble was, but got him to admit that his family talked of the Walker/Granites families as 'the enemy'. And the reason he went to Little Sisters was to fight the enemy, right?

'Yes,' answered Basil Jurrah, without the assistance of the interpreter, but immediately returning to speak through him, he again resisted all of Tippett's propositions that he and his companions intended to fight and had armed themselves. He maintained to the end that Liam Jurrah had hit him twice on the head with a machete: 'It was him that hit me', 'When I fell I saw him', 'It was him', 'Even though I was drunk and dizzy, it was him, I saw him.'

Basil Jurrah's long pauses as he gave evidence appeared to prompt Chief Justice Riley to speak to the jury about Aboriginal witnesses. He said his remarks were not intended to apply to Basil Jurrah specifically, but they were made halfway through his evidence. The chief justice spoke of the 'daunting prospect' for anyone of giving evidence in the Supreme Court with all its formality, but it was especially so for a 'relatively unsophisticated' Aboriginal person 'from a remote location'. He then referred to the 'substantial silences' from some Aboriginal witnesses before they gave their answers. In someone from a different background, the jury might think this was because they were 'fudging', but for some Aboriginal witnesses, significant silences might be their 'natural way of speaking … in ordinary conversation'. As with witnesses who kept their eyes averted (not the case with Basil Jurrah who quite often grimly fixed Tippett with his gaze), this might be 'cultural' rather than 'evasive', said the chief justice.

I thought that Basil Jurrah's silences were more significant. They seemed to clearly signal that a proposition from Tippett had gone too far into Warlpiri business. His resistance was just as clear when responding to the prosecutor: asked what trouble had led him to go to Little Sisters, Basil Jurrah heaved a big sigh. He leaned in to whisper to the interpreter who then told the court, 'He doesn't want to talk about that.' The message seemed to be, this was business over which the court had no jurisdiction.

Other witnesses also wanted the court to keep its nose out of 'the trouble'. Fear of retribution might have been a factor for some, and the threat seemed real enough. On day five of the trial the female interpreter complained about intimidation by a member of the Granites family, who had warned her not to take sides. The incident had occurred during the lunch break and was reported by the prosecutor to the chief justice before the jury came back in: the interpreter had gone to him in a state of extreme anxiety and was unwilling to go on with her duties. The Granites woman was still outside in the lobby. The chief justice had her brought in and spoke to her sternly, warning her of the possibility of being charged with contempt of court and going to gaol. Did she understand? Yes, she nodded. The interpreter was satisfied and resumed her place alongside the witness. By the end of the trial, all seemed forgotten. On the day of the verdict she sat happily in the public gallery, ensconced between Warlpiri relatives, all of them Liam Jurrah connections. 'Congratulations,' she said to him in English with a big smile, as he walked from court a free man.

She interpreted for Freda Jurrah, the first witness to be called. The prosecutor established that Freda had relatives on both sides of the feud. One of her children had married into the Walker/Granites family. On the other hand, it was to support the Watson family that she had come into Alice Springs from her home community of Nyirripi.

In cross-examination Tippett put to her that the Watson family was 'blaming' the Walker/Granites family for Kumunjayi Watson's death.

No, said Freda Jurrah.

The Watson family was 'angry' with the Walker/Granites family, he said.

Objection.

There was 'trouble' between the Watson family and the Walker/Granites family, he tried.

Yes.

And through a number of further propositions he attempted to lead her into agreeing that the Watsons 'blame' the Walker/Granites family for Kumunjayi's death.

No answer. Then a whispered exchange with the interpreter who told Tippett, 'She can understand but she doesn't want to tell you.'

Tippett wouldn't let it go, not even when Freda Jurrah said that it was 'another trouble' at play on the night of 7 March at Little Sisters. He went through all his propositions again.

No, no, no, answered Freda.

'Oh!' he finally said with exaggerated irony, before moving on to another line of questioning.

'That Jon Tippett!' a court staffer muttered as we broke for morning tea. 'Everyone is trying to quell the trouble and he just tries to bring it all up again.'

A member of the jury was concerned too. He or she sent a note to Chief Justice Riley suggesting that the court be cleared when 'cultural reasons' for the fighting were being explored: witnesses might feel subject to influence from people in the public gallery. The chief justice declined to do so. He would consider such a move only in an 'extreme case', not on the basis of a 'speculated possibility'. He had been watching the gallery during questioning and had not seen anything to concern him.

Tippett continued to dig into 'the trouble' with Freda Jurrah's daughter, Ingrid White. She agreed to his proposition that during the fighting at Little Sisters she was part of the group 'on the Watson side'; she agreed that the two sides had been fighting each other 'since the young man died'; that it had been going on for 'many months'. Whenever the two sides came together, they argued, he put to her.

Objection.

'I won't press it,' said Tippett but he did, going on to list the people present in her circle that night on the Watson side.

'They weren't involved with that problem,' she cut in.

Tippett persisted, but Ingrid White was firm: 'We wasn't involved with that problem so I don't want to talk about it.'

Before the fighting began Ingrid had been sitting with her mother, sister, brother and others around a fire out the front of Murray Woods's house, Number One, at Little Sisters. Although the parents of Kumunjayi Watson stay with Murray Woods when they're in Alice Springs, he told the prosecutor that people from the Walker/ Granites side are 'part of my family too … I'm in the middle of them two families.'

The other poignant evidence about being in the middle came from Liam Jurrah himself in the interview he had given to police.

The uncontested victim of serious harm on the night was his cousin, Basil Jurrah. How did two Jurrahs end up on opposing sides of the feud? Although he consistently denied wanting to fight and rejected utterly the proposition that he had hit Basil Jurrah, Liam Jurrah did admit to getting angry at Little Sisters. He said he was at the back of the group 'rushing in' when he 'heard someone calling my name. That's when I got angry but I didn't have any fight with no-one.'

What was he getting angry at, asked Senior Constable Aila.

'They was saying I didn't respect anybody, I don't want to know my old man as well and my grandfather. All you want to do is to come here and be with your mother's family.'

Is that rude? asked Aila.

'It sort of made me feel …'

Frustratingly, the recording was inaudible for the rest of this answer, but 'rude' didn't seem to be quite the right term. The taunts had hit a real sore point. Any observer of Aboriginal life in Central Australia begins to understand something of the defining importance for an Aboriginal person of whom they are related to. In Liam Jurrah's case, he seems to have largely missed out on a close relationship with his father and father's family.

Anthropologist Yasmine Musharbash describes the Warlpiri ideal of a stable marriage where children grow up in their parents' camp, but she says this ideal is 'rarely the norm' today. So children often live in jilimi, women's camp, 'sometimes with their mothers, or more regularly with their grandmothers'.[9] The paternal grandmother relationship has a special status and it is 'emotionally often close, caring and comfortable', writes Musharbash. Again, this is an ideal, how Warlpiri people say it should be, but in reality many children are raised by their maternal grandmothers.[10] So it was for Liam Jurrah: it was his maternal grandmother, Cecily Granites, who raised him.

Tall stature and good looks seem to run in the family. Although she has arthritis, Cecily Granites appears youthful for a great-grandmother. She and Liam are clearly close. When he first moved to Melbourne to play professional football, she went with him and took the opportunity to enrol in a course to improve her English – '*your* language', she stressed with a smile when telling me this, as we sat in the lobby one day, waiting for the trial to resume. She used to work as a teacher at the Yuendumu school but the feud had completely disrupted her life. Her house in Yuendumu was destroyed during a rampage by the opposing family and she told me she had recently been spending most of her time in Adelaide. Liam had been staying with her at the Alice Springs visitors park on the night of the fighting. She was often present in court during the trial along with many other members of her extended family. As Liam was free to come and go from the courthouse, he almost always took his breaks with them. He'd come to life in their company, talking, laughing, cuddling babies, playing gentle tussling games with the little kids and electronic games with the older adoring boys.

During the committal one of his relatives, senior Warlpiri man, Rex Granites Japanangka, had distributed to reporters a single typed page, headed 'Statement regarding Liam Jurrah Jungurrayi'. He signed it and gave his qualifications: 'BA, Education; Elder, Mediator and Interpreter.' It was a call for help, wanting the government and the court to 'support the authority of family elders'. He described Liam Jurrah as an example of young Aboriginal men not listening to their elders. Liam's 'young father' had 'left his family early in Liam's life, and he did not have a strong male role model in his family to provide discipline', he said. 'We elders taught Liam the basics of ceremony, but he still has a lot to learn.' He wrote of 'several young men who have been misbehaving' and they had asked Liam to help: 'Liam made the decision on his own … He did not consult us.'

This gives perhaps some idea of the emotional context for Liam Jurrah's reactions in the escalating situation at Little Sisters. The taunts began again.

'They started calling out, I'm "not Jurrah",' he told Aila in his police interview.

'That made you mad?'

'I'm a Jurrah,' he said with emphasis, then attempted to explain: 'It's pretty complicated between Jurrah versus Jurrah.'

The fighting at Little Sisters was not only 'a tale of two Jurrahs'. Everyone or almost everyone involved was related, to Liam Jurrah and to one another. How long have you known Liam Jurrah? they were all asked.

'He's my nephew,' said Freda Jurrah.

'He's my cousin, I talk to him anytime,' said her son, Samuel White.

'My uncle,' said her granddaughter, Philomena White.

Philomena had grown up in Yuendumu as had Liam. She said she saw him hit Basil Jurrah twice on the head with a machete. In cross-examination Tippett made much of the dark conditions and suggested that she may have confused Liam with Josiah Fry.

Didn't Fry have a haircut like Liam's, wasn't he tall like him?

'Little bit.'

Didn't he have the same build?

'No' – she was quite clear about that.

Daphne White had known her cousin Liam a 'long time'. She gave evidence of him being armed with an iron bar, running towards her together with others.

How did she recognise him in the dark, Tippett challenged.

'He was taller than them.'

Didn't she have trouble seeing in the dark?

'I could see.'

Tippett persevered: she couldn't see who was fighting because it was too dark.

'I can see the fighting, I was busy fighting too,' Daphne insisted.

I was reminded of Musharbash in the jilimi at night: 'When we sat around the fire telling stories and someone or other came towards us in the dark, I used to be perplexed by everybody but me recognising who was approaching long before I could see their faces in the firelight. However, it was not Warlpiri people's night vision that was superior to mine, but their knowledge of others, and of others' bodies.'[11]

Though she warns against making too much of this – there is time for observation around a campfire and this may be different in a fight[12] – Crown prosecutor Stephen Robson made much the same point in his summing up. The eyewitnesses were 'all family, blood or skin way'. They knew Liam Jurrah very well, he argued. Even apart from him being a tall man, they would have been 'very familiar with his voice, his physique, the way he walked'. They hadn't just seen him, they'd recognised him. Daphne, even as she was busy fighting, said she heard Liam's voice. 'Let's hit her,' he was saying in Warlpiri. Several witnesses spoke of hearing Christopher Walker call out from the darkness. They all said they recognised him by his voice.

There were some attempts to explore the Warlpiri distinctions between 'blood' and 'skin' relationships in the trial. Murray Woods, the old man 'in the middle of them two families', described Liam Jurrah as his 'grandson'. Was it this relationship that led Liam to show him some consideration during the fighting? Murray said he saw Liam try to hit Murray's son, Lemiah, on the head and saw him actually hit the windscreen of Murray's car. But he also spoke of when he, Murray, was hit and punched from behind and became dizzy: Liam 'got hold of me and sat me down in a chair'. Then Liam took him away from the fighting, to a neighbouring house: 'He made sure I was all right.'

Murray's grandfather relationship to Liam may have been 'skin way', meaning a classificatory relationship within the Warlpiri kinship system; it was not specified in court. But when thirty-four-year-old

Allan Collins, a companion of Basil Jurrah's on the night, described himself as Liam's 'young grandfather', Tippett wanted clarification: 'There are blood relationships and other relationships.' Chief Justice Riley was also uncertain about the term – 'except in relation to myself', he quipped. Prosecutor Robson tried to elucidate with further questions.

'I'm Leo Jurrah's young uncle,' said Collins – Leo being Liam's father.

'Blood way or skin way?' asked the prosecutor.

'Skin way.'

'I'm not sure we can do better than that,' said the chief justice.

In his summing-up, prosecutor Robson tried to draw some conclusions about what people's interconnection might mean, although he was generalising about 'Indigenous Australians', not Warlpiri. Tippett had tried from the outset to suggest that the testimony against his famous client was an attempt to 'bring him down' because he was 'a standout', 'head and shoulders above' the rest. Robson refuted this 'tall poppy syndrome' argument. Isn't it 'a cultural nuance' associated with European Australia? he asked. He urged the jurors to consider it in the light of their own life experience, but he hadn't seen too many Indigenous Australians 'wanting to cut down one of their own'. Tippett expressed concern that Robson was trying to 'get in as an expert on Indigenous culture'. Chief Justice Riley also seemed to think it was dangerous ground and told Robson to 'tread carefully'.

There are degrees and degrees of being 'one of their own'. Essau Marshall gave devastating evidence about his 'countryman' Liam Jurrah. He spoke for himself, not through an interpreter, in a clear, deep voice, meeting both prosecutor and defence with a steady gaze. He said Liam was 'pounding' Basil Jurrah with a machete, 'celebrating' as he did so, chanting 'BJ, BJ, BJ!'

'Countryman' in Aboriginal English, according to Musharbash, translates Warlpiri concepts that can include family connection, long-term cohabitation or belonging to a certain place.[13] But in the events on 7 March Marshall's loyalty was explicitly to his 'cousins', Allan Collins and Basil Jurrah. At Little Sisters he'd prepared to fight 'just to defend my two cousins', he said. When he ran off into the scrub, 'thinking to my two cousins' had caused him to turn around, which is how he saw the attack on Basil Jurrah.

Liam Jurrah's interview with police was peppered with relationship references. He seemed to prefer to talk about people in this way. Even when asked to name them, which he would, he would then revert to the relationship designation. So when he was talking of being down the creek drinking, he spoke of one of his companions as 'one of my cousins married to other cousin'. This was Josiah Fry, whom he consistently referred to as 'cousin', even when other cousins were in the picture. The relationships Liam spoke of included 'my little cousin' (un-named); 'my little nephew' who was hit on the head (named); 'my sister', the nephew's mother (un-named); Basil, of course ('my cousin'); 'my little uncle' (named) and 'my little cousin' (named), to both of whom he claimed to have given the axe that he'd wrested from Fry's hand; 'my cousin' (named), a woman who took the injured 'little nephew' in her car back to the visitors park from where he was conveyed to hospital; 'other families' (not specified); 'my aunty Freda' – the only time he joined a given name to the relationship designation.

Naming people by their kin relations is the way Warlpiri 'describe everyday realities', says Musharbash. Because of the emphasis that this seems to put on relationship, it might be assumed that a special closeness is implied. But, as Musharbash says, a 'multitude of gradations exist within these relations, involving a range of interactions ... most Warlpiri can trace genealogical links to each other one way or another, and all of them can trace a classificatory link, but not all of them live together – or even like each other, for that matter'. She draws attention to 'the fact that Warlpiri relationships, and often especially close relationships, are fraught with tensions'. This can lead to relations slowly deteriorating or they can be 'ruptured swiftly and suddenly'.[14]

Despite all the obvious tensions of the long-standing feud and within the Jurrah family, Liam Jurrah still cited his relationship to Basil Jurrah as the reason for throwing down his weapon: 'As soon as I saw Basil, I threw it away. He's my cousin.' When he went back to the visitors park after the fighting, he said he tried to calm everyone down 'but I was worried about Basil as well 'cause he's my cousin'.

~

When Chief Justice Riley sentenced Peter Hudson for the assault on Daphne White, he commented on the 'tragically commonplace' nature of the crime – 'a drunken Aboriginal man violently [assaulting] his drunken Aboriginal wife or some other vulnerable person'. He also expressed a sense of futility in his role: imposing severe sentences 'is to address the problem after the damage has been done'. An obvious step, in his view, 'would be to limit the flow of alcohol' to people like Hudson. But this wasn't being done, or not adequately, and in his experience, the situation was getting worse: 'The terrible problems we now see are destined to be repeated in the next generation. It seems it is all too hard.'

He had cause to make similar comments when just a few days later he sentenced Christopher Walker and Josiah Fry for their part in the fighting at Little Sisters. Both had been drinking – in great quantity, according to Liam Jurrah in his police interview – and both had, according to the sentencing remarks, long-term drinking problems. The chief justice regarded Walker's prospects of rehabilitation as poor, but he had more hope for Fry, ordering him into residential rehab immediately upon release from gaol. Walker got four years and six months, with a non-parole period of three years; Fry got two years, suspended after ten months.

The chief justice gave a brief account of both men's lives to date. Josiah Fry was born in Adelaide and began school there. His parents separated when he was ten because of his father's heavy drinking. He moved with his mother to Alice Springs and again went to school. He could read and write English although he left school at thirteen after his Warlpiri initiation. He could play keyboards and guitar and had been a good footballer in the past. His mother worked, including in 'responsible employment', but he had never worked. His father worked 'sporadically'. Fry began drinking when he was eighteen, regularly getting 'full drunk' although he claimed not to have been so affected on 7 March. He had convictions for traffic offences including driving under the influence. He also had convictions for going armed in public, damaging property, breaching a DVO, engaging in violent conduct and breaching bail.

Christopher Walker had spent his early years at Yuendumu until his parents separated when he was three or four. His mother took him to Adelaide for a while, then gave him to his maternal grandmother to look after at Hermannsburg. His paternal grandmother sometimes had him too, at various places including Murray Bridge in South Australia. He was returned to his father when he was thirteen (a typical age for initiation although it was not mentioned in his case). He spent significant periods living with family at Warlpiri town camp in Alice Springs. He went to school only occasionally, but spoke English reasonably well. He had had some work with a Community Development Employment Program.

Walker had a history of increasingly serious violence, all of it associated with excessive drinking. In March 2006 he was sentenced to six months for an aggravated assault, and to eighteen months for causing grievous harm. In July 2006, he was again convicted of aggravated assault and sentenced to three months. In October 2007 he was released on a good behaviour bond for threatening with a weapon. He pleaded guilty to the September 2010 aggravated assault on Kumunjayi Watson's brother and was sentenced to fourteen months, suspended after five. He'd been out of gaol just over a week when he assaulted Basil Jurrah at Little Sisters.

'It seems you did not learn a lesson from your time in prison,' the chief justice said.

Walker's other criminal history went back to a first conviction in the juvenile court in 2005. It included unlawful entry of buildings, stealing, unlawful use of a motor vehicle, breaching orders for release, failing to comply with a restraining order and traffic matters.

Warlpiri elder Rex Granites Japanangka, in his statement of July 2012, asked 'the court to help us restore our traditional role of teaching and disciplining young men so they will grow up in the next generation and stop these cycles of family problems'. It was not clear how he thought this could be done though he did take a swipe at 'a new system of authority based on money' introduced since the settlement of Australia.

'We teach our young people, but they don't have to listen because they can get what they want from the government. That includes grog and drugs,' he said.

Meanwhile, the 'next generation' already has another on the way. Liam Jurrah was twenty-four years old at the time of his trial and had a six-year-old son, whom he saw but did not live with. Walker was the same age, and had two children, aged six and four. He'd been in and out of gaol for all of their lives and wouldn't be out again for at least two years. Fry at twenty-one was also the father of a child. His wife intended to stand by him and move to the remote community north-east of Alice where he was ordered to live after completing rehab. There, a long way from Warlpiri lands but with the support of his mother and a maternal aunt, the chief justice hoped he would begin to 'make a life' for himself and his family.

ORDEAL

Approaching Alice Springs from the south, the land stretches flatly east and west, some low hills in the distance, the wall of the range rising massively in the north. Most of the townspeople, black and white, live north of the range. On the south side apart from 400 or so rural blocks, there's a new suburb – at present just a few houses behind a fancy sign and a tin fence – and five town camps. The one known as New Ilparpa is set back a little from the highway. The town's only commercial radio station borders it on one side; Yirara College, a boarding school for Aboriginal secondary students, on the other.

On the night of 18 February 2013, some time after 8.30 pm, J Pollard was walking with his wife along the gravel road leading into the camp. He had been out of gaol for only a few days. The night was hot. He was wearing jeans, no shirt, no shoes. A car turned up, stopped, and four men jumped out, shouting threats. Pollard ran. The four chased him, a fifth followed in the car. They caught him at the college fence and started beating him, with sticks, a metal pole, fists, enough to make him bleed and render him semi-conscious. He was put in the back seat of the car, across the laps of some of the men. They stripped off his jeans and threw them out the window as they headed back into town. Pollard's wife called police at 9.09 pm.

The men's destination was Charles Creek, not the town camp, but a drinking camp in the sandy creekbed out front, a stone's throw from the intersection of Schwarz Crescent with the highway. The sobering-up shelter is just across the road, Hungry Jack's is on the corner. Pollard was dragged from the car. A mob formed around him. He was prostrate, naked. More people joined in the continued beating. He was stabbed numerous times. Petrol was poured on his genitals and lit, though the flames were quickly put out. He was beaten with a star picket, punched in the face, hit with sticks. A bottle was thrown at his head. His sternum was fractured; so were his jaw and a rib; his femoral artery was transected.

At times he called out for help. The mob clapped and cheered. Only one woman among them tried to put a stop to the ordeal. When he eventually appeared lifeless, he was wrapped in a blanket, put back in the car, taken a little north of the town and dumped in a ditch just off the highway. The car was torched. A call to 000 at 11.58 pm reported the car well ablaze.

Pollard's decomposing body was not discovered until two days later on the evening of 20 February. The autopsy followed the next day. Cause of death was stated as 'multiple traumatic injuries', including twenty-three stab, puncture or laceration wounds. Some detail of how Pollard died was made known by police a week later, after their arrest of several men. Rumours far more gruesome than the sufficiently terrible facts were soon circulating. It was also suggested that the killing was a 'payback' for the death of the young woman who had been attacked at Abbott's Camp on Christmas Day 2012.

Pollard's family members, through their victim impact statement to the court, would eventually give their view of the payback motive for his death, but they didn't wait till then to let their anger be known. When the committal hearing began a little more than a year later they hurled abuse at the accused men, prompting a complaint from their lawyers. The magistrate told the family he understood 'how sad and upset' they must be but he would have to close the court if they didn't 'behave'.

There were then seven men in the dock – six accused of murder and one of being an accessory after the fact. The Crown prosecutor referred to the suggestion by some witnesses that the men had been motivated by payback but he would not be setting out to establish this.

'Payback' became my shorthand for the case in reports for the *Alice Springs News Online*, but I was taken to task for it. In a comment on the site a member of a prominent local Aboriginal family accused me of 'completely and unnecessarily sensationalising the matter'. 'Compared to the facts of the case, it is hardly sensational,' I replied, to which he came back: 'I am not qualified to discuss Payback, and neither [is] the Alice News. Therefore, stick to the facts.'

Then other readers joined in:

'Payback is a common term widely used. These reports should be read in all the communities, particularly by youths, where it remains important to raise awareness, strengthen caution, concerning how easily a few drinks may end or change lives, with consequences affecting lives of relatives and friends not directly involved.' (This from a reader married into a Western Desert Aboriginal family.)

'Drunken thuggish violence is just that, it has absolutely nothing at all to do with "payback" as per traditional law. No attempt should be made to try and associate this kind of behaviour with traditional law. It is not! ... All too often it seems to me "culture" is being used as an excuse for behaviour that has nothing at all to do with "culture". Time for Aboriginal people who are aware of this to point these things out so that "culture" cannot be used as an excuse to brutalise your families and loved ones.' (This from a town councillor.)

My critic replied to the councillor: 'Your opening line was exactly my point, and I couldn't have put it better myself.'[1]

What can a local layperson know of payback? As one of the commenters says, it is a widely used term, yet the publicly reported instances and resultant debates are only sporadic. The debate usually reflects the issues that Pollard's death raised – around the role of alcohol in exacerbating the violence, around the intervention of mainstream justice that puts offenders in gaol, out of reach, and by leaving the sense of injury festering, leads to someone else being made to pay in the offender's place. A case reported in the *Alice Springs News* in 2000 had all these features. Residents of Abbott's Camp complained about a payback that had a man running for his life through the camp, pursued by several attackers armed with knives and nulla nullas. He was caught outside on the banks of the Todd, had his right thigh slashed and suffered a stab wound to the scalp. Another man and a woman were also stabbed in the attack. Camp leaders said the dispute came from out of town and implored the perpetrators to stay away, to fight in their own community. The perpetrators were drunk, they said, and it was suggested the 'wrong' victims had been chosen: the 'right' ones were in gaol. The leaders' forthright comments were part of their determined campaign for a more peaceful existence at Abbott's Camp. Long before the federal government's Intervention led to a ban on all drinking in town camps, the leaders of Abbott's Camp were asking for it to be declared 'dry'. At the time two applications before the Liquor Commission had been rejected. They were finally granted in 2005.[2]

Debate was sparked again in 2003 when the NPY Women's Council invited anthropologist Peter Sutton to come to town. The council, an advocacy and service organisation which has its central office in Alice, was lobbying for a greater police presence in the Ngaanyatjarra, Pitjantjatjara and Yankunytjatjara lands straddling the

Northern Territory, Western Australia and South Australia where the two states and the Territory meet. It was deeply concerned about the high level of violence in the region, going unchecked by the rule of law, and wanted Sutton to address a meeting between its staff and members and senior police from all three areas. At this stage Sutton's 2001 essay 'The Politics of Suffering' was circulating widely on the internet. It caused a furore among many in anthropological and progressive political circles for its critique of cultural relativism and 'tragedy tolerance';[3] others, like Marcia Langton who wrote the foreword to Sutton's 2009 book of the same title, welcomed its 'sharp clear view of the problems that face Aboriginal citizens of the inland gulags and outback ghettoes of remote Australia' and hoped that its 'humanist reasoning' would be more widely applied.[4] When the essay came to our notice at the *Alice Springs News* in February 2002, we prepared a detailed summary of its key ideas to publish in our weekly edition.[5] It was game-changing for the local debate, this deeply informed challenge to what had become mantras of self-determination, this emphatic compassionate demand that priority be given to the wellbeing of the more vulnerable, especially children, at the expense of the old traditions and power structures. In May the following year when Sutton addressed the women's council, we led the edition with a lengthy report. It began: 'To keep on with laws and policing that are not working for the most vulnerable members of society – children, old people, women – "is to have blood on your hands". Violent crime, rampant in remote areas where police presence is minimal, should be dealt with entirely under "Australian law" – without regard to Aboriginal customary law.' At the time customary law was the subject of a government-appointed inquiry in the Territory, but Sutton took 'a very dim view of judges who think it is okay to send someone off to have a spear put in their leg'. Customary violence was appropriate, he said, in a stateless society where people could only exercise self-redress:

There was no external authority, there were no police, no judges, no courts, it was you and them. Sometimes old people would be drawn in to adjudicate, but only on some matters – matters of religion, matters of marriage. Those were two areas where there could be a kind of communal will above kinship politics. Even then executions are known to have been used in an abusive way [on occasion] by people who claimed sacrilege or desecration. That is said to still go on, it is the most feared thing [in this] region. Particularly women and young men are terrorised by fear of execution. They won't utter certain words, won't mention certain things. That is traditional religion, but you can't separate out that and the spearing in the leg for misdemeanours of various sorts from a general culture of the association of power and authority with the execution of violence. That is the principle that has got to shift, in my view, in order for children to be protected.[6]

Sutton was forceful in his analysis and the NPY Women's Council agreed with him.

Just a few years later the federal government put paid to any accommodation of customary law with its Northern Territory Emergency Response legislation.[7] That didn't stop the debate, however. In December 2009 there was an Alice Springs screening and discussion of a film, *Bush Law*, exploring the possibilities of a 'dual legal system' to address sky-rocketing Indigenous crime rates.[8] The eight-member all-Aboriginal discussion panel included only one woman, Rosalie Kunoth-Monks, who had become a leading critic of the Intervention. 'We want our law recognised,' she said. 'We have never ceded our language, our country.' She looked back with some reverence at ceremonial killings during her lifetime: 'If a really bad transgression took place, and there had to be a death, that had nothing to do with all of us, it was the feather boot, or feather foot, that was out there. Unknown to us, it was the senior of seniors who did that, and carried out that action.'

Other people at the screening didn't like the term 'payback', it was seen as 'vulgar', but they variously evoked payback practices conducted by the Old Men as cleansing, absolving, a ceremony of forgiveness, clearing the slate, soothing, preventing a festering sore, bringing that peace, settling the community down, assuaging the aggrieved, a speedy and simple resolution of conflict.

Kunoth-Monks later qualified her remarks for the *Alice Springs News*: 'That action took place in the bygone years. The Aboriginal people have gone more than half way to comply with the so-called dominant culture. They do it in such a way that the great majority of people are happy those days of ceremonial killings are over. We agree that life should not be taken.'[9]

Psychologist Craig San Roque had intensive experience of these issues in the years 1993 to 1997, when he and others worked with senior Warlpiri men and women assisting magistrates in bush courts to consider certain aspects of customary law in adjudication and sentencing matters. Japaljarri Spencer and Japanangka Williams were key on the Warlpiri side. They had full cooperation from the police, Correctional Services were involved, and the then minister, Country Liberal Eric Poole, was attentive. There were problems, though, and the efforts were closed down after a national outcry that San Roque says was 'uninformed and hysterical', leaving the issues suppressed but unresolved.[10]

Responding to coverage of the *Bush Law* screening, San Roque commended Kunoth-Monks and others on the panel for recognising:

> ... the value of (all) people following their cultural forms and customary procedures of trauma resolution, rather than leaving resolution to the court system alone – which may have other

priorities. This is a practical humane problem which has to be solved every time there is a violent crime …

They placed the matter into the field of community social health, making the case that if the Indigenous justice system is perverted in its process (from within) or obliterated by the Western system (from outside), then the result, in fact, is not the desired order and social peace but an insidious kind of repetitive disorder and complicating chaos.

The failure to sort out victim / perpetrator relationships after a crime creates a culture of anxiety in the region, requiring more and more policing.

Careful ceremonial inter-family reparation can settle everyone down. Due settlement is at the heart of the customary law system.

Whether grievous bodily harm is used or not is a vexed question. The Rabbi Jesus introduced a form of forgiveness into the old Judaic law. Contemporary Aboriginal law people might find new ways to carry out the repair and break this deadlock.[11]

After the online exchange criticising me for using the term 'payback', I asked my anthropologist friend about it. She doesn't worry about what term is used but too often now, she lamented, it is invoked to cover unregulated, intoxicated violence and so reduces the credibility of Aboriginal cultural law – much the same point as the town councillor was making and that my critic agreed with.

Traditionally, said the anthropologist, dispute resolution by payback was supervised, witnessed and regulated (we didn't discuss lethal payback for sacrilege, as described by Peter Sutton). In this way it redressed injury, restored balance between the parties and reduced violence. Other family members could be paid back in the offender's stead, but this too would have been negotiated and supervised. These days, it is far more likely that payback will be delivered in an impulsive, opportunistic way by members of the aggrieved family who are unauthorised, unsupervised and in all likelihood drunk. When that happens, she said, it is no more acceptable under Aboriginal law than vigilante action is under non-Aboriginal law.[12]

This is similar to comments made by Arrernte woman Margie Lynch Kngwarraye in a letter to the editor of the *Centralian Advocate*. She was writing to rebut statements reportedly made from the bench by then Chief Justice Brian Martin in a 2010 case involving threatened rather than actual payback.[13] He was said to have expressed the view that it was time Aboriginal families in Central Australia 'grew up and learnt how to solve their arguments lawfully' – a view she saw as lacking in understanding of 'a judicial system involving two very different cultures'.

'There is a distinction,' she wrote, 'between a managed and controlled "payback" and tribal punishment served to settle disputes, which most Aboriginal families enter into and where justice is served in accordance with Aboriginal law, and the chaos of violence erupting from payback without management, tribal punishment not served and "revenge" situations inundating the courts under Australian law.'[14]

If the killing of Kumunjayi Pollard was motivated by payback, the evidence, as court proceedings unfolded, showed it to be of the unmanaged, uncontrolled kind, erupting in a 'chaos of violence', to use Kngwarraye's words.

~

Clarinda Dixon was the only witness to the events in Charles Creek who was not drunk at the time. She arrived in court with bare feet, looking very young and slight. Her boyfriend, Silas Raggett, whom she called Chicka, was one of those accused of murder. The others were Kasman Andy, Lawrence Collin, Christopher Daniel, Grant Inkamala and Mervyn Wilson. The seventh man, the accused accessory, was Robert Daniel. When I first saw these men, during a video-link mention, I was shocked by their apparent age. I was expecting Pollard's killing to have been at the hands of reckless, terribly drunk young men. Only Kasman Andy looked young to my eyes. He had a big soft body and face and a doleful expression. Robert Daniel had grey-white hair and beard, while Mervyn Wilson and Lawrence Collin were greying. I put Robert Daniel in his sixties, Wilson and Collin in their fifties, Christopher Daniel in his forties and Silas Raggett in his thirties. At sentencing a year later I discovered I had to take a decade off all my estimates. Christopher Daniel was only twenty-nine when Pollard died, and Silas Raggett just a young man at twenty-two. There seemed nothing youthful about them.

They all sat grim-faced through Clarinda's evidence, none more so than Silas (Chicka), permanently frowning, and often leaning forward, arms on his legs, hands clasped, eyes fixed on the floor.

Clarinda found it hard to be in the witness box. At first she stared straight in front of her but soon and for most of the rest of a wearying two and a half hours she too stared at the floor, sometimes sinking her head almost to her chest, her bleached hair hanging over her face, speaking in a tiny voice and mostly through an interpreter. She never looked at the defendants.

At the time of the killing she and Chicka had been together for only a couple of months – they were 'boyfriend/girlfriend' rather than married, she told the Crown prosecutor. She also corrected parts of her statement to police, including this – that she had started to cry when she heard that Kumunjayi Pollard had passed away.

'Did you start to cry?' the prosecutor asked.

'No,' she said.

During the day of 18 February, Clarinda had seen Chicka hot-wire a car, a blue Commodore, owned by the sister of a man drinking in the creek. It was used to go and buy grog. In the evening she was in the car with him but was told to get out when the men decided to go to Ilparpa Camp. Chicka was going to drive them. Clarinda stayed behind in the creek with Rosemary James, wife of Mervyn Wilson. She was still sitting with her when the men returned.

Kumunjayi Pollard walked from the car, she said, and as he walked 'they was punching him'.

Mervyn Wilson's lawyer wanted to know how people were disposed at this point. He drew two pictures for her, one showing people walking in a line, the other showing people in a circle around a figure in the middle. Which one represented what she saw? She couldn't have looked more unhappy, pointing to the picture of the circle.

She heard Kumunjayi say, 'Don't hit me, uncle.' And again: 'Uncle, can you help me?' His uncle was Mervyn Wilson.

Where was Mervyn when Kumunjayi said this?

He was there, sitting close to him, hitting him.

With a weapon or his hand or what?

With his hand.

Clarinda was standing then, alongside Rosemary. When Rosemary threw a bottle at Kumunjayi, he was on the ground, face up, surrounded. At one point, she said, he was in the lap of a woman, Petrina Andy Marshall: 'She was telling them to stop.'

She said she saw Kumunjayi stabbed by Christopher Daniel.

Where?

Maybe in the leg.

But after further questioning, she couldn't be sure as Petrina was there, in the way, trying to stop it all. She said she saw Kasman Andy holding a 'silver pocket knife'.

Was it open or closed?

'A little bit bent, a little bit sharp.'

As for Chicka, she said she called to him when the men arrived back at the creek and he came over. He told her that he had hit Kumunjayi at Ilparpa, but she didn't see him strike a blow at Charles Creek. She said they were standing together, apart from the mob.

When Chicka's grandmother came over from the sobering-up shelter across the road, the three of them walked off, heading for Hidden Valley town camp.

'Where's my grog?' Mervyn Wilson sang out as soon as he got out of the car back in Charles Creek.

He was calling to his wife, Rosemary James. Her gait as she walked to the witness box had the tremor of a heavy drinker though she did not appear to be drunk.

Before she began, the magistrate explained that she could object to giving evidence against her husband. An interpreter was present but Rosemary mostly answered the magistrate directly, as he tried with several questions to satisfy himself that she understood her choice.

It could have an impact on your relationship with your husband, he finally suggested.

'It'll be okay … I can talk,' she said.

There were aspects of her statement that incriminated her. The prosecutor asked that the paragraph dealing with them 'not be read in evidence', but they did come up in cross-examination. (At the time she had not been charged with any offence but later a warrant was issued for her arrest.)

On the night of 18 February by the time her husband arrived back at the creek, Rosemary had already drunk a bottle of chardonnay on her own. She was feeling 'half drunk', she told the court, though in her statement she had put it at 'full charged'. Clarinda was sitting with her for company but the young woman didn't drink. Rosemary had more wine hidden in the scrub. She fetched it – a two-litre cask, or 'box' as she called it. She sat down to pour it into a bottle, before starting to drink it with Mervyn. Kumunjayi Pollard was swearing at her, she said. 'Rotten vulva' was the interpreter's literal translation of the abuse. Rosemary got up, telling Kumunjayi – and in the court she now spoke in English – 'I didn't brought you here' and struck him with the bottle.

Kumunjayi had been 'pulled' and 'dragged' from the car: 'They were all stabbing him and punching him near the car and he was still alive.'

She said Mervyn punched Kumunjayi in the face. He was lying down when Mervyn hit him. Other men were punching him as well, but she never saw Mervyn with a weapon.

She said she saw Christopher Daniel with a knife, 'swinging' it across Kumunjayi's stomach and side, although under questioning she couldn't say what kind of knife it was. She said in English, 'I could see his hand swinging.' (The autopsy showed no stab wounds to the front of the torso, but eight to the back.)

Two more people from Napperby joined in, 'kicking Kumunjayi as well'. She heard him calling for help – 'Uncle, help me'. Then Petrina Andy came and tried to help.

A bit later, Rosemary said, she heard her husband say to stop hitting Kumunjayi and to take him to Abbott's Camp, where he had family, or to hospital. She could also remember Lawrence Collin saying the same and 'Leave it'.

Petrina Andy Marshall had spent the day drinking, half of a Jim Beam 'four corner' on top of beer. Her evidence around the time of the day (as her mobile phone was flat) was calculated by bottle shop opening and closing times: the morning drinking was at the Peanut Bar, which opens at ten; the take-away grog was bought at the adjoining bottle shop, which opens at two and she drank it in the park near Centrelink; she later went back to the bottle shop but saw it was closed, so she knew it was after 9 pm when she got back to Charles Creek. 'Full drunk' by then, she sat down with a group of eight, a few metres from Clarinda and Rosemary, at the same time as the carload of men arrived.

Petrina was assertive in the witness box, insisting that she had 'put the right stories' to the police. On discrepancies between the statement and what she said now, she preferred her present recall of events: 'I didn't put it in the statement, I saw it with my eyes.' Under persistent questioning, she would back down sullenly. She had not had access to an interpreter when she made her police statement, although she spoke mostly through one in court.

She said Mervyn Wilson hadn't wanted to go to Ilparpa – 'they was forcing him'. Back in the creek, she saw him walk towards Rosemary, saying that he had hurt Kumunjayi. She also heard him ask, 'Where's my grog?' She said he joined in the beating in the creek, with a weapon. She demonstrated him raising his hands over his right shoulder and bringing a star picket down on Kumunjayi's back, twice. She said Rosemary hit Kumunjayi three times with the bottle in her hand (as opposed to throwing it at his head, the action which would eventually become part of the agreed facts). Kumunjayi was calling out to Mervyn, 'You my uncle, why you hitting me?' and to her, 'Petrina, help me, help me.' She was saying, 'Enough, enough.'

She said she had seen – 'with my eyes', pointing to them – Christopher Daniel siphon petrol from a car into a beer can and use it to burn Kumunjayi 'in the private areas'. She was the only witness to talk about this and some doubt was raised in the committal about whether the burning had actually taken place. A locum forensic pathologist said he had not detected any sign of it, but after the committal the prosecution took it further, obtaining expert evidence from a forensic chemist that became part of the eventually agreed facts: Kumunjayi's pubic hair had indeed been 'damaged due to direct exposure to heat / flames', though it could not be established who had done this, nor who had stopped it. Petrina said Mervyn Wilson put out the flames, with water he'd fetched from a nearby house. Like Rosemary, she too said that in the end he had told the others to stop hurting his nephew, to take him back to Abbott's Camp.

When she tried to help Kumunjayi, she said she got pushed away by three of the accused. Under questioning she admitted that she may have been mistaken about two of them, but insisted that 'I seen Christopher's hand pushing me'.

At first Petrina said she saw Christopher stab Kumunjayi twice. She backed away from this to agree that it may only have been once and in the buttock rather than in the back or shoulder as she had told police. She saw Lawrence Collin stab him in the head, using the same knife Christopher had. But she also heard him trying to stop the attack, suggesting Kumunjayi be taken to Abbott's Camp or hospital. Kasman Andy had 'an iron' (peg or star picket) and 'he hit him everywhere as well'. Under questioning she specified that it was twice, to the back of the head. (The autopsy showed multiple stab wounds and lacerations to the head but no internal haemorrhage.) She had Robert Daniel hitting Kumunjayi too. She was challenged on all of these propositions, given how drunk she was. Sometimes she retreated, but sometimes she remained insistent: 'Even though I was drunk, I could easily see the people, there was a big mob of them.'

These were the key witnesses with a story to tell about the events in the creek that night. A man told of a 'big mob' around Kumunjayi, 'cheering happy way'. Others went to things they had heard said by the accused, such as 'We killed him', or to having seen Pollard, naked, assailed, but with little further detail, their recall apparently clouded by how drunk they all were. Some backed away from their statements under cross-examination (as to who they saw doing what, when), and some reaffirmed them under re-examination. Some lived in Alice Springs, others moved between town and Western Desert communities – Papunya, Mount Liebig, Kintore. One woman was in custody, wearing a prison-issue t-shirt with the slogan 'No Joke! Quit the smoke!'; one man was in rehab. Sometimes cross-examination could sound like drinking was the offence being pursued, yielding little other information (the point being, of course, to cast doubt on the credibility of whatever might have been relevant).

So you started drinking at two o'clock?

Yes, at the Riverside.

Inside?

No, in the creek.

What were you drinking?

Two twenty-four packs of VB and a Jim Beam and three bottles of Coke.

What kind of Jim Beam?

A 'big mumma'.

Who did you share the grog with?

My missus.

This was Jason Cooper talking, a youngish man who stood straight-backed with strong arms folded across his chest. He took the questioning in his stride, often smiling.

After drinking in the bed of the Todd in front of the Riverside pub, he and his wife got a taxi to Charles Creek, he said. The grog was finished while it was still daytime. Was he full drunk by then?

Little bit, only little bit.

You consumed the alcohol pretty quickly?

Yes.

He went back to Riverside to buy more. He ran into family and they got two thirty-packs of VB.

Where did you go to drink the second lot of beer?

24 Hour Shop.

You mean the park nearby?

Yes.

It was 'a bit late' when he walked back to Charles Creek.

Were you full drunk by then?

Yes.

Had you had any food that day?

No.

~

As the Crown prosecutor summarised his brief on the fourth day of the committal, we heard of some of the admissions made by the accused men.

Kumunjayi Pollard had been hunted 'like a kangaroo', Lawrence Collin had told police. He admitted to being at Ilparpa Camp where Pollard was captured, to kicking him and hitting him on the shoulder with a stick. He claimed to have said eventually 'that's enough' – but then he added, damningly, that Pollard could be taken 'to that mob now in the creek', referring to the Andy 'mob'.

(The court had been expecting to hear from Paul Andy – 'an important witness' – but he could not be found. The defendants certainly wanted him in court: in a surprising intervention from them the day before, as they were being led away, they called out in chorus that Paul Andy had been there.)

Christopher Daniel at first denied any involvement with the events. Two days later he admitted – 'by a process of small steps' – that he was present during the events at both Ilparpa and Charles Creek. He admitted to kicking Pollard four times and hitting him four times when he ran to the Yirara College fence. He admitted to using a stick to strike him at Charles Creek. He also referred to petrol being poured on Pollard's groin and lit, though not by him. He denied having stabbed him, and also claimed to have tried to stop the attack.

Robert Daniel, accused of being an accessory after the fact, had walked into the Alice Springs police station on 21 February and given a voluntary statement. He admitted to being involved in disposing of Kumunjayi Pollard's body. The prosecution contended that there was a 'degree of minimisation' in his statement. What the court didn't hear at the committal, but would learn in Daniel's eventual plea hearing, was that in the early hours of 19 February, the morning after the attack, he had rung the doorbell of the sobering-up shelter and told a staff member that a man might have been killed across the road, that he had wrapped the man's body in a blanket and put it into a car. The information was passed to the police who went to Charles Creek. When they couldn't find the body they put it down to a false alarm. (Police later gave me a more detailed explanation of their initial investigation.)[15]

Kasman Andy had gone with Robert Daniel to the police station. At first he told police he had been sleeping in the car. They arrested him. While he was being cautioned he went further, saying he had driven the car and offering to show police where the body was (not knowing, apparently, that it had already been found).

Grant Inkamala in a police interview said he saw Kumunjayi Pollard 'sleeping' at Charles Creek before he took himself off to drink elsewhere. Around midnight he was picked up by the car bearing Pollard's body. He said the car ran out of fuel on the north Stuart Highway; when it was torched he walked away. He did not admit to taking part in the attack on Kumunjayi.

Mervyn Wilson, Kumunjayi's uncle, admitted that he was with the group at Ilparpa Camp but claimed not to have been involved at Charles Creek. He said he had gone to Ilparpa to 'teach his nephew a lesson'. He said he had hit him on the head with a stick and on the leg with an iron bar. When Kumunjayi called to him, 'Uncle', he replied, 'You're the one who wanted to fight me.' He claimed he told Kasman Andy to take Kumunjayi to the hospital on the way back to Charles Creek. He said at Charles Creek Grant Inkamala had tried to cover Kumunjayi's face with a sheet and he told him not to; he claimed that at that point Kumunjayi was still alive, although he was 'talking very slowly'.

Silas Raggett, aka Chicka, did not give a police interview. But a forensic scientist identified his DNA on the jeans found on the highway not far from Ilparpa Camp, thought to be the jeans stripped from Pollard. Pollard's DNA and blood were also found on the front of Raggett's shorts.

Pollard's blood and DNA were found on Kasman Andy's jeans, his DNA on Andy's shoes. His blood and DNA were also found on a stick at Ilparpa, with Andy's DNA on the other end.

Christopher Daniel's DNA was found on the end of a metal pole at Ilparpa as well as on a piece of broom, with Pollard's DNA on the other end. Daniel's DNA was also on a stick at Ilparpa that had Pollard's hair on the other end. Pollard's blood and DNA were found on Daniel's boot and on the front of his jeans.

Pollard's DNA and blood were found on Mervyn Wilson's thongs and shirt.

These men were arrested between 21 and 26 February; Pollard died on 18 February. In the intervening days they had made no attempt to dispose of the clothes they were wearing during the attack; indeed it seems they were still wearing those clothes. Lawrence Collin had changed. A shirt worn by him during the attack was later found but it did not yield any forensic results. Nor were there any forensic findings for Robert Daniel and Grant Inkamala.

The men were committed to stand trial and almost another full year passed.

~

Until just a few days before the trial was due to commence this had been a murder trial listed for forty days with six men in the dock. Carpenters had been in over the summer to enlarge the dock in readiness, taking space from the public gallery. Now pleas to reckless manslaughter had been negotiated for four of the men, and for one of them, a plea to aggravated assault. Grant Inkamala had joined Robert Daniel in pleading to accessory after the fact and these two had already been dealt with. Six QCs – from Darwin and interstate – had dropped eight weeks' worth of income, some with a bit more notice than others. On 3 March 2015 two turned up to handle the plea hearing for their clients. They put a bright face on it; the banter was about holidays in Bali and fast driving and drinking sessions.

The clock was ticking towards ten. Wigs went on, papers were shuffled, but the Crown prosecutor had yet to arrive.

'Prosecuting must be so easy in a place like this,' remarked one of the QCs.

'If it was easy this wouldn't be a manslaughter plea,' replied a seasoned local barrister.

Four men were brought into the dock. There should have been five. Christopher Daniel had been left behind at the gaol. Guards went to fetch him – a forty-kilometre round trip. The hearing got under way a little over an hour later. Justice Stephen Southwood was on the bench.

The charges were read and Kasman Andy, Lawrence Collin, Christopher Daniel and Mervyn Wilson each stood to plead guilty to engaging in conduct causing the death of J Pollard, reckless as to causing the death. Then Silas Raggett stood. His charge was now aggravated assault. His lawyer had suggested that because of Raggett's rudimentary English he might have to enter the plea on his behalf, but Raggett spoke for himself: 'Guilty.'

Robert Daniel's and Grant Inkamala's plea hearings had already taken place. It was accepted that they had been involved only in the disposal of Pollard's body, not in the attack. Both suggested, through their lawyers, that they had gone along with it because they felt 'intimidated' by what the principal offenders had done to Pollard. Daniel was sentenced to nine months; a reduction of six months acknowledged his early plea, and cooperation with police and the prosecution. Inkamala got twelve months, a lesser discount reflecting his more limited cooperation. They had both already been on remand for much longer, close in fact to the maximum penalty for their offence. The many months of liberty lost to them is known in legal parlance as 'dead time'. It seems rather shocking, but perhaps as they walked free from the court the two men counted themselves lucky that out of that terrible night they had not had to face more serious charges.

The agreed facts for Robert Daniel stated that the five principal offenders had 'formulated *a plan to kill* [Kumunjayi] in retaliation for the death of a female member of their family at the hands of a relative of the victim in December 2012'. For Inkamala, the seriousness of his offending was said to be qualified by him being 'unaware of the earlier events at Ilparpa and of the *plan to abduct and kill* the deceased'. The emphasis is mine. Had the prosecution been confident of proving beyond reasonable doubt this level of premeditation for the principal offenders, it would be reasonable to expect that the charge would have been a murder and the QCs would have had their trial.

Observers of open court are never privy to plea negotiations. They would have been exceptionally complicated in this case, with its great tangle of evidence and about a dozen lawyers involved on behalf of (initially) six defendants facing mandatory life if convicted of murder. Just a few days earlier, when Paul Andy had finally come before the Magistrates Court for his assault on Kumunjayi (he admitted one punch to the face), the prosecutor had described the case as one where 'the Crown could not possibly unravel the detail of what happened at Charles Creek'.

All we could know now was that the agreed facts stated that five men made a plan to go to Ilparpa Camp 'to find and beat' Kumunjayi Pollard 'for unknown grievances'. The intention to abduct and kill had gone; so had the payback motive. At Ilparpa it was agreed that all five were responsible for each other's conduct. Silas Raggett aside, the other men were aware that 'members of their extended family group were present at Charles Creek and there was a substantial risk of other persons becoming involved in the beating of the deceased. Each offender was also aware of a substantial risk of the deceased dying as a result of being subjected to a further beating at Charles Creek.'

~

Particularly gruelling, as the facts were read onto the record, was the summary of forensic evidence, for its sheer volume of damage done to one man. Those who inflicted it deserved to be sent to gaol for life, never to receive visitors, said Kumunjayi's family. They had submitted a hand-written victim impact statement, signed by several of them. Also handed up at their request, to become an unconventional part of the court's file, was a colour photo collage that included an image of Kumunjayi with his son and daughter and one of his sisters.

This 'trouble' had caused a lot of problems for them, said the family. They didn't go into detail but passed rather to Kumunjayi's life. He had been raised in Kintore, a community far to the west of Alice Springs, until he was nine. When both parents passed away he went to live with family at Mount Liebig. (This was also the home community of Sebastian Kunoth, who had fatally attacked his wife in Abbott's Camp.)

Kumunjayi had fathered two children; he had been a good football player, even travelling to Port Hedland to play: 'The family are very sad about losing him. We are always thinking about him and he is always in our memories.'

They went on to talk about the motivation for the attack: 'What those men did to him was wrong and really bad. He was not responsible for that trouble that happened before at Abbott's Camp. Those men had no reason to blame him or hurt him like they did.'

They thus confirmed the widespread view – in the community, if not pursued in court – that the killing was in revenge for the death of Kunoth's wife, but the payback victim had been wrongly chosen.

In her victim impact statement Kumunjayi's wife recalled having been there when her husband was chased down and attacked at Ilparpa Camp: 'I was really upset and crying and yelling for them to stop. I feel really sad and lonely without my husband. Our daughter ... is going to grow up without her father and that makes her very sad.' She said she was missing the financial support Kumunjayi gave her for their child, and would miss the future in which they were 'going to live happy together'.

In submissions on behalf of the men their lawyers offered various explanations for the crime, though none seemed to have much substance.

Kasman Andy had been 'unable to provide a clear account' of what he did, so 'severely intoxicated' was he. His drunkenness did not mitigate his actions but it helped 'explain why a twenty-four-year-old without a history of violence should become involved'. He was 'taken up by the motivation of others in the setting of that drunkenness', contended his lawyer, and that motivation related to 'the death of another person'.

For Kumunjayi's uncle, Mervyn Wilson, the explanation was unrelated to the payback: he wanted to teach his nephew a lesson for disrespecting him, his lawyer said. Wilson had heard that Kumunjayi, while he was in prison, had said 'cheeky' things about him. (The word 'cheeky' has a much stronger, more aggressive connotation in Aboriginal English than in standard English.[16])

Lawrence Collin had lived some of his life at Mount Liebig and his wife was from there. Nonetheless, there was no mention of the payback as his reason for getting involved. It was said rather that he felt 'humiliated and upset' after an earlier physical altercation with Kumunjayi.

Silas Raggett's involvement was linked 'probably unjustifiably' to the 'matters raised in the victim impact statement from Kumunjayi's family members', said his lawyer, going to some length to avoid saying anything too explicit. He added, though, that it seemed that the woman killed at Abbott's Camp was a cousin of his client.

Christopher Daniel's lawyer could not even go that far. He was 'not able to put anything by way of explanation' for his client's involvement.

The complete silence on motive from Daniel, or rather from his lawyer, and the vagueness or paltriness of reasons proposed on behalf of the others was disturbing to hear. It was difficult to have a shred of sympathy for them, Pollard's death had been so cruel, yet they seemed so deeply alienated, these men. The hold over them of Aboriginal law was impenetrable for me, but no Aboriginal voice was raised in their defence, scarcely even their own. As for settler law, it might have had them in its grasp physically, but it did not seem to touch them.

The Crown prosecutor sought to 'clear the air' about the payback motive, pointing out that Kumunjayi Pollard was not and could not have been present at the Abbott's Camp killing: he was in gaol at the time and not released until a few days before his own death. He added that as far as he was aware, Kumunjayi was not even related to the perpetrator of the Abbott's Camp killing, although the two had grown up in the same community (Mount Liebig). The prosecutor's logic on these points appeared similar to that of Kumunjayi's family.

Even if payback were accepted as a motive, what could explain the prolonged ordeal Kumunjayi was put through? The prosecutor suggested a 'pack mentality' had taken over, an idea supported by the difficulty in drawing a line between the actions of principals and of aiders and abetters. He argued that very little weight could be given to intoxication as a mitigating factor. On the contrary, in his submission it was an aggravating factor.

The strongest submissions on intoxication as a mitigating factor were put by Mervyn Wilson's lawyer, Russell Goldflam of NT Legal Aid. The level of alcohol abuse in the whole 'sub-community' of which his client was a part should be taken into account, he argued, 'at least to some extent'. He described the drinking by all civilian witnesses on the night (bar Clarinda Dixon) as 'nothing less than astonishing'.

He wanted to hand up as an aide-mémoire a de-identified table he had prepared that summarised the quantities drunk. The prosecutor challenged its usefulness to the court in this form, and Goldflam was asked to resubmit it with identification. He later released the de-identified summary to me. It included not only the staggering quantities consumed by each of the twenty-eight individuals, but where the grog was purchased. No surprise – given the proximity to Charles Creek – that most of it came from the Riverside (Todd Tavern) bottle shop, though one witness bought a two-litre cask 'privately', paying $40 to a profiteer named Troy. The summary also had a note emphasising the date of the drinking – a Monday in February, not Christmas Day or anyone's birthday. Just a normal day. The evidence showed too that many of the witnesses came together around the Riverside the next day, to drink again and talk over the events of the night before. These details may not be of much judicial value but they are telling of a situation that preoccupies many in Alice Springs, especially those who have to deal with the aftermath.

At the time of Pollard's death the Banned Drinkers Register – which might have prevented some or all of these witnesses from legally purchasing alcohol – had been dumped by the relatively new Country Liberal government. There remained a regime of restricted hours for take-away sales, but it was clearly not enough to prevent the extraordinary levels of consumption that this case revealed. It would take another year before the Territory government backed drastic action initiated by police in Alice Springs, stationing officers in Temporary Beat Locations (TBLs) at all bottle shops. Police have the power to seize any open or unopened container of alcohol if they believed an offence might be committed by the purchaser – such as drinking in a restricted area, which in Alice Springs, as we've seen, comprises the entire public area of the town, all the town camps, including their dwellings, and any suburban house declared to be 'dry' (an enforceable arrangement made by some to protect themselves from the depredations of drinkers).

In practice, the police at bottle shops mostly pre-empted purchases by asking where the would-be customer intended to drink and for proof of residence. Either way, had it existed at the time, the measure would have prevented almost all of the drinking in the creek on the night of Kumunjayi's death.

There was and is concern that the measure targets Aboriginal people. If there were any doubt of that, the signs at the TBLs dispel it. They use a graphic showing a black crow, depicted against a field of dots in the desert Aboriginal style. Indeed, the image is a detail from a painting by a then serving Aboriginal Community Police Officer for use in another context. Police have ignored protests over its use, as the government did the early marches and rallies protesting 'racist alcohol policies'. It has been hard for this protest to gain momentum because the TBLs seem to work. The local lobby group People's Alcohol Action Coalition – made up mainly of professionals, and of which Goldflam is a member – did not take long to make public statements acknowledging the policy's benefits: 'Although there are many concerns about this approach it has made a large difference to violence, alcohol-related hospital presentations and public drunkenness.'[17]

Soon after, the Aboriginal-controlled health service, Congress, released data showing a 'dramatic reduction' in alcohol consumption by clients in their rehab program, which they attributed largely to the TBLs. They also noted police data showing a 50 per cent reduction in assaults since the TBLs began, and similar drops in both alcohol-related emergency presentations at the Alice Springs Hospital and referrals to the Women's Shelter. Although they had concerns that the strategy was discriminatory, and had a less discriminatory alternative to suggest,[18] they supported its continuation 'for its positive effect on Aboriginal people in Alice Springs'.[19]

The strategy, renamed Point of Sale Intervention, when it was applied across all outlets, continued to make gains in reducing both consumption and harms and is likely to remain a key plank of the town's alcohol management plan. A 10 per cent drop in consumption was recorded in the 2014 calendar year, and from June 2014 to end of May 2015 alcohol-related assaults dropped by 22 per cent, while over the same period alcohol-related family violence assaults decreased by 23 per cent. However, gaps in the coverage of outlets in Alice Springs appear to have eroded some of these gains, with alcohol-related assaults and family violence rising again in the latter half of 2015.[20]

All this came too late for Kumunjayi Pollard.

Mitigating or aggravating, intoxication was overwhelmingly present in his death and the actions and lives of those who caused it. Kumunjayi himself had been drinking that night. His post-mortem blood alcohol reading was .129, most of it due to 'ingestion' in the opinion of the pathologist.

Of Kumunjayi's assailants, none seemed more woefully affected by the grog than his uncle, Mervyn Wilson. He was now forty-five years old. He had been drinking since his first flagon of wine at age sixteen, encouraged by his older brother. Their mother was not a drinker; their father liked a beer after work but had no problem with grog. Both parents had recently passed away. Wilson had fathered three sons with a 'girlfriend' from Papunya and later a daughter with a woman who died from the grog. His present wife, Rosemary James, was an alcoholic like him. They had two children together, aged about eleven and twelve, who were in foster care. A desire to see the children brought the couple into Alice Springs back in February 2013, but they were refused access because of their drinking. They had nowhere to stay in town and were camping in the river under the Stott Terrace bridge.

Goldflam detailed Wilson's state of health: he was being treated for latent tuberculosis; his eardrums were perforated, his hearing terrible; unsurprisingly, given his years of excessive drinking, he had a fatty liver which needed to be treated; he had sustained a lot of injuries, many of them inflicted by Rosemary James, including a stabbing to his left arm which had required surgery and rendered the limb permanently weakened. This violence he had returned. One of several convictions for assault against her took place later on the very night of the death of Kumunjayi Pollard.

Kasman Andy was very drunk on the night, although there was no evidence that the twenty-six-year-old, then twenty-four, had a chronic drinking problem. His issue was more one of chronic ill health due to the rheumatic fever he had contracted at age ten. (This disease is associated with disadvantage, its prevalence in Northern and Central Australia is one of the highest reported in the world.)[21] On the day Andy went to the police station with Robert Daniel he was very unwell. Police dropped their questioning of him to send him to hospital, where he stayed for a week being treated for a rheumatic episode. He had suffered twelve such episodes since 2006. While on remand he was taken to Adelaide for surgery to repair damage to his aortic valve. His prognosis was good but, said his lawyer, his long-term illness had had a significant impact: his shortness of breath, chronic fatigue and obesity had meant that he hadn't developed good self-esteem and assertiveness. His education had been interrupted; he had little English, minimal literacy and remained very reserved, lacking in confidence. The implication of all this was that Andy was easily led.

We didn't hear much about Silas Raggett's drinking. Submissions about him were fairly cursory, due in part to the language barrier between him and his lawyer,[22] and in part to his lesser involvement in the violence, having walked away from the attack once he got back to Charles Creek. (He would be sentenced to eighteen months; the excess of his time on remand had not been 'dead', however, as it had helped account for the sentence received for a separate aggravated assault he had committed five days before the attack on Pollard.)

Christopher Daniel was drunk on the night, having started early in the evening, as the evidence showed, said his lawyer. But what's to be made of it? asked Justice Southwood. It affects judgment, put the lawyer, though this was not an excuse for what he had done. His client accepted that he would face a significant period of imprisonment, but a parole period should allow him to prove to Kumunjayi's family that he can behave himself as 'a grown initiated man, not a drunken thug'.

Lawrence Collin had an ongoing problem with alcohol, said his lawyer. Back in February 2013 he had come into Alice Springs for a holiday, on leave from his job with the shire, but in town he was unable to 'self-regulate', getting into an 'unfortunate culture of drinking', an underlying factor in his prior assault convictions, including two with a weapon. The victim was his wife. He was drinking on the day of Pollard's death.

Collin stood and spoke in Luritja to express his remorse to Kumunjayi's family seated in the public gallery. His words were received in stony silence. The court did not hear a translation. His lawyer asked that this be accepted as a 'genuine expression of contrition' and that he be given due credit for it.

The apology from Christopher Daniel, said to speak English 'fairly well', was brief: 'I want to say I am sorry for what happened.' His lawyer tried to make the best of it: the statement was 'laconic' but had the merit of not being 'lawyer's words' that had made their way 'into a prisoner's mouth'. He asked that it be accepted as indicating some remorse – 'not any higher than that'.

The lawyer for Kasman Andy had less than this to go on. He asked that Andy's admissions at the police station be accepted as demonstrating remorse.

An apology from Mervyn Wilson to Kumunjayi's family – some

of whom, at least, are his family too – was the first matter addressed by Goldflam. After hearing their victim impact statement, Wilson had written: 'To those family I have to say sorry. I say sorry to my nephew. I felt shamed to see him naked. He was saying, "Don't hit me, I'm your nephew".' His remorse was not a recent invention, said Goldflam. Wilson told police in his interview, conducted with an interpreter, that he felt bad when he realised Kumunjayi had been stabbed, because he was his nephew. He had made similar statements on other occasions during his two-year remand.

What could be his prospects for rehabilitation, this man whose life had been so subsumed in drink? He knew, said Goldflam, that he would spend a good part of the years remaining to him in gaol, but still he had formulated the desire to reform: to stay away from drink and from family who drink, to get a job, make some money and provide some support for his family. He had done some work in the past – driving a grader, manning the petrol bowsers at the Papunya store, night patrol, rubbish pick-up, repairing cars in a mechanic's workshop. He could read. (During the committal I had watched Wilson study the various witnesses statements provided to him by Goldflam.) In gaol he had started reading the Bible. He had talked with Goldflam about its lessons – that you should 'love everyone, love your enemies'.

Kasman Andy's prospects for rehabilitation were good, his lawyer argued. He was young, he had not been in gaol before, and following his heart surgery could look forward to better health. He had family support: his parents were in court. (How difficult it must have been for them in the crowded public gallery, hard up against the anger of Kumunjayi's family.) His father had acted as his 'prisoner's friend'; other significant family figures were his grandmother and his cousin Geraldine, to whom he had confided that he had hit Pollard, as she reported during the committal. In gaol he had been working in the laundry, had completed the 'Safe and Sober' course, and attended some anger management lectures (though a translator was not present – three exclamation marks in my notebook).

Lawrence Collin, thirty-eight, was raised by both his parents. He went to school to Year Seven but could not read and write. He understood basic English. He liked hunting and painting. In Papunya and Mount Liebig he worked at various jobs in their Community Development Employment Program (CDEP). In 2011 he and his family had had to leave Mount Liebig because of unspecified family trouble. They moved to Kintore where he got work with the shire council. He had married young and until his arrest was still living with his wife. She was in court for the plea hearing. They have three daughters.

Christopher Daniel, thirty-one, had been working in gaol as a 'block cook' but his past employment had been scant – some CDEP work in 2007. Despite his fairly good command of spoken English and staying at school till the age of sixteen, he could not read and write. He is initiated (we didn't hear about this in relation to the others but that doesn't mean they are not). He was married but the relationship ended in 2009. He has three children. As a single man, he went back to live with his parents. The family had come into Alice Springs when his father's leg had to be amputated, but they had since returned to Papunya.

Daniel's father's name was mentioned. I recognised it from reporting on his situation back in 2008. After his amputation he had been allocated a house in Charles Creek town camp, but it burned down, leaving him and his family without shelter. They were camping in the open nearby, going into the burnt-out shell to fetch water and to shower. Months went past like that, although the water got cut off – tough in a wheelchair.[23] I remembered taking photographs and searched them out.

I see a young man pushing the old man, trouser leg dangling, through the creek sand. They stop in the shade of a tree, a sunlit rocky hill behind them. The nuggety physique is right for Daniel, but the man takes care for his face not to be caught by the camera, sinking his head so that it is covered by the peak of his baseball cap, or else turning his back. It's of no import, it may not even be Daniel, but it expresses something of the way he remains obscure to me.

~

How would Justice Southwood find his way through the tangle of evidence to apportion guilt? Christopher Daniel 'understands he will be sentenced on the facts', his lawyer submitted, but 'there will never be clarity regarding some aspects of the facts'. The Crown prosecutor said that it was 'difficult to draw a real distinction' between the acts of the principal offenders and the aiders and abetters; that a 'pack mentality' had developed. In this context, how too would Justice Southwood view the role of intoxication?

The 'objective seriousness' of the crime was how he put it all into perspective. He hammered out the facts of Kumunjayi's ordeal: the humiliation and degradation, the cheering and clapping of the merciless mob, the drawn-out brutality, sadistic and torturous. The principal offenders might have been drunk, 'yet they were capable of organising themselves to obtain a car, go to Ilparpa Camp, beat and deprive the deceased of his liberty, take him to Charles Creek ... beat him again ... dump his body in a gully off the Stuart Highway, burn the car and walk away.' The fact that they might not have inflicted all of the injuries leading to Kumunjayi's death mattered little in the context of their reckless manslaughter: 'The four offenders were not merely faced with a set of circumstances where the risk of death materialised in the moment, but by their conduct they created and promoted the risk from start to finish.'

He apparently accepted the assertions of the prosecution and of Kumunjayi's family, bluntly rejecting any notion of traditional payback being involved: 'The offenders engaged in very lawless and violent behaviour. It was not in accordance with Aboriginal custom. The deceased had done nothing to provoke the attack on him, nor had he caused harm to any of the offenders or their relatives. It appears that the offenders may have been acting under a misapprehension about what had occurred to a relative at Abbott's Camp.'

A little later he invoked authorities on 'one of the historical functions of the criminal law' – 'to discourage victims and their families and friends from resorting to self help, and the consequent escalation of violent vendettas between members of the community'.[24]

Had the payback been conducted in accordance with Aboriginal law, had the offenders put that forward as a traditionally sanctioned motive for their conduct, Justice Southwood might have been troubled. The judiciary is at present constrained from taking customary law into account even for the purposes of sentencing. This was brought about by section 91 of the *Northern Territory National Emergency Response Act 2007*. When that Act was repealed in 2012, the provision was incorporated in the Commonwealth's *Crimes Act 1914*, as section 16AA, applicable only to offences committed in the Northern Territory.[25] In a decision in 2009 (*The Queen v Wunungmurra*) Justice Southwood made clear his critique of the effect of that provision. His concern was precisely around the way it interfered with assessment of the 'objective seriousness' of an offence. Ordinarily this assessment includes consideration of the reason for the offence. Yet if the reason goes to acting in accordance with customary law (as was being proposed on behalf of Wunungmurra), the Aboriginal offender is precluded from having 'his or her case considered individually on the basis of all relevant facts'. This 'distorts the well established principle of proportionality, and may result in the imposition of what may be considered disproportionate sentences,' Justice Southwood said then.[26]

In sentencing Pollard's killers, he was saved from this dilemma.

Even where payback had been alluded to as a reason for their conduct, it had been only in the vaguest of terms. The offenders themselves – or perhaps I should say their defence counsel – had not seemed to believe it.

Justice Southwood dismissed the argument for intoxication to be considered a mitigating factor as put by Goldflam for the chronically alcoholic Mervyn Wilson. Rather he saw the need, given Wilson's record of violent offending while drunk, for specific deterrence and protection of the community from him. He drew on legal authorities dealing with cases involving social disadvantage including endemic alcohol abuse,[27] and with Aboriginal offenders and victims,[28] to make his point on the necessity of holding serious violent offenders to account, however disadvantaged and however drunken, and thereby offering the protection of the law to their victims. In assessing the personal moral culpability of an offender he had to take into account the alcohol abuse common in their environment, but he also had to balance that with the seriousness of the offending. He had to avoid treating drunken violence done to an Aboriginal victim as less serious just because it had been perpetrated within their own society.

'The objective seriousness of this case overwhelms any consideration which might otherwise have been given to Mervyn Wilson's chronic addiction to alcohol,' he concluded. 'In his drunken state he made a deliberate decision to engage in the joint enterprise. It is not suggested that he did not appreciate that what he was doing was wrong or that he was unable to control himself.'

Earlier, his general comments on mitigation had showed where his thinking was heading.[29] While mitigating factors had to be given appropriate weight, it could not be accepted that 'Aboriginal offenders are in general less responsible for their actions than other persons'. To do that would be 'to deny Aboriginal people their full measure of human dignity', assigning them 'to a particular category of persons who are less capable than others of decent behaviour'. And the victim of an Aboriginal offender was no less 'in need or deserving of such protection and vindication as the criminal law can provide'.

Pollard's killers violently, cruelly took his life. A just sentence would accord him due recognition of his human dignity, said Justice Southwood. That he was an Aboriginal man in no way changed this. To do otherwise would be to treat him as a second-class citizen, and not as equal before the law.

Heavy sentences were coming, not as heavy as Kumunjayi's family would have had them, but long years in gaol nevertheless.

Justice Southwood did not accept that Kasman Andy played a significantly lesser role in the violence: 'They were all equally involved in the conduct that they embarked upon following the making of their plan.' He found Andy's assistance to police 'was minimal', but together with the plea it was 'demonstrative of some remorse'. By way of mitigation he would take into account Andy's age, his prior character and his plea of guilty: 'The offending is out of character and he has some prospects of rehabilitation.'

Andy's co-offenders, by contrast, he saw as 'dangerous' men with extensive criminal records. Christopher Daniel's went to six pages, with four prior convictions for crimes of violence and two for being armed with or possessing an offensive weapon. We also learned that on 19 February 2013, the day after Pollard's death, he had assaulted his own mother, while armed with an offensive weapon. Lawrence Collin had a ten-page criminal record (typically there are half a dozen offences per page). It included nine crimes of violence. Mervyn Wilson's was seven pages, with seven priors for crimes of violence, including two for serious harm and two for assault police. Most of his crimes had been drunken and most had been against his wife, Rosemary James. In 2006 he had hit her with a rock, breaking her leg. In 2007 he had assaulted her while he was on parole.

For Daniel, Justice Southwood took into account the utilitarian value of his plea. It indicated a 'willingness to facilitate the course of justice': 'While I am not satisfied that [he] is truly remorseful, he has accepted responsibility for this crime.'

He acknowledged Collin's apology to Pollard's family in court and that he had 'accepted responsibility for his actions since August 2013 when plea negotiations commenced'.

For Wilson, though, he had little indulgence. This would not be reflected in a harsher penalty but he roundly rejected the instances of his supposed remorse, on the night and in his interview with police – his various claims that he felt bad about the attack on his nephew, that he had said to take him to hospital. 'I don't accept any of that,' said Justice Southwood. He also commented on Wilson's motive for attacking Kumunjayi (that he'd heard of him saying 'cheeky' things about him) – 'an extraordinarily casual approach to engaging in violent conduct'.

Overall, he did not think there was much by way of mitigation for any of the offenders. He did not accept that any of them 'showed any concern for the deceased on the night that he was beaten to death'. Nor was he satisfied that any of the offenders were truly remorseful as yet: 'However I do accept they are starting to gain some insight into what they have done. They have started to undertake appropriate rehabilitation courses and by their pleas they have accepted responsibility for what they have done and they have assisted in the administration of justice.'

He sent all four to gaol for sixteen years. Andy was distinguished from the others only in relation to his non-parole period – eight years as opposed to their ten.

If Collin's apology to Kumunjayi's family was received in stony silence, so too were these sentences. I caught nothing of the usual dread. It was all too inevitable and depressing. I looked over at the men. Wilson and Collin both had long curly hair. When they had arrived that morning it was wet from their showers. It was still damp now as their fate was settled. Back in gaol it would be cut.

Kumunjayi's family straggled out through the lobby and into the hot day. There was hardly a murmur among them.

Months later as I began to write this account, I found myself feeling flattened by its misery, wondering what the account could offer. Then I reread the family's victim impact statement and resolved to set down as much as I'd grasped.

'This has caused trouble for more than this family and this community,' they wrote in their concluding sentences. 'The true story needs to be heard by everyone so it stops any more trouble. We are still sad about this. It is always there with us, that memory about what happened. We are upset all the time. It never finishes.'

EPILOGUE:
COMING THROUGH THE GAP

The season was turning and I had almost finished work on this book when Liam Jurrah came before the court again, facing two charges of aggravated assault and two for breaching domestic violence orders (DVOs). The alleged victims were women, his former partner and his recent partner. After almost two months on remand he was pleading guilty.

The wattles in bloom along the roadside cheered me a little as I headed into town for the hearing on 4 September 2015. It was more than sad to see the apparent downward spiral of this still young man whose football talent, fine looks and trajectory from a remote desert community into A-league stardom had so captured hearts around the country.

As I was driving, I found myself thinking of the end of San Roque's essay, 'A long weekend in Alice Springs', where he evokes the Dreaming's wild dog, an intruder, approaching town as I was, 'along the bitumen strip from the south': 'He trots through the gap in the range and on into town. He is sniffing the wind. A fight is brewing. It will always be brewing. He will keep coming through the gap forever. This mythic dog will outlive generations of humans.'[1] I had puzzled over that ending, wondered why it seemed to offer little hope. I should have realised that's not San Roque's way, he wants you to do the mental work. In considering how a 'cultural complex' might operate in Alice Springs, he quotes from Thomas Singer's definition: 'Cultural Complexes structure emotional experience … tend to be repetitive, autonomous, resist consciousness and collect experience that confirms their historical point of view … provide a simplistic certainty about the group's place in the world in the face of otherwise conflicting and ambiguous uncertainties.'[2] Now I was starting to get it, that we are mostly blind to the ways in which today keeps laying down tomorrow, we defend and promote them even as we witness their failure. Today it is a mongrel dog that trots along the bitumen, in other words all of us, damaged offspring of settlement, sniffing the air of our times. And so it will go, 'repetitive, autonomous', unless … I was still thinking about the next step when I parked the car by the river. 9.55 am. I would have to hurry in case Jurrah was up first.

He cut a different figure now. Gone were the stylishly trimmed beard and hair, the well-cut suit that he wore during the 2013 trial. His beard was full and his curly hair tousled; he wore a loose-fitting black t-shirt, baggy track pants and sports shoes, no doubt the clothes he was arrested in. Yet his demeanour remained confident. He had tried to obtain bail on two recent occasions, representing himself, his lawyer having withdrawn for want of evidence to support the applications. It's no easy matter to represent yourself, even for minor matters in the Magistrates Court, unless it's simply to plead guilty and take what comes. Jurrah's preparedness to do so struck me as a measure of his confidence, but perhaps also of a certain unconcern for the judgments being made against him. Being held on remand is a kind of judgment.

Now we heard about why.

On 16 June 2015 in Hermannsburg he drunkenly assaulted his former partner, punching her with a clenched right fist to the face, which fortunately was protected from the full impact by the hood of her jacket. He also kicked her in the back and was shouting at her, when a witness told him to stop. Jurrah then left.

He had gone to see her, apparently at her invitation, despite the full 'no contact' order against him. The victim later complained to police. Jurrah had been convicted of an aggravated assault against her in the previous year, earning a five-month sentence, suspended after three. For this new assault he handed himself into police but declined to answer questions or take part in an interview. After coming before a magistrate he was bailed.

Less than one month later on 11 July, while still on bail, Jurrah again got drunk and went to see his then partner in an Alice Springs town camp where she was living with their infant son. Both mother and baby were named as protected persons in a DVO specifying no contact if Jurrah was intoxicated.

Jurrah yelled at the woman to come home with him, then jumped the fence and punched her in the face. When she tried to run away, he grabbed her by the hair and dragged her towards the gate. She struck out at him. He smashed a beer bottle to create a jagged edge and tried to hit her. Other people stepped in. He was still able to grab a steel-framed chair and hit her in the back of the head with it. The blow left an eight-centimetre laceration. Her forehead was also bruised. The arrival of police put an end to the attack. Jurrah was arrested and this time bail was refused.

His lawyer said Jurrah had been told by the woman the day before that she wanted no further contact. It was the prospect of not seeing his little boy that particularly upset him, although Jurrah told the lawyer the woman had also hit him in the face. This was the context of the offending, said the lawyer, though it was not put by way of excuse: there can be 'no excuse to resort to violence'.

For the assault against his former partner in Hermannsburg, mandatory imprisonment for a minimum three months applied as it was a 'Level Three' offence – a subsequent aggravated assault. (Mandatory minimum sentencing for repeat violent offenders had been introduced by the Country Liberal government elected in 2012 in fulfilment of an election promise.) For the assault on his more recent partner in Alice Springs the greater degree of injury and the involvement of a weapon raised the issue of whether it was a more serious 'Level Five' offence, which would earn a mandatory minimum of twelve months' 'genuine gaol time'.[3] Did the injury interfere with the victim's health to the requisite degree? asked Jurrah's lawyer. She quoted from the victim impact statement: the victim was 'sad and upset' but said, 'I don't think my life will change.' While the head wound had required eight sutures and there was some blood in evidence on photos submitted to the court, there was no further information about the victim's health. The paucity of evidence made the level of the offence an open question, she said. There would be no getting away from some time in custody, but she argued for partial suspension and orders to undertake rehabilitation for alcohol and anger management: her client acknowledged that he 'needs help'.

That's also what his second victim thought. The police prosecutor wanted the assault on her to be seen as a Level Five offence but perhaps undermined the argument when he too quoted from her victim impact statement: she wanted Jurrah to go to gaol *and* to get treatment.

The prosecutor argued that Jurrah knowingly breached the DVOs against him: 'The man does understand the consequences of a breach, the court has explained the consequences,' he said. (Although thought for the consequences are not often heeded when a person is drunk, drunkenness could not be used as an excuse.)

While these submissions were being heard, more than once Jurrah turned around, making hand signals to family members sitting in the back row of the gallery: his older brother, a cousin, some women too, but not his grandmother. The matter was stood down while a Community Corrections officer made an assessment of Jurrah's suitability for supervision and rehab.

As I left the building to find some lunch, I glanced down at the graffiti, 'This is the front line.' On any day, as we've seen, there are many battles on many fronts taking place inside, but the big one that sends so many Aboriginal people, especially men, to gaol, and leaves so many Aboriginal people, especially women, injured, traumatised or dead, nobody seems to be winning. While police stationed at bottle shops, when there is full coverage of all outlets, has led to a very welcome marked decrease in assaults, it is hard to see that enforcing discriminatory drinking laws will be able to hold the line in the long term.

Judges are all too aware of the issues. Chief Justice Trevor Riley clearly acknowledges that his job comes after 'the damage has been done' and has repeatedly exhorted government and the community to do more to 'limit the flow of alcohol'. At a public meeting about family violence, held in Alice Springs in September 2013 and attended by hundreds, black and white, Justice Jenny Blokland went further, pointing out that half of the inmates in the Alice Springs gaol were men who were there for having assaulted their intimate partners. She was one of the people gaoling them, she said, but it gave her no pleasure; it was a protective measure, often short term, and didn't solve the problem. Other speakers put forward possible causes – alcohol and all the reasons people might choose to 'drown conscience' in a bottle. Justice Blokland acknowledged the very difficult social problems in Alice but this did not explain the 'gendered nature' of the violence: 80 to 90 per cent of perpetrators were men. She agreed that reduction in the supply of alcohol would have 'the biggest impact at the least cost', but more was needed, including teaching young people about 'respectful relationships'.[4]

Something like this would no doubt be tried with Liam Jurrah, I thought as I waited for the sentencing, expecting that his second victim's call for gaol time *and* treatment would be heeded. His case attracted a lot of easy judgment. People commenting on the *Alice Springs News Online* coverage were keen to vent against him: 'I am sick of seeing "news" about this woman basher,' one 'Disgusted' would write after my report of the sentence. 'He is a has-been! He blew his chance to be a positive role model. I don't know why the media keep acting like he is some kind of success story! HE ISN'T!'[5] But I couldn't help thinking of the mongrel dog of our times on its seemingly endless cycle when I learned that while Jurrah was serving his sentence in 2014, his father was also in gaol. And so was his mother.[6] Alongside his football and other opportunities, including his 2013 acquittal, that too was a measure of the 'chance' he had had.

It was after 4 pm when Jurrah was brought back into court. While the magistrate, a woman, read the Corrections report, we could hear the clock ticking. It had a kind of metaphoric weight, for it is time that the court deals in. Jurrah again turned round and hand-signalled to his family.

Community Corrections were prepared to supervise and the magistrate had decided that the second assault was a Level Three. Jurrah was young for sentencing purposes, she said, and he should be given the opportunity to rehabilitate. If he didn't, she warned him, he would have to serve the balance of the partially suspended sentences she was about to impose and the court would be less inclined towards leniency next time.

The difference in seriousness of the two assaults was calculated as one month. With concurrency (including for the restored balance of the 2014 sentence and the penalties for breaching the DVOs) the effective sentence was nine months, to be suspended after four. He had served two on remand, so he would be out in another two.

There were orders to not drink alcohol, to undertake rehab and a family violence program, to not leave the NT, but also to not remain in Alice Springs without permission.

I could only speculate on what it all meant to Jurrah. He stood with his chin tilted, hands behind his back, immobile, as I'd seen him stand before when things were difficult. But the sentence was intended too as a message to the community. The magistrate duly recited the mantra: 'Alcohol-fuelled violence, especially against women, is not acceptable.' This did not seem to be the main take-away for Jurrah's supporters. Outside the court his cousin ('skin brother') Kasman Spencer, coach of the Yuendumu Magpies, told an ABC reporter that they were disappointed: they were hoping to have Jurrah freed to play football that weekend.[7] That was never going to happen.

Two days later the Magpies won the Country Division One Grand Final, played in Alice Springs. In his post-match comments Spencer was reported to have 'paid tribute' to the gaoled Jurrah.[8] If there was any thought of the women his cousin assaulted, or the trouble (the ongoing trouble) that his cousin was in, it didn't seem to be at the forefront of his mind.

The post-match photos checked for a bit this rueful thought of mine. For one thing, they were sent to the *Alice Springs News* by Bess Nungarrayi Price, one of the country's most prominent Aboriginal voices raised against domestic violence. At the time of writing she is MLA for the electorate of Stuart, which takes in her home community of Yuendumu, and a minister in the Northern Territory government. She was photographed with the Magpies and their supporters. Their joy was transfiguring – they all looked magnificent. Everyone needs a bit of forgetting, I thought.

But not too much. Remembering, bringing to consciousness, doing the mental work is what it takes to stop the mongrel dog on its track. 'A man can choose,' said a man who knew. This was San Roque's collaborator, the late A Japaljarri Spencer, the man whose question about a story for intoxication had led to the *Sugarman* project. Japaljarri was also the uncle of Kasman Spencer, Jurrah's skin brother. He passed away as I was thinking about these things. Tributes flowed at the news of his death; he was widely respected and admired. In his younger years, though, in a drunken rage, he had killed a close family member. He was punished, under both Aboriginal cultural law and Australian law. Then he made a choice, he changed his life. For decades he worked with Australian law as an Aboriginal Community Police Officer as well as within Aboriginal law, delicately managing the many obstacles and conflicts of such a difficult path. He thought deeply about how to communicate the lessons he had learned and produced an important series of instructional paintings, with subjects such as *Family Breakdown*, *Sad Boys Are Sniffing*, *Thinking about Young People* and, more recently, *Eagle and Crow*, which 'shows the life of a man' in our times:

> You see him born into his father's Jukurrpa, his family all around looking at him, singing. He follows his spirit and his Jukurrpa to bush camp. He becomes a man. The eagle, Walawaru, comes. 'Come with me – I will show you all your life.'
>
> Eagle lifts him high in the sky. Eagle shows him a strong way for a man living in these times. He shows him how to work the white way and the black way together. Eagle gives him a clear sharp mind. He follows Jukurrpa. His vital spirit, Kurunpa, stays strong and intelligent. He learns many things, he works for people. Jukurrpa, Kurunpa and Mapanpa (power) run inside him. He learns and works in two cultures, English and Indigenous. He keeps his family together. They have a good time.
>
> Karnka Crow is jealous. He calls out. 'You come with me, have a good time, plenty of grog, plenty of women. Don't listen to that eagle.'

The man changes tracks. He looks into Karnka country. 'I'll be okay, Crow won't suck my blood.'

He sits down in drinking camps. He gets lazy. He gets lost in town. He learns ganja culture, his mind changes, he kills women, he forgets Jukurrpa, Kurunpa slides away, he loses power, he lies down. Karnka sucks his blood. There he is, sick.

Walawaru comes again and lifts him up high. Eagle says, 'This is your life. Use your brain. A man can choose. Which way will you go?'

'I will stick with you,' says the man.

This is the story of any man. This is the parable of Eagle and Crow.[9]

~

Trouble erupts on days that are like other days in almost every respect, until those moments from which there is no turning back. This is part of what I've realised as I've been going into court, that the context of most crime, even the most serious, is ordinary, which is not to say untroubling. In Central Australia's ordinary there are things we have in common – such as a culture of excessively heavy drinking – and things that are peculiar to us as individuals, families, and broader social and cultural groupings. This is obvious yet seems to need stating in the face of the blunt instruments of law and order responses, including mandatory sentencing. Each case, as these stories reveal, is particular – each victim, each perpetrator, each set of circumstances, each violent act. Up close, as women and men die or are injured at the hands of another, categories and generalities disappear. Victims and perpetrators know this starkly. Lawyers and judges know it by long exposure. The general public and the politicians who seek their favour should take heed and stop trying to tie the hands of the courts.

This goes for the complex matter of consideration of Aboriginal law too, by which I mean a cultural setting far broader than, and in the twenty-first century necessarily excluding, the tribal corporal punishment which those words conjure. It is clear from the stories in this book that there is an evolving relationship between many Aboriginal people in Central Australia and the Australian settler law: they seek its protection, its vindication of their rights, its adjudication in serious matters, even though they may not be satisfied with the outcome, even as it locks up their men in such great number, even while they seek its reform. Evolving too is the co-existing governance of their everyday lives by their own law and mores. No amount of social and cultural bludgeoning from without is going to eliminate that. The devastating impact of their more ready resort to violence – especially violence inflicted with a weapon, in extreme disproportion by men upon women, and under the exacerbating influence of alcohol – is being recognised and examined among them. We have seen the local examples, the NPY Women's Council, the Stop the Violence actions, the leadership shown by impressive individuals such as Wenten Rubuntja, Margaret Kemarre Turner, Japaljarri Spencer, among others. They should be given all the support they may require. The courts meanwhile need to be able to consider the whole person, the whole context insofar as they are able. The suppression by fiat of any consideration of Aboriginal law is highly artificial given the realities of people's lives outside and thus the realities of what the courts have to deal with. There is surely everything to gain by working with people as they are and are becoming, rather than expecting them to leave a significant part of themselves at the door and forcing judges to look at them with blinkers on.

For a too brief period a therapeutic court was tried in Alice Springs and Darwin, working intensively to support the power of individual choice and to keep people out of prison.[10] It was called the SMART Court (SMART stood for 'Substance Misuse Assessment and Referral for Treatment') and operated similarly to other so-called drug courts in Australia and the US. Sentencing of offenders with serious alcohol and/or drug problems was deferred while they were given a chance, a six- to twelve-month window, to turn their lives around. Total abstinence, involving clinical testing, was required and a range of other disciplined efforts, especially around work or training. It wasn't easy, but the 'clients' were effectively supported according to their various needs. If they fell off the wagon or got into other kinds of trouble, even skipped court appointments, there would be consequences, measured in units of gaol time additional to the ultimate sentence for the crime they had committed. But they could 'earn' this gaol time back as well as other rewards, including less frequent clinical testing for substance use and less frequent visits to court. There were also rewards that were not easy to measure: words of encouragement, smiling affirmation, congratulation. The atmosphere was informal. Clients could remain seated while they spoke for themselves, if they chose, directly to the magistrate.

Everyone was waiting for the magistrate to arrive; there was banter with the client, about his tattoos, his girlfriend, his new job. They all joined in, the legal aid lawyer, the court clinician, the police prosecutor and the correctional services officer. He was an open-faced, smiling young man in his twenties.

When the magistrate entered, the good cheer continued. He spoke directly to the young man who remained seated and responded for himself. The tone was conversational. Property offences not drug offences had brought him before the court, but his drug use had been deemed a significant factor in his offending.

'So you haven't had a smoke for four weeks,' said the magistrate, reading off the results of the defendant's urinalysis: 'You'll be clean soon.'

The young man agreed, sure that at his next visit the readings would be near zero.

He'd started his new job that week. The magistrate wanted to know where and what the hours were. He was pleased with what he heard: 'What reward would you like?'

Everyone laughed – they were all pleased. The young man hesitated.

Perhaps he'd like to not have to come to court so often, suggested the magistrate, that would help him settle into his new job.

'Excellent!'

'I'll give you a go at a month.'

His testing would continue fortnightly. If his levels got to zero, the regularity of the testing would drop as well.

'Keep it up,' urged the magistrate, and with another 'Excellent!' the young man left.

Next on the list entered. He'd been charged with driving offences, including high-range drink-driving, as well as contravening a DVO. He was older and at a glance appeared to have had a tougher life. He had also had 'bad luck' recently, the magistrate noted, having been involved in a car crash.

'You weren't tempted to have a steadying drink?'

Tempted, yes, he admitted, but he hadn't given in and the tests confirmed it. For the time being he'd be kept on a schedule of fortnightly visits to court, which could 'loosen up' later. He didn't have a job but otherwise was doing well. Despite the accident, 'you haven't been stressed into drinking or doing drugs, well done', said the magistrate.

The following man had been charged with similar driving offences and failing to obey the direction of a police officer. He agreed with the magistrate that he was doing well.

'Is it a struggle any more?'

'No, not at all, Your Honour.'

The first couple of months had been difficult. Now he was on monthly court visits and weekly testing: 'I'll stick with that,' he said.

'You seem to be cruising through the whole process. People have different levels of struggle but you seem to be doing as well as anyone.'

The man looked gratified: 'Thank you, Your Honour.'

Those three were all Caucasian. The next man was Aboriginal, in his late thirties, early forties perhaps, charged with drug offences. The upbeat mood continued.

'Your urine tests are going down,' noted the magistrate.

'No worries, ey!'

'You haven't been tempted?'

'Nuh, keeping myself busy, doing a course.'

He'd been on weekly urine tests; he was rewarded by going to fortnightly. If everything was tracking well at the next visit, his court appearances would be spaced out to monthly.

'Thank you, Your Honour, have a good day!'

It was not only the demeanour of offenders that changed in the SMART Court. That of the whole program team but none more than the magistrate, David Bamber, was remarkably different. Gone was the weary monotone of his interventions and judgments from the bench; in its stead, a kindly warmth, genuine interest, good humour. It seemed like the repair work of this court was going both ways.

As they worked through the list, not surprisingly some cases were more difficult.

A young Aboriginal woman came in. She'd been charged with possession of methylamphetamines and cannabis. This was her first review. She'd missed one appointment, but had kept one; her tests weren't clean. She admitted she was still smoking and using 'a bit of meth'.

Her agreement with the court was not to consume, the magistrate reminded her: 'This is a zero program.'

She said she'd been told by a program worker that she could cut down gradually, as it's 'hard to go cold turkey'.

The magistrate asked the team whether she was getting mixed messages. The court clinician said there could be issues for some people in going cold turkey safely.

But sanctions were imposed: she earned one day's gaol time for the cannabis use, one for the amphetamines, one for missing an appointment. All three were suspended. The magistrate noted that she had cut down and that she'd been honest – 'That's good.' He smiled encouragingly and got a little smile back from this otherwise anxious-looking young woman.

An Aboriginal man came in. He was middle-aged, his hair starting to turn grey. His charges were high-range drink-driving and driving while disqualified.

After a 'bad start' he was doing well: 'You've kept all your appointments, you've been enthusiastic, you're feeling well.'

Did he want to say anything?

'No,' he whispered.

For his earlier breaches he'd earned ten days' gaol time, suspended. Now he was rewarded for total compliance by getting three days back.

An Aboriginal woman appeared. She'd been charged with medium-range drink-driving and driving while disqualified.

She'd started a job that week, as a kitchenhand. She'd negotiated with her employers to get Thursdays off and work Saturdays, so that she could attend court fortnightly and in the alternate week go to counselling.

A lawyer spoke on her behalf: she'd made a slow start, but the barriers had been identified and strategies put in place.

'I understand it's difficult ...' began the magistrate.

'I can stick to it,' the woman said in a firm voice. 'I go back to work tomorrow.'

~

The SMART Court was around for long enough to see its first graduates.[11] One woman in Alice had turned from regular heavy drinking – of up to thirty cans of full-strength beer in a sitting and this over more than two decades – to being sober, taking on full-time employment, progressing in her job, looking after family, aspiring to rent her own flat. She had been charged with high-range drink-driving and driving while disqualified, and these were not her first drink-driving offences. At graduation Magistrate Bamber had to consider sentencing. Ordinarily for those offences and her record he would have felt obliged, in line with Supreme Court directions, to impose gaol time. However, given that the program was rewards-based and that she had done 'everything a person could', he imposed a conviction and good behaviour bond for two years. Other graduates on the day were two young men who had had cannabis habits, one of them the smiling young man I had seen on my first visit. Clean now and with their lives on track, they were both given twelve-month good behaviour bonds. A cake was brought into court to celebrate the achievements of the three. It was a bit awkward, pushing the files aside and cutting it up on the bar table, but everyone was beaming.

The success and value of the program, as Magistrate Bamber noted, lay not only in people completing it, but in them being able to 'get on with their lives' afterwards. The true test was going to be in the months and years to come. Once they had emerged from the structured program and had to leave behind the support of the team, some people would no doubt have found it harder to keep on the straight and narrow. But a hopeful start had been made.

The program was not available to violent offenders, although then Chief Magistrate Hilary Hannam, who had overseen its establishment, argued that it should be: not for all or even any serious violent offenders, but she wanted magistrates to have the discretion. If it were properly resourced and available to the widest range of offenders, she believed it would be an effective tool in dealing with much of the criminal conduct in the Northern Territory. Substance misuse does not cause crime, but there's a correlation between the two and the relationship appears to be particularly strong for violent crime, she argued. 'There is also a great deal of evidence that suggests that alcohol plays a major role in much of the offending by Indigenous people.'[12]

Far from being extended, after just eighteen months of operation the SMART Court was scrapped in December 2012 by the Country Liberal government, without ever being evaluated (the same fate as suffered by the Banned Drinkers Register). Absence of an evaluation did not stop Attorney-General and Justice Minister John Elferink from asserting that the court was 'ineffective and inefficient',[13] a view he had held from Opposition when he spoke against its introduction, classifying it as a 'soft on crime' approach and disparaging the capacity to change of most people who would come before it.[14] In his rigorous examination of what works and what doesn't in responding to Indigenous offending, criminologist Don Weatherburn emphasises the importance of proper evaluation, of only pursuing what is proven to work and persisting with it. The evidence for drug courts he found was 'generally very favourable'.[15]

Even if the SMART Court had survived and been extended to violent offenders (as was originally intended),[16] it would not have been available for the serious kinds of offences coming before the Supreme Court, about which I have mostly been writing. However, many of these offenders had long-standing histories of substance abuse and long criminal records of escalating seriousness that had been cycling them repeatedly through court orders and terms in prison. The mongrel dog had been coming through the gap for years.

ACKNOWLEDGEMENTS

Many conversations over many years stand behind this book. I thank my friend, and friend of Central Australia, the writer Barry Hill for his long-term encouragement of my work, his generous support for this project in particular, his vital insights and challenges as it developed and wonderfully helpful suggestions on writing matters. I thank my brother, the historian Mark Finnane, for setting me on the course of writing it. I first saw its possibility when he asked me in 2011 to collaborate with him on an article about responses to the killing of Kwementyaye Ryder. His own work on criminal history, including the history of Indigenous crime and settler law, his skill as a writer and his keen interest in Central Australia made his feedback on this text invaluable. I am indebted to my friend the senior Alice Springs lawyer Russell Goldflam for many careful explanations on points of law, contributions of his own insights and analysis, and perceptive comments on my account of contexts with which he is intimately familiar. The enriching influence on the book of the thinking and writing of Craig San Roque is clear; I thank him too for his friendship and long-standing gracious support of my work. For their generosity, warmth, wisdom, example and patient answers to my questions, I am deeply grateful to Doris Kngwarraye Stuart and Margaret Kemarre Turner.

Many other family members, friends and acquaintances have offered me much valued encouragement and support, over the years and for this project, including as perceptive readers and contributors of their own professional, cultural and personal knowledge and perspectives. I thank them all and in particular (in alphabetical order) Alison Anderson MLA, Margaret Carew, Janet Chlanda, Bob Durnan, Susan Fielding, my sisters Antonia Finnane, Francine Finnane, Gabrielle Finnane and Rebecca Finnane, Dick Kimber, Jane Lloyd, Greg McAdam, Blair McFarland, Jennifer McFarland, Pip McManus, Mary-Ann Marshall, Eli Moss, Rod Moss, Tim Rowse and Jennifer Taylor.

Mike Gillam has my deep appreciation for his fine cover photograph and generous friendship.

I am grateful to editors Julianne Schultz at *Griffith Review* and Peter Browne at *Inside Story* for publishing, respectively, earlier versions of the chapters 'Warlpiri versus the Queen' and 'Race in the dock II'.

For their friendly professional assistance I thank Courts Liaison and Education Officer Malika Okiel, Criminal Registrar Shane Slattery (and staff), and Mavis Welsh at Court Recordings (formerly Merrill Corporation, now DTI).

To the team at UQP my deep appreciation for shepherding this book along its way to publication: to publisher Alexandra Payne, my thanks in particular for her early interest and enthusiasm, for championing it through to acquisition and for warm support as we crossed each hurdle; and my special thanks to editor Nikki Lusk, for fine-tuning the text, with queries, challenges and suggestions as well as her sharp editorial eye and to project editor Jacqueline Blanchard for her sustaining commitment through to the end.

My decades in Central Australia have taken me a long way from my family of origin yet, together with my family of creation, they are my anchor in the world. My dear late father, Peter Finnane, would have read this book with great attention. I know my mother, Patricia Finnane, in her ninety-first year will be among the first to do so. I have much to thank them both for, not least for imparting from the first an awareness of the people and world around us and a commitment to a fairer, kinder society. Above all I thank them for the gift of a loving family that sustains me through all my endeavours.

My children, Jacqueline Chlanda and Rainer Chlanda, could not have been more devotedly supportive of this book and of me as I wrote it. I have been privileged to have them also for insightful readers, their perspectives finely honed by growing up in Central Australia and by the adult paths they have taken.

As founder and editor of the *Alice Springs News*, my husband, Erwin Chlanda, has had a large role in forming me as a journalist, exemplary in his persistence, his tough but fair approach to often difficult subjects, his independence of mind, commitment to the practice of his craft and to Central Australia. My work over the years has benefitted greatly from his challenging critiques, matched only by his unwavering appreciation. This book owes its greatest debt to his professional and material support, but more than that, to his loving daily presence.

NOTES

INTRODUCTION: ONE STONE ROOM

1   The forum was organised as part of Shifting Ground, a 2007 program produced and curated by Kieren Sanderson exploring 'how the arts could reimagine people's lived relationships with "place", "community", "culture" and the "environment".' See Kieran Finnane, 'Incubating ideas', catalogue essay in *Shifting ground – Art in public places in Alice Springs*, Ipomea Press, Alice Springs, 2008; Kieran Finnane, 'Icons, living and dead', *Griffith Review*, 44, pp. 244–53.

When on 8 December 2015 I spoke to Kemarre Turner about this reference to the tree she had more to say: 'The family, past and present, belongs to that foundation. It can never be cleared away with anything, rain, wind, storm. It's a sacred tree, people can't push it away. It will never vanish, it lives for the generations.' 'When it's very old the tree will die,' I said, as gently as possible. 'No,' she said firmly. 'The new plant comes up from the roots.'

2   Kieran Finnane, 'Northern end of the mall reopens', *Alice Springs News Online*, 20 July 2013, http://www.alicespringsnews.com.au/2013/07/20/northern-end-of-the-mall-reopens/, accessed 30 October 2015.

3   Preparation of the rollout of the National Broadband Network in Alice Springs has led to the mapping of more than 600 sites. See Erwin Chlanda, 'IT and ancient lore, how will they get on?', *Alice Springs News Online*, 26 November 2015, http://www.alicespringsnews.com.au/2015/11/26/it-and-ancient-lore-how-will-they-get-on/,   accessed

26 November 2015.

4 David Brooks (for Mparntwe People), *A town like Mparntwe: a guide to the Dreaming Tracks and Sites of Alice Springs*, IAD Press, Alice Springs, 2003 (first published as *The Arrernte landscape* in 1991), pp. 17–20. See also Erwin Chlanda, 'Sites issue hotting up', *Centralian Advocate*, 4 February 1983.

5 Quoted in *Site seeing*, catalogue for an exhibition, paintings by Carol Ruff, photographs by Jon Rhodes, main text by David Brooks, published by Jon Rhodes, Thora, NSW, 1994.

6 Kieran Finnane, 'Poisoned sacred trees to remain', *Alice Springs News*, 1 October 2009, in online archive at http://www.alicespringsnews.com. au/1635.html, accessed 30 October 2015.

7 Brooks, p. 9.

8 *Hayes v Northern Territory*, http://www.austlii.edu.au/cgi-bin/sinodisp/au/ cases/cth/federal_ct/1999/1248.html, accessed 30 October 15.

9 Typescript courtesy Doris Kngwarraye Stuart.

10 Kieran Finnane, 'Aboriginal interests buy Kmart complex for $16m', *Alice Springs News*, 8 July 2010, in online archive at http://www.alicespringsnews. com.au/1723.html, accessed 30 October 2015.

11 *Performance Audit of Centrecorp Aboriginal Investment Corporation*, a report of the former Office of Evaluation and Audit (Indigenous Programs), 1 November 2008, http://www.anao.gov.au/uploads/documents/Performance_Audit_ of_Centrecorp_Aboriginal_Investment_Corporation_Pty_Ltd.pdf, accessed 2 September 2011.

12 See, for example, Erwin Chlanda, 'Administrators untangle web of native title group's businesses', *Alice Springs News Online*, 10 April 2014, http:// www.alicespringsnews.com.au/2014/04/10/administrators-untangle- web-of-native-title-groups-businesses/, accessed 30 October 2015.

13 There has been some progress towards preparing the ground for private home ownership in just one camp, Ilpeye Ilpeye. See 'Private home ownership for town camp', *Alice Springs News Online*, 22 June 2013, http://www.alicespringsnews.com.au/2013/06/22/letter-private-home- ownership-in-town-camp/, accessed 26 November 2015; 'Construction brings jobs to Ilpeye Ilpeye residents', NT Department of Local Government and Community Services, newsroom, 15 September 2014, http://www. dlgcs.nt.gov.au/about_us/newsroom/newsroom-docs/2014/construction_ brings_jobs_to_ilpeye-ilpeye_residents, accessed 26 November 2015.

14 Australian Bureau of Statistics (ABS), 2011 Census of Population and Housing, *Aboriginal and Torres Strait Islander Peoples (Indigenous) Profile* (Catalogue number 2002.0): *Alice Springs Town Camps* (IARE701002); *Alice*

exc. Town Camps (IARE701001).

15 Kieran Finnane, 'Mother's assault on toddler not what it seemed', *Alice Springs News Online*, 7 November 2011, http://www.alicespringsnews. com.au/2011/11/07/mothers-assault-on-toddler-not-what-it-seemed/, accessed 30 October 2015.

16 Erwin Chlanda & Kieran Finnane, 'The Desert Knowledge upstairs-downstairs dilemma', *Alice Springs News Online*, 5 July 2012, http://www. alicespringsnews.com.au/2012/07/05/the-desert-knowledge-upstairs-downstairs-dilemma/, accessed 30 October 2015; and Kieran Finnane, 'Dealing with a drift that became a wave', *Inside Story*, 18 May 2011, http:// insidestory.org.au/dealing-with-a-drift-that-became-a-wave, accessed 30 October 2015.

17 Kieran Finnane, 'We share the land', *Alice Springs News Online*, 13 July 2015, http://www.alicespringsnews.com.au/2015/07/13/we-share-the-land/, accessed 30 October 2015; and personal communication with Mervyn Rubuntja, 2 July 2015.

18 See, for example, the views of criminologist Thalia Anthony reported in Kieran Finnane, 'Driving offences sky-rocket: bad drivers or more police', *Alice Springs News*, 21 October 2010, in online archive at http://www. alicespringsnews.com.au/1738.html, accessed 30 October 2015.

19 *Alice Springs News*, 11 March 2010, in online archive at http://www. alicespringsnews.com.au/1706.html, accessed 30 October 2015.

20 Rod Moss, *One Thousand Cuts*, University of Queensland Press, St Lucia, 2013, p. 163.

21 National Homicide Monitoring Program, *Homicide in Australia 2010–12*, report no. 23, http://www.aic.gov.au/publications/current%20series/ mr/21-40/mr23/04_homicide-2010-12.html, accessed 23 October 2015.

22 Northern Territory Crime Statistics, November 2015, http://www.pfes. nt.gov.au/Police/Community-safety/Northern-Territory-crime-statistics/ Statistical-publications.aspx, pp. 39 & 41, accessed 15 February 2016.

23 ABS, *Recorded crime – offenders, 2013–14 – Northern Territory.* http://www. abs.gov.au/ausstats/abs@.nsf/Lookup/4519.0main+features312013-14, accessed 5 December 2015.

24 Northern Territory Government, *Northern Territory crime statistics*, November 2015, p. 41.

25 Steven J Skov et al., 'How much is too much? Alcohol consumption and related harm in the Northern Territory', *Medical Journal of Australia*, vol. 193, no. 5, 6 September 2010, pp. 269–72.

26 Dennis Gray et al., 'A longitudinal study of influences on alcohol

consumption and related harm in Central Australia: with a particular emphasis on the role of price', National Drug Research Institute, Curtin University, October 2012, table 9, p. 28.

27 Anthony Morgan & Amanda McAtamney, 'Key issues in alcohol-related violence', *Research in practice*, no. 4, Australian Institute of Criminology, http://www.aic.gov.au/publications/current%20series/rip/1-10/04.html, accessed 24 October 2015.

28 Northern Territory Government, *Northern Territory crime statistics*, November 2015, pp. 46-47.

29 Morgan & McAtamney.

30 Northern Territory Government, Department of the Attorney-General and Justice, *Northern Territory Annual Crime Statistics*, issue 1, 2011–12, figure 10, p. 16, http://www.nt.gov.au/justice/policycoord/documents/statistics/nt_annual_crime_statistics_2012.pdf, accessed 5 December 2015.

31 Don Weatherburn, *Arresting incarceration – pathways out of Indigenous imprisonment*, Aboriginal Studies Press, Canberra, 2014, p. 55.

32 ABS, *Prisoners in Australia 2014: Northern Territory snapshot*, http://www.abs.gov.au/ausstats/abs@.nsf/Lookup/by%20Subject/4517.0~2014~Main%20Features~Northern%20Territory~10021, accessed 5 December 2015; and *Prisoner characteristics Australia*, http://www.abs.gov.au/ausstats/abs@.nsf/Lookup/by%20Subject/4517.0~2014~Main%20Features~Prisoner%20characteristics,%20Australia~4, accessed 5 December 2015.

33 ABS, *Recorded Crime – Victims, Australia 2014 – Northern Territory*, http://www.abs.gov.au/ausstats/abs@.nsf/Lookup/by%20Subject/4510.0~2014~Main%20Features~Northern%20Territory~34, accessed 5 December 2015.

34 Carly Ingles, 'Overflow: why so many women in NT prisons?', presentation to a conference of the Criminal Lawyers Association of the NT, 26 June 2015, p. 2, http://clant.org.au/images/images/the-bali-conference/2015/InglesPaper.pdf, accessed 26 October 2015.

35 F Al-Yaman et al., *Family violence among Aboriginal and Torres Strait Islander peoples*, 2006, Australian Institute of Health and Welfare, Canberra, quoted by Weatherburn, p. 56.

36 Australian Institute of Health and Welfare, *National hospital morbidity database*, 2011/12, quoted by People's Alcohol Action Coalition (Dr John Boffa on behalf of) in their submission to the House of Representatives Standing Committee on Indigenous Affairs Inquiry into the Harmful Use of Alcohol in Aboriginal and Torres Strait Islander Communities, 24 April 2014, p. 11.

37 The history of this engagement is succinctly traced in Russell Goldflam,

'The (non-)role of Aboriginal customary law in sentencing in the Northern Territory', *Australian Indigenous Law Review*, vol. 17, no. 1, 2013, pp. 72–80.

For a detailed Australia-wide history with frequent focus on the Northern Territory, comparisons with other post-colonial states, and concerned particularly with jurisdictional responsibility for responses to violence, see Heather Douglas & Mark Finnane, *Indigenous crime and settler law: white sovereignty after empire*, Palgrave MacMillan, Houndmills, Basingstoke, Hampshire (UK), New York (USA), 2012. In Chapter 7, '"Benign Pessimism": A National Emergency', they consider the post-Intervention context, arguing that the very need for the Intervention's customary law prohibitions 'emphasised the reality of the persistence of custom and the continuing problem of governance over Indigenous *inter se* violence', p. 214.

38 Russell Goldflam, 'Where's my interpreter?', presentation to *Language and Law II*, a conference of the Supreme Court of the Northern Territory, 28–30 August 2015, p. 8, http://www.supremecourt.nt.gov.au/conferences/documents/presenter-info/Russell%20Goldflam%20-%20Where's%20my%20interpreter.pdf, accessed 26 October 2015. Goldflam is also a senior lawyer with the NT Legal Aid Commission in Alice Springs.

39 ibid., pp. 9–10.

IN THE MINDS OF MEN

1 Kieran Finnane, 'Problem drinkers and the rest of us', *Inside Story*, 22 June 2011, http://insidestory.org.au/problem-drinkers-and-the-rest-of-us, accessed 31 October 2015.

2 Jennifer Turner-Walker (aka Jenny Walker, Jenny McFarland), personal communication 11 June 2015, and 'Clash of the paradigms – Night Patrols in remote central Australia', thesis for the degree Master in Criminal Justice, University of Western Australia, 2010, http://www.fare.org.au/wp-content/uploads/research/Thesis+complete+2.pdf, accessed 31 October 2015.

3 However, see Goldflam, 'The (non-)role of Aboriginal customary law ...', for his discussion of an exceptional instance in 2012 of cultural matters being explored, under a particular section of the *Sentencing Act*. Evidence from an anthropologist, about kinship obligations and traditional demand sharing in the contemporary context, was taken into account for sentencing purposes, p. 76.

Carly Ingles also comments on the case. She notes that the finding of exceptional circumstances was not challenged on appeal, adding: 'It highlights, though, the potential deficiencies of sentencing where the same level of expert opinion is not sought', p. 10.

4   Lisa M Jamieson et al., 'Hopitalisation for head injury due to assault among Indigenous and non-Indigenous Australians, July 1999 – June 2005', *Medical Journal of Australia*, vol. 188, 2008, pp. 576–79, quoted in Peter Sutton, *The politics of suffering: Indigenous Australia and the end of the liberal consensus*, Melbourne University Press, Carlton, 2009, p. 101.

Anthropologist Jane Lloyd, who has worked for more than two decades on domestic violence issues in Central Australia, has observed: 'The nature, extent and intent of the violence by the offenders is evident in the use of the upper end of moderate to severe force to deliberately cause injuries to the head, face and torso.' See J Lloyd, 'Violent and tragic events: the nature of domestic violence-related homicide cases in Central Australia', in *Australian Aboriginal Studies*, vol. 1, 2014, pp. 99–110 at p. 103.

5   Northern Territory Police, 'Serious assault arrest', media release, 27 December 2012, http://www.pfes.nt.gov.au/Media-Centre/Media-releases/2012/December/27/Serious-Assault-Arrest-Alice-Springs.aspx, accessed 31 October 2015.

6   Northern Territory Police, 'Serious assault charges', media release, 28 December 2012, http://www.pfes.nt.gov.au/Media-Centre/Media-releases/2012/December/28/Serious-Assault-Charges-Alice-Springs. aspx, accessed 31 October 2015.

7   Northern Territory Police, 'Murder charges expected today', media release, 28 December 2012, http://www.pfes.nt.gov.au/Media-Centre/Media-releases/2012/December/31/Murder-Charges-Expected-Today. aspx, accessed 31 October 2015.

8   Robyn Lambley, 'Statement on death in Alice Springs', Northern Territory Government, media release, 31 December 2012, http://newsroom.nt.gov.au/mediaRelease/7718, accessed 31 October 2015.

9   Nigel Adlam, 'List lapse lets murder accused back on grog', *NT News*, 3 January 2013, http://www.territorystories.nt.gov.au/bitstream/10070/243816/2/ntn03jan13002x.pdf, accessed 31 October 2015.

10   Bob Durnan, 'Death, violence and politics in the festive season', *Alice Online*, 3 January 2013, http://aliceonline.com.au/2013/01/03/death-violence-and-politics-in-the-festive-season/, accessed 18 June 2014.

11   Northern Territory Police, 'Call for public assistance – murder investigation – Alice Springs', media release, 25 February 2013, http://www.pfes.nt.gov.au/Media-Centre/Media-releases/2013/February/25/Call-for-Public-Assistance-Murder-Investigation-Alice-Springs.aspx, accessed 31 October 2015; 'Six charged in relation to murder – Alice Springs', 26 February 2013, http://www.pfes.nt.gov.au/Media-Centre/

Media-releases/2013/February/26/Six-Charged-in-relation-to-Murder-Alice-Springs.aspx, accessed 31 October 2015; 'Seventh man charged in relation to murder', 27 February 2013, http://www.pfes.nt.gov.au/Media-Centre/Media-releases/2013/February/27/Seventh-man-charged-in-relation-to-Murder-Alice-Springs.aspx, accessed 31 October 2015.

12 Emma Sleath, 'Five men charged with murder', ABC Alice Springs, http://www.abc.net.au/local/audio/2013/02/26/3698760.htm, accessed 31 October 2015.

13 Northern Territory Police, 'Murder charge', media release, 21 February 2013, http://www.pfes.nt.gov.au/Media-Centre/Media-releases/2013/February/21/Murder-Charge-Alice-Springs.aspx, accessed 31 October 2015.

14 Anderson subsequently left the Country Liberals taking other disaffected Aboriginal members with her. She sat for a while as an independent member before joining, then leaving the Palmer United Party. At the time of writing she is once again an independent.

15 Paul Serratore, 'Minister walkout sinks safety summit', ABC Alice Springs, 4 March 2013, http://www.abc.net.au/local/stories/2013/02/28/3700485.htm?site=alicesprings, accessed 31 October 2015.

16 Personal communication with Russell Goldflam by email, 26 November 2015, speaking in his capacity as President of the Criminal Lawyers Association of the Northern Territory.

17 Dean puts her finger on issues also observed by Jane Lloyd, who writes: 'Many children have been socialised in an environment where they have witnessed their mothers or other women being violently abused. From the 15 confirmed domestic-related homicides and two suspected homicides reported in this paper, at least 27 children are now orphaned. They have all witnessed and experienced the fear, trauma, loss and grief associated with this level of violence. Their social and emotional development and well-being is compromised by the violence they have witnessed and the uncertainty surrounding the continuity, stability and predictability of their future care and protection', pp. 106–7. 'Orphaned girls were especially vulnerable to harms such as child and sexual abuse and to forming unsafe and violent relationships in their early teens and they struggled to nurture and protect their own children', p. 108.

18 'There are still many Aboriginal communities in which virtually all deaths, other than those of infants and, in some cases, the elderly, are either attributed to sorcery committed by members of near or distant groups, or result from personal violence ... The sorcery analysis not only provides a

cause for the death, it deflects blame and rage away from the participants and to the social outside, emphasises insider solidarity, and plays a critical function in maintaining external inter-group hostilities or suspicions.' Sutton, pp. 89–90.

19 Weatherburn, pp. 86–7.

20 Margaret Kemarre Turner, *Iwenhe Tyerrtye: What it means to be an Aboriginal person*, IAD Press, Alice Springs, 2010, pp. 14–15.

21 Nicolas Peterson,'Other people's lives: Secular assimilation, culture and ungovernability', in Jon Altman & Melinda Hinkson (eds), *Culture crisis: Anthropology and politics in Aboriginal Australia*, UNSW Press, Sydney, 2010, p. 255.

22 Craig San Roque, 'A long weekend in Alice Springs', in Thomas Singer & Samuel L Kimbles (eds), *The cultural complex: Contemporary Jungian perspectives on psyche and society*, Routledge, New York, 2004, pp. 46–61. The essay was later adapted and drawn as a graphic novel by Joshua Santospirito, titled *The long weekend in Alice Springs*, San Kessto Publications, Tasmania, 2013. In this form its ideas reached a broad audience in Alice Springs.

23 ibid., p. 56.

24 ibid., p. 48.

25 ibid., p. 51.

26 ibid., p. 59.

27 ibid., p. 54.

28 See comments to Kieran Finnane, 'Final act in a history of violence', *Alice Springs News Online*, 15 April 2014, http://www.alicespringsnews.com.au/2014/04/15/final-act-in-a-history-of-violence/, accessed 31 October 15.

TROUBLE AT THE TURN-OFF

1 The name of the community is also sometimes spelled as Alekarenge. It refers to the Dog Dreaming of the Kayteye traditional owners. In the 2011 Census the total population, based on usual place of residence, was reported as 536.

2 Useful national and jurisdictional data on domestic violence-related homicides cannot be disaggregated to a regional level (Lloyd, p. 99). For the Central Australian cross-border region Lloyd records that 'Between 2000 and 2008, in a population of 6000 Indigenous people, fifteen women were killed by their husbands or boyfriends and another two women were officially reported as missing, suspected of being killed by their partners. Six of the homicides occurred between May 2007 and November 2008 … In contrast to the national and international trend and recent data

on Indigenous homicides in other jurisdictions ... fewer men (less than seven) were victims of homicide from this region over the same eight-year period', p. 102. It is noteworthy that in some of the case studies reported by Lloyd, the women died while far away from their families, living at town camps in Alice Springs, pp. 104–5.

3 Ingles, pp. 2, 10. Men are still the vast majority of offenders at 92 per cent, women at 8 per cent. In 2013–14 the NT female prison population grew by 27 per cent, the male prison population by 16 per cent. Statistics are identified by gender or race but not both so it is difficult to be precise about the number of Indigenous women involved. However, combined with a review of Supreme Court cases, it is clear that the increase in female prisoners disproportionately involves Indigenous women (Ingles, p. 2).

See also Lloyd, p. 102: 'in regions such as Central Australia women's violence against women and men is different. First, women's violence is often enacted in public and is more likely to be witnessed and subject to an intervention by a third party, a relative or an outsider. Second, while women's violence can be fatal, the nature of the violence is very different and the victims are only inflicted with a minimal number of wounds rather than multiple wounds from a prolonged assault with force, which is the case with many of the male-on-female homicides.'

4 At the time of writing, both premises are subject to restricted hours of trade for take-away purchases, Sunday to Friday inclusive 10 am – 10 pm, Saturday and public holidays 9 am – 10 pm. Different product restrictions apply. For Wycliffe Well the regime is twelve cans (375 ml) of light beer per person per day; or eight of mid-strength beer; or six of full-strength beer; or six of RTDs (with alcohol content not greater than 5 per cent). For Wauchope Hotel (renamed Devils Marbles Hotel) the restriction is only on cask wine or fortified wines, which may not be sold in containers larger than two litres. Personal communication by email from Communications Manager, Department of Business, 4 December 2015.

5 Diana Eades, *Aboriginal ways of using English*, Aboriginal Studies Press, Canberra, 2013, pp. 142–43. She describes Aboriginal English, of which there are many examples in this book, as rule-governed dialectical varieties of English. Standard English is 'simply the dialect of English which is spoken by the more powerful, dominant groups in society', p. 78.

6 Maggie Brady, *Indigenous Australia and alcohol policy: meeting difference with indifference*, UNSW Press, Sydney, 2004, pp. 55, 111.

7 Kieran Finnane, 'Years in gaol for six perpetrators of alcohol-fuelled killings', *Alice Springs News Online*, 27 July 2011, http://www.alicespringsnews.com.

au/2011/07/27/years-in-gaol-for-six-perpetrators-of-alcohol-fuelled-killings/, accessed 31 October 2015.

8 Nicholas Abercrombie, Stephen Hill & Bryan S Turner, *The Penguin dictionary of sociology*, London, 1994, pp. 17–18.

9 Émile Durkheim, *Suicide*, translated by John A Spaulding & George Simpson, The Free Press, New York, 1951 (original French edition published 1897), p. 257.

10 In John Cameron (ed.), *Changing places: re-imagining Australia*, Longueville Books, Double Bay, 2003, pp. 159–69.

11 ibid, p. 164.

12 ibid, p. 164.

13 Wenten Rubuntja with Jenny Green, *The town grew up dancing: the life and art of Wenten Rubuntja*, Jukurrpa Books, Alice Springs, 2002, pp. 105–6.

14 Margaret-Mary Turner (as she was then known), 'Alice Springs – where to in the new millennium?', *Alice Springs News*, 2 February 2000, in online archive at http://www.alicespringsnews.com.au/0705.html, accessed 30 October 2015.

15 Dennis Gray & Tanya Chikritzhs, 'Regional variation in alcohol consumption in the Northern Territory', *Australian and New Zealand Journal of Public Health*, February 2000, vol. 24, no. 1, pp. 35–38, this figure on p. 37.

16 The Tennant Creek campaign and achievements significantly influenced the debates, campaigns and ultimately policies and strategies adopted in Alice Springs in the following decade, though the town never went so far as having a grog-free day.

17 Quoted in Alexis Wright, *Grog war*, Magabala Books, Broome, 2009 (first published 1997), pp. 70–71.

18 Brady, p. 111.

19 ibid., p. 99.

20 ibid., p. 82.

21 ibid., p. 82.

22 ibid., p. 113.

23 With the lifting of race-based prohibition, the right to drink became an enduring symbol of equality and status for Aboriginal people (ibid., p. 58). Race-based prohibition was progressively repealed by the states between 1957 and 1972: Brady, 'Out from the Shadow of Prohibition' in Jon Altman & Melinda Hinkson (eds), *Coercive reconciliation: stabilise, normalise, exit Aboriginal Australia*, Arena Publications Association, North Carlton, 2007, p. 185. In the Northern Territory it ended in 1964, following the grant of voting rights in 1962, Brady, 2004, p. 19.

24 Brady, *Indigenous Australia and alcohol policy*, p. 83.

25 See also Douglas & Finnane: 'While law reform commission reports have consistently recognised customary law as a feature of daily life in many Indigenous communities, they have avoided categorical definitions of customary law ... This approach poses a dilemma. On the one hand, this refusal or inability to codify customary law contributes to uncertainty about what customary law is and how the state and its institutions should respond to it. At the same time, to define customary law, to write it, is to lose it', pp. 187–98. This situation has 'allowed Indigenous custom to preserve its distinction and to maintain a more complex relationship with "the" law', pp. 217–18.

26 Turner-Walker.

27 Kieran Finnane, 'Centre "worst in the world" for stabbings', *Alice Springs News*, 7 December 2006, in online archive at http://www.alicespringsnews. com.au/1349.html, accessed 30 October 2015. The source for the report was AO Jacob, F Boseto & J Ollapallil, 'Epidemic of stab injuries: an Alice Springs dilemma', *ANZ Journal of Surgery*, vol. 77, 2007, pp. 621–25, doi:10.1111/j.1445-2197.2007.04174.x.

28 Anne Barker, 'Stabbing rate in Alice halves', ABC Radio, *PM*, 4 April 2008, http://www.abc.net.au/pm/content/2008/s2208598.htm, accessed 22 January 2015.

29 ABS, 2006 Census of Population and Housing, Community Profile series, Laramba (Indigenous Location).

RACE IN THE DOCK I

1 Cameron Boon, 'WANTED: Do you know this man?', *Centralian Advocate*, 31 July 2009, p. 1.

2 *The Queen v Joachim Golder* (sentence), The Supreme Court of the Northern Territory, Kelly J, transcript of proceedings, 2 September 2010, SC 20921764.

3 Brooks, pp. 6–7.

4 Elisabeth Attwood, 'Booze, litter, begging, violence: native title holders say "Enough"', *Alice Springs News*, 23 November 2005, in online archive at http://www.alicespringsnews.com.au/1247.html, accessed 30 October 2015; and 'Kids are targets for protocols', *Alice Springs News*, 23 March 2006, http://www.alicespringsnews.com.au/1312.html, accessed 30 October 2015.

5 Katrina Bolton, 'Plan to strip blankets from Alice homeless', ABC News, 28 July 2009, http://www.abc.net.au/news/2009-07-28/plan-to-strip-blankets-from-alice-homeless/1369246, accessed 30 October 2015.

6   Kieran Finnane, 'Clark on her own', *Alice Springs News*, 6 August 2009, in online archive at http://www.alicespringsnews.com.au/1627.html, accessed 30 October 2015.

7   Kieran Finnane, 'Heated meeting fails to resolve council by-laws', *Alice Springs News*, 20 August 2009, in online archive at http://www.alicespringsnews.com.au/1629.html, accessed 30 October 2015.

8   On these intentions and provisions of the Intervention see, for example, 'Brough juggernaut rolls on', 9 August 2007, *Alice Springs News*, in online archive at http://www.alicespringsnews.com.au/1427.html; and Erwin Chlanda, 'Grog ban in parks', *Alice Springs News*, 24 July 2008, http://www.alicespringsnews.com.au/1525.html, accessed 30 October 2015.

9   See, for example, Kieran Finnane, 'Rates, roads, rows?', *Alice Springs News*, 15 February 2007, in online archive at http://www.alicespringsnews.com.au/1402.html; and Chlanda, Erwin, 'Govt. revolution in bush', *Alice Springs News*, 6 November 2008, in online archive at http://www.alicespringsnews.com.au/1540.html. Both accessed 1 November 2015.

10 Kieran Finnane, 'Grieving family urges calm', *Alice Springs News*, 6 August 2009, in online archive at http://www.alicespringsnews.com.au/1627.html, accessed 30 October 2015.

11 Sara Everingham, 'Alice death sparks fears of race hate', ABC Radio, *AM*, 28 September 2009, http://www.abc.net.au/am/content/2009/s2697935.htm, accessed 30 October 2015.

12 'Hundreds farewell a brother', *Centralian Advocate*, 21 August 2009, p. 2.

13 Reported by *Alice Online*, quoted in Everingham.

14 Everingham.

15 Alex Barwick, 'Leaders restore burnt cross', ABC Alice Springs, 1 October 2009, http://www.abc.net.au/local/stories/2009/10/01/2701928.htm, accessed 30 October 2015.

16 *Centralian Advocate*, 2 October 2009, p. 18.

17 Barwick.

18 'Friends farewell "extraordinary" Ed', ABC Alice Springs, 9 April 2009, http://www.abc.net.au/news/2009-04-09/friends-farewell-extraordinary-ed/1646774, accessed 23 November 2015.

19 Kirsty Nancarrow, 'Candle, not racists, set fire to Alice memorial', ABC Alice Springs, 20 October 2009, http://www.abc.net.au/news/2009-10-20/candle-not-racists-set-fire-to-alice-memorial/1109882, accessed 30 October 2015.

20 For example, Jennifer Mills, 'The Trouble with Alice', *New Matilda*, 8 June 2010, https://newmatilda.com/2010/06/08/trouble-alice/, accessed

30 October 2015.

21 Wright, p. 8.

22 Kieran Finnane, 'Music saw him through', *Alice Springs News*, 4 November 2010, in online archive at http://www.alicespringsnews.com.au/1740.html, accessed 30 October 2015.

23 Kieran Finnane, 'Comic take on clash of cultures', *Alice Springs News Online*, 21 April 2015, http://www.alicespringsnews.com.au/2015/04/21/comic-take-on-clash-of-cultures/, accessed 1 November 2015, and personal communication with Trisha Morton-Thomas, 17 April 2015.

24 Kieran Finnane, 'Briscoe Inquest: reduce supply of excess alcohol from take-away outlets, says Coroner', *Alice Springs News Online*, 17 September 2012, http://www.alicespringsnews.com.au/2012/09/17/briscoe-inquest-reduce-supply-of-excess-alcohol-from-take-away-outlets-says-coroner/, accessed 30 October 2015.

25 'Alcohol meeting in chaos and under heavy guard', *Alice Springs News Online*, 5 October 2012, http://www.alicespringsnews.com.au/2012/10/05/alcohol-meeting-in-chaos-and-under-heavy-guard/, accessed 1 November 2015.

26 Dan Moss, 'A town's day of tears', *Centralian Advocate*, 27 April 2010, p. 5.

27 Kieran Finnane, 'Racial divide no surprise', *Alice Springs News*, 20 May 2010, in online archive at http://www.alicespringsnews.com.au/1716.html, accessed 30 October 2015.

28 Alex Hope, 'Segregation damages our Alice community', *Centralian Advocate*, 2 October 2009, p. 6.

29 Margie Lynch Kngwarraye, 'Who needs to grow up here?', *Centralian Advocate*, 30 April 2010, p. 6.

30 Liz Jackson, 'A Dog Act', ABC TV, *Four Corners*, first broadcast 29 July 2010, program transcript at http://www.abc.net.au/4corners/content/2010/s2958043.htm, accessed 13 March 2015.

31 Chris Graham, 'Racism alive and well in the Alice', ABC TV, *The Drum*, 29 September 2010, http://www.abc.net.au/news/2010-07-20/35382, accessed 24 March 2015.

32 Michael Brull, 'The more things change', *Overland*, 2 September 2010, https://overland.org.au/2010/09/the-more-things-change/, accessed 24 March 2015.

33 Jackson.

34 Kieran Finnane, 'Appeals from Spears, Kloeden rejected', *Alice Springs News*, 19 August 2010, in online archive at http://www.alicespringsnews.com.au/1729.html, accessed 30 October 2015.

35 Jackson.

36 'Mother's tears for a stolen son', *The Australian*, 24 April 2010, http://www. theaustralian.com.au/news/nation/mothers-tears-for-a-stolen-son/story-e6frg6nf-1225857639483, accessed 1 November 2015.

37 Will Storr, 'Australia's dark heart', *The Guardian*, 3 October 2010, http:// www.theguardian.com/world/2010/oct/03/alice-spring-murder-racism, accessed 6 February 2015.

38 Graham.

39 Michael Brull, 'Top blokes, totally out of character: when five white men beat an Aboriginal man to death', *Overland*, 14 May 2010, https://overland. org.au/2010/05/top-blokes-totally-out-of-character-when-five-white-men-beat-an-aboriginal-man-to-death/, accessed 25 March 2015.

40 Jackson.

41 Storr.

42 Brull.

43 *Grivell & Mackley v The Queen*, Court of Criminal Appeal of the Northern Territory [2008] NTCCA 06, 15 May 2008.

44 Kloeden and Spears sought leave to appeal against the severity of their sentences but their applications were refused.

45 Kieran Finnane, 'Ryder family are satisfied with court outcome', *Alice Springs News*, 23 April 2010, in online archive at http://www.alicespringsnews. com.au/1713.html, accessed 30 October 2015.

RACE IN THE DOCK II

1   An earlier version of this chapter was published on *Inside Story*, 14 October 2013, http://insidestory.org.au/race-in-the-dock, accessed 2 November 2015.

2   Jonathon Howard, 'Boxer Ed fell for Alice', *Centralian Advocate*, 7 April 2009, p. 2; victim impact statement of Sarah Woodberry, 25 March 2011, read onto the record by Woodberry in the Supreme Court of the Northern Territory at Alice Springs.

3   Kieran Finnane, 'Hargrave murder accused say they can't get fair trial', *Alice Springs News*, 23 September 2010, in online archive at http://www. alicespringsnews.com.au/1734.html, accessed 30 October 2015.

4   Russell Goldflam, affidavit, 26 May 2010, in *The Queen v Graham Woods*, Supreme Court of the Northern Territory at Alice Springs, no. 20912126.

5   *Centralian Advocate*, 7 April 2009, pp. 1–2.

6   Jonathon Howard, 'Hargrave Mum and Dad's plea: Don't let this happen again', *Centralian Advocate*, 17 April 2009, pp. 1–2.

7   'Friends farewell "extraordinary" Ed', ABC Alice Springs, 9 April

2009,   http://www.abc.net.au/news/2009-04-09/friends-farewell-extraordinary-ed/1646774, accessed 12 December 2015.

8 'Desert racer honours murdered friend', ABC Alice Springs, 2 June 2009,   http://www.abc.net.au/news/2009-06-02/desert-racer-honours-murdered-friend/1700884, accessed 12 December 2015.

9 Dan Moss, 'DNA found on knife', *Centralian Advocate*, 4 December 2009, pp. 1–3.

10 Kieran Finnane, 'Grieving family urges calm', *Alice Springs News*, 6 August 2009, in online archive at http://www.alicespringsnews.com.au/1627.html; Kieran Finnane, 'Racial divide no surprise', *Alice Springs News*, 20 May 2010, in online archive at http://www.alicespringsnews.com.au/1716.html, both accessed 30 October 2015.

11 'Justice Blokland: Trial judge can overcome difficulties', *Alice Springs News*, 23 September 2012, in online archive at http://www.alicespringsnews.com.au/1734.html, accessed 30 October 2015.

12 Kieran Finnane, 'Trials in Alice and Darwin delayed as jury array quashed by full court', *Alice Springs News*, 30 September 2010, in online archive at http://www.alicespringsnews.com.au/1735.html, accessed 30 October 2015.

13 Russell Goldflam, 'The white elephant in the room: juries, jury arrays and race', p. 9, presentation to a conference of the Criminal Lawyers' Association of the NT, 2011, http://clant.org.au/images/images/the-bali-conference/2011/Goldflam,%20Russell%20-%20The%20White%20Elephant%20in%20the%20Room%20-Juries,%20Jury%20Arrays%20&%20Race%20(2011).pdf, accessed 30 October 2015.

14 Federal Court biographical information at http://www.fedcourt.gov.au/about/judges/current-judges-appointment/current-judges/reeves-j, accessed 24 July 2015; Gwen Byrnie, 'Introducing the first Northern Territory-based Federal Judge', Crikey, 24 September 2007, http://www.crikey.com.au/2007/09/24/introducing-the-first-northern-territory-based-federal-court-judge/, accessed 24 July 2015.

15 Goldflam, 'The white elephant in the room', p. 9.

16 This figure is for Central Australia in 2009, after more than a decade of licensing restrictions. It equates to 13.9 litres of pure alcohol per capita for persons aged fifteen and over. At least it represents a drop from 1.76 times the national average in 2000: Dennis Gray, et al., 'A longitudinal study of influences on alcohol consumption and related harm in Central Australia: with a particular emphasis on the role of price', National Drug Research Institute, Curtin University, October 2012, table 9, p. 28.
The excessive consumption is seen in both Aboriginal and

non-Aboriginal people in the NT, although the estimates are higher for Aboriginal people: in 2006–07, 16.1 litres of pure alcohol per annum for Aboriginal drinkers, as opposed to 13.8 litres for non-Aboriginal people, in contrast with a national figure of 9.88 litres: Steven J Skov, et al., 'How much is too much? Alcohol consumption and related harm in the Northern Territory', *Medical Journal of Australia*, vol. 193, no. 5, 6 September 2010, pp. 269–72, see box 1, p. 270.

17 'Court told of fatal stabbing', *Centralian Advocate*, 8 March 2011, pp. 1–2.

18 Goldflam, 'The white elephant in the room', p. 10.

19 Graham Woods appealed his sentence on the basis of how Justice Reeves dealt with the issue of excessive self-defence. The Court of Criminal Appeal found that Reeves had erred in finding that it could not be a matter in mitigation. But the burden of proof was on Woods to establish that he had acted in self-defence, and that burden had not been discharged. The appeal was dismissed. Woods then applied for special leave to appeal to the High Court but was refused. Proceedings were finalised on 5 October 2012, three and a half years after Hargrave's death: Goldflam, personal communication, 12 May 2013.

20 Personal communication on 31 May 2011.

WARLPIRI V THE QUEEN

1 An earlier version of this chapter was published under the same title in *Griffith Review*, 41, Spring 2013.

2 Marcia Langton, 'Medicine Square' in Ian Keen (ed.), *Being black; Aboriginal cultures in settled Australia*, Aboriginal Studies Press, Canberra, 1988, pp. 201–25, this reference on p. 221.

3 Marcia Langton, 'The end of "big men" politics', *Griffith Review*, 22, November 2008, https://griffithreview.com/articles/the-end-of-big-men-politics/, accessed 13 October 2015.

4 Reported by Erwin Chlanda, 'Picture of lawless Alice served to national audience, again', *Alice Springs News Online*, 26 July 2012, http://www.alicespringsnews.com.au/2012/07/26/picture-of-lawless-alice-served-to-national-audience-again/, accessed 2 November 2015.

5 The feud itself received national media coverage well before the events at Little Sisters involving Liam Jurrah. See for example Rosemary Neill, 'A sorry tale of sorcery and payback in Yuendumu', *The Australian*, 2 October 2010, http://www.theaustralian.com.au/national-affairs/a-sorry-tale-of-sorcery-and-payback-in-yuendumu/story-fn59niix-1225933040018, accessed 16 April 2013. The feud is also the most recent example considered

by Douglas & Finnane of the incomplete exercise of jurisdiction over Indigenous *inter se* violence, see pp. 214–17. They write: 'The practical reality for many Indigenous Australians is that individuals' lives and deaths and conditions of living are a subject of the jurisdiction of some kind of law but not the law of the state; plurality of law is the condition', p. 219.

6   See, for example, Bob Gosford, 'They took our culture, now there is no law', *Overland*, vol. 202, Autumn 2011, https://overland.org.au/previous-issues/issue-202/essay-bob-gosford/, accessed 17 October 2015.

7   See, for example, Kieran Finnane, 'Chief Justice condemns ongoing revenge attacks at Yuendumu', *Alice Springs News Online*, 17 October 2012, http://www.alicespringsnews.com.au/2012/10/17/chief-justice-condemns-ongoing-revenge-attacks-at-yuendumu/, accessed 2 November 2015.

8   Erwin Chlanda, 'Yuendumu manual for healing community troubles', *Alice Springs News Online*, 17 August 2013, http://www.alicespringsnews.com.au/2013/08/17/yuendumu-manual-for-healing-community-troubles/, accessed 2 November 2015.

9   Yasmine Musharbash, *Yuendumu everyday*, Aboriginal Studies Press, Canberra, 2008, p. 52.

10 ibid., p. 66; and personal communication with Yasmine Musharbash by email, 11 December 2015.

11 ibid., p. 98.

12 Personal communication with Yasmine Musharbash by email, 11 December 2015.

13 Musharbash, pp. 34–35.

14 ibid., pp. 143–44.

ORDEAL

1   See comments to Kieran Finnane, 'Payback: six in court accused of beating man to death in Alice Springs', *Alice Springs News Online*, 31 March 2014, http://www.alicespringsnews.com.au/2014/03/31/abuse-hurled-at-men-accused-of-payback-killing/, accessed 14 May 2015.

2   Erwin Chlanda, 'Payback in Alice Springs', *Alice Springs News*, 13 September 2000, in online archive at http://www.alicespringsnews.com.au/0737.html, accessed 30 October 2015; Jane Vadiveloo quoted in Eve Vincent & Clare Land, 'Clueless white males', *New Matilda*, 31 May 2006, https://newmatilda.com/2006/05/31/clueless-white-males, accessed 30 July 2015.

3   Sutton, p. 77.

4   Langton in Sutton, p. vi.

5   Kieran Finnane, 'Noted anthropologist calls for massive change', *Alice Springs News*, 20 February 2002, in online archive at http://www.alicespringsnews.com.au/0903.html, accessed 30 October 2015; Sutton's essay was published in *Anthropological Forum*, vol. 11, no. 2, 2001, pp. 125–73.

6   Sutton quoted in Kieran Finnane, 'Blood on our hands', *Alice Springs News*, 14 May 2003, in online archive at http://www.alicespringsnews.com.au/1015.html, accessed 30 October 2015.

7   Russell Goldflam, 'The (non-)role of Aboriginal customary law in sentencing in the Northern Territory', *Australian Indigenous Law Review*, vol. 17, no. 1, 2013, pp. 72–80.

8   Danielle Loy, the filmmaker, quoted in Erwin Chlanda, 'Should tribal law become part of Australian law?', *Alice Springs News*, 3 December 2009, in online archive at http://www.alicespringsnews.com.au/1644.html, accessed 30 October 2015.

9   ibid.

10 Craig San Roque, personal communication, 4 December 2015.

11 Craig San Roque, 'Could new ways be found to repair crime?', letter to the editor, *Alice Springs News*, 10 December 2009, in online archive at: http://www.alicespringsnews.com.au/1645.html, accessed 21 May 2015.

12 Turner-Walker.

13 Rajiv Maharaj, 'Grow up: Judge raps payback culture', *Centralian Advocate*, 16 April 2010, pp. 1–2.

14 Kngwarraye, Margie Lynch, 'Who needs to grow up here?', *Centralian Advocate*, 30 April 2010, p. 6.

15 Police had heard the night before from Kumunjayi Pollard's wife, in a call to 000, that her husband had been taken captive from Ilparpa Camp. On the information heard in open court, it seemed there was no further action until they were alerted to a decomposing body by a passing cyclist on the evening of 20 February. However, responding to enquiries from me, police gave a fuller account of their investigation:

At Ilparpa Camp on 18 February Pollard's wife told them that her husband had been chased by a group with weapons but he had run away, was hiding and did not wish to talk to police. She said the car full of people with weapons was waiting for him outside the camp. Police conducted numerous patrols in the area but could not locate any vehicles or 'persons of interest'. They told Pollard's wife to call straightaway if the group returned. When they heard of Robert Daniel's report in the early hours of 19 February, there was nothing to suggest a link between the two reports. Their search of the creekbed included waking numerous campers, all of whom said there had been no fighting or incidents that evening.

Late in the night of 20 February, following the discovery of Pollard's as yet unidentified body, police were dealing with an unrelated disturbance, at which relatives of Pollard expressed concern for his welfare. They gave more detail of the assault at Ilparpa and spoke of jeans with blood on them believed to be his, sighted by the Stuart Highway. When police went back to Ilparpa, they were told further specific details of what had happened on 18 February. Personal communication by email from a Public Information Officer for NT Police, Fire and Emergency Services, 6 August 2015.

16 Diana Eades gives the Aboriginal English meanings of 'cheeky' as 'dangerous, poisonous, unpredictable'. See 'Aboriginal English: implications in legal contexts in the Northern Territory', a paper given to the Northern Territory Supreme Court Language and Law II Conference, 28 August 2015, http://www.supremecourt.nt.gov.au/conferences/index. htm, accessed 27 November 2015.

17 Dr John Boffa, 'NTG should release Alcohol Mandatory Treatment review', letter to editor, *Alice Springs News Online*, 24 June 2014, http:// www.alicespringsnews.com.au/2014/06/24/ntg-should-release-findings- of-alcohol-mandatory-treatment-act-review/, accessed 15 June 2015.

18 A new Alcohol Management Plan (AMP) for the whole of Alice Springs is in draft form at the time of writing. It does not include population-wide supply reduction strategies long lobbied for by Congress, such as a floor price for take-away alcohol set at the price of beer, nor a take-away alcohol- free day linked to payday for Centrelink benefits. It does give consideration to a point of sale identification system to enforce the same restrictions and orders as currently enforced by the TBLs (renamed POSIs). The draft AMP is available at http://www.dob.nt.gov.au/gambling-licensing/ alcohol-policy/amp/Documents/as-draft-amp-2015-2017.pdf,   accessed 5 December 2015.

19 'Cops at bottlos a winner, says Congress', *Alice Springs News Online*, 24 August 2014, http://www.alicespringsnews.com.au/2014/08/24/cops- at-bottlos-a-winner-says-congress/, accessed 15 June 2015.

20 'Gaps in bottlo policing blamed for rise in assaults', *Alice Springs News Online*, http://www.alicespringsnews.com.au/2016/02/14/gaps-in-bottlo- policing-blamed-for-rise-in-assaults/, accessed 15 February 2016. Northern Territory Crime Statistics, November 2015, http://www.pfes.nt.gov.au/ Police/Community-safety/Northern-Territory-crime-statistics/Statistical- publications.aspx, pp. 39 & 41, accessed 15 February 2016.

21 RHD Australia, Menzies School of Health Research Darwin, media release and backgrounder, 11 May 2015.

22 We didn't hear in court why this could not have been overcome with the assistance of the interpreter service, but in his paper 'Where's my interpreter?' Russell Goldflam reports that the interpreters needed for this case had 'gone to ground' ahead of the trial: 'It was a work health and safety issue: no-one could guarantee the safety of the interpreters, who felt threatened, perhaps by the family of the deceased, or perhaps by the families of the accused, or perhaps by both. Rumours reached me that threats had actually been made, but whether or not that had indeed happened, the interpreters were spooked', p. 6. Had the trial gone ahead this may have presented some real issues for fairness, for the accused and for the witnesses.

23 Kieran Finnane, 'Life's better with income management, say men and women from town camps and bush', *Alice Springs News*, 6 March 2008, in online archive at http://www.alicespringsnews.com.au/1505.html, accessed 30 October 2015.

24 *Munda v Western Australia* [2013] HCA 38 (2 October 2013).

25 Goldflam, 2013, p. 74.

26 Southwood J, *The Queen v Wunungmurra* [2009] NTSC 24, Supreme Court of the Northern Territory, 9 June 2009, SCC no. 20824528.

   See also discussion of this case in Douglas & Finnane, pp. 210–12: 'Although the judge accepted the prosecution's submission that the statement [of cultural evidence] could be used neither to reduce nor increase the defendant's sentence, he found that the statement was able to be read for the other purposes identified by the defence counsel.' These were that it provided context and explanation for the offence, established Wunungmurra's character, his prospects of rehabilitation and his lack of predisposition towards domestic violence. The authors continue: 'it seems that the judgment still leaves it open for a judge to consider exculpatory cultural evidence in sentencing decisions'.

27 *Fernando v The Queen* (1992) 76 A Crim R 58 by the New South Wales Court of Criminal Appeal (NSWCCA).

28 *Munda v Western Australia*.

29 These comments on mitigation drew on the statement on sentencing principles by Brennan J in *Neal v The Queen* (1982) 149 CLR 305.

EPILOGUE: COMING THROUGH THE GAP

1 San Roque, 2004, p. 60. San Roque drew on the public versions of the Dog Story published in Brooks (for Mparntwe people), pp. 8–9.

2   ibid., p. 48.

3   John Elferink, NT Attorney-General and Minister for Justice, Sentencing Amendment (Mandatory Minimum Sentences) Bill 2012, second reading speech, 29 November 2012, NT Hansard, http://notes.nt.gov.au/lant/hansard/hansard12.nsf/WebbySubject/4F84E713E3F06F1F69257B270005 4889?opendocument, accessed 17 January 2016.
    Offending and re-offending dropped following the introduction of mandatory minimum sentencing for violent offences, but the drop was thought to be related rather to police being stationed outside bottle shops (POSIs) as a crime reduction strategy in Alice Springs, Tennant Creek and Katherine. See C Whyte, J Yick, D Vahlberg, & L Swart, 2015. Review of the *Northern Territory Sentencing Amendment (Mandatory Minimum Sentences) Act 2013*. Department of the Attorney- General and Justice, Darwin, pp. 2 & 31-32, http://www.fru.nt.gov.au/justice/policycoord/researchstats/documents/Review%20of%20the%20 Northern%20Territory%20Sentencing%20Amendment%20Mandatory%20 Minimum%20Sentences%20Act%202013.pdf, accessed 21 February 2015.

4   Kieran Finnane, 'Aboriginal men "need to reinvent" themselves: forum', *Alice Springs News Online*, 11 September 2013, http://www.alicespringsnews.com.au/2013/09/11/aboriginal-men-need-to-reinvent-themselves-forum/, accessed 18 October 2015. See also Justice Blokland's paper for the 2013 CLANT conference in Bali, 'Unnecessary Suffering: Violence against Aboriginal Women in the Northern Territory; a Discussion of Contemporary Issues and Possible Ways Forward', http://clant.org.au/images/images/the-bali-conference/2013/Blokland.pdf, accessed 28 October 2015.

5   http://www.alicespringsnews.com.au/2015/09/04/jurrah-gets-nine-months-supended-after-four/, accessed 7 December 2015.

6   Jake Niall, 'Inside the world of Liam Jurrah', *The Age*, 30 May 2014, http://www.theage.com.au/afl/afl-news/inside-the-world-of-liam-jurrah-20140530-zrtim.html, accessed 16 October 2015.

7   Sally Brooks, *ABC TV News*, broadcast 4 September 2015.

8   Jordan Gerrans, *NT News*, 8 September 2015, http://www.ntnews.com.au/news/centralian-advocate/yuendumu-clinch-cafl-division-one-premiership-flag/story-fnk4wgm8-1227517541646, accessed 17 October 2015.

9   A Japaljarri Spencer with Rob Burdon, Des Rogers and Craig San Roque, text for a poster reproducing Japaljarri's painting, *Eagle and Crow*. Quoted in full in Japaljarri's obituary by San Roque, 'Eagle and Crow: Andrew Spencer Japaljarri', *Alice Springs News Online*, 8 December 2015, http://www.alicespringsnews.com.au/2015/12/08/eagle-and-crow-andrew-spencer-japaljarri/, accessed 10 January 2016.

10 Kieran Finnane, 'Court of good hope', *Alice Springs News Online*, http://www.alicespringsnews.com.au/2011/11/10/court-of-good-hope/, accessed 9 December 2015.

11 Kieran Finnane, 'SMART court gets first graduates … and first romance', *Alice Springs News Online*, http://www.alicespringsnews.com.au/2012/02/04/smart-court-gets-first-graduates-and-first-romance/, accessed 9 December 2015.

12 Kieran Finnane, 'Court of good hope', *Alice Springs News Online*, http://www.alicespringsnews.com.au/2011/11/10/court-of-good-hope/, accessed 9 December 2015.

13 'Strengthening Justice, Strengthening Our Community', Budget 2013 media release, http://www.territorystories.nt.gov.au/bitstream/10070/244889/1/Elferink-140513-Strengthening_justice_strengthening_our_community.pdf, accessed 17 January 2016.

14 Elferink, Alcohol Reform (Substance Misuse Assessment and Referral for Treatment Court) Bill, second reading debate, 5 May 2011, in NT Hansard, http://notes.nt.gov.au/lant/hansard/hansard11.nsf/WebbySubject/258D865F20508F9D692578A2000E31B5?opendocument, accessed 17 January 2016.

15 Weatherburn, p. 103.

16 Hilary Hannam, 'Current issues in delivering Indigenous justice: challenges for the courts', a paper delivered to the AIJA Indigenous Justice Conference, 19 July 2013, p. 8. Available at http://www.aija.org.au/Ind%20Courts%20Conf%2013/Papers/Hannam.pdf, accessed 17 January 2016.